How to Sell Without Selling

Step-By-Step Marketing Formula to Attract Ready-to-Buy Clients…Create Passive Income and Make More Money While Making a Difference

By Terry Dean

Step-By-Step Marketing Formula to Attract Ready-to-Buy
Clients…Create Passive Income and Make More Money While
Making a Difference
Copyright © 2017 by Terry Dean
ISBN 978-0-9778671-2-7
Published By:
MyMarketingCoach, LLC
10380 SW 48th AVE
Ocala, FL 34476
http://www.mymarketingcoach.com

Table of Contents

Introduction

Marketing has changed. If you're still trying to sell to customers using old, worn-out hard close techniques that worked decades ago, you will soon be as extinct as the dinosaurs. You can't 'trick' a customer into a sale. And no matter what you've heard from some online marketers and sales trainers, there is no need for mind control techniques. Good marketing is not manipulation. You'll sell more by serving your customers and clients than you ever will by taking advantage of them.

If you're like me, and many of the clients I've worked with over the years, those old sales techniques made you uncomfortable anyway. You got into business to bring value to others. And that's why you're going to love the methods I'll be sharing throughout this book.

These methods allow you to guide, encourage, and share value with your customers before they ever spend a single penny with you. Subscribers regularly email me and tell me how much they appreciate the value that I've shared with them, even if they haven't purchased yet. This same principle applies with blogs, podcasts, videos, and social media. You don't have to wait for someone to become a customer before adding value to their life.

Today's customers are better informed than ever before. They research products. They compare you to the competition. They're even researching the new breakthroughs occurring in your field. If you're following old sales techniques based on tricking people into buying your products or services, then a highly educated customer is a negative to you. But if you're focused on serving your customers, this will be a game changer for you.

I've worked with clients in hundreds of markets over the years. They include authors, consultants, coaches, restaurant owners, chiropractors, CPAs, e-commerce websites, SaaS (software as a Service), marketing agencies, and more. We found time and time again that an educational and often entertaining approach is much more effective in today's market than worn-out sales techniques.

You may have heard the term 'content marketing' before, and you'll see some similarities to the approach being shared here. You're going to be sharing content with your audience through emails, blogs, podcasts, videos, webinars, and possibly even live presentations. You may have even tried some of these techniques before, but you likely didn't achieve the results you were looking for.

Most content marketing is ineffective because it's sharing the wrong type of content and doesn't have a systematic strategy behind it. We're not going to be sharing content for contents sake. You're never going to persuade anyone to buy from you just by sharing a large volume of random content. Everything you do and everything you share will have a specific purpose behind it.

You're going to discover a simple five step system for persuasion. It works just as well for converting a friend to your way of thinking as it does for selling your products or services. It works for emails, websites, webinars, and even one-on-one conversations. It is a basic foundation for everything you do with your marketing. It becomes a golden thread that ties together many of the techniques you're soon going to be using in your daily life.

Next we'll investigate and identify your ideal client. Throughout this book, I'm going to be using the word 'client' and 'clients' instead of customers. If you're in a retail business, I'm not leaving you out. You may currently be using the word customers, but I want you to start thinking about them as clients. You're not just a provider of products. People come to you because they want to improve their lives in some way. If you're a men's clothing retailer, men are coming to you because they want to look good. They want to look professional. They want to appear confident and in control. When we boil it all down, they want to feel better about themselves. Think of yourself as a consultant they bring in to achieve the best results in their life.

It doesn't matter what business you're in. Your clients have a problem they want to solve or they have a desire they want to see fulfilled. They come to you for help. You have an ethical obligation to help them make wise choices to produce their desired outcome. As your client, they're under your protection. You will guide them, coach them, and make it your mission to achieve the highest and best results for them.

You will discover how to identify your ideal client and fall in love with them again. One of the biggest mistakes business owners make is falling in love with the product or service they're selling. Instead, you want to fall in love with your client. First, you have to get to know them. If you have a lot of day-to-day interaction with them, you probably already have pretty good insights into what makes them tick. If you're new in the market or you're trying to expand into a different market, I'm going to give you techniques that allow you to quickly identify the exact language that motivates your ideal clients to take action.

From here we will move to The Strategic Myth. This goes beyond an origin story because it integrates in with everything you do. Your clients aren't just purchasing the products and services you offer. They're not even just purchasing the benefits. They're buying from you because they identify with your story, your mission, and your community. Knowing The Strategic Myth behind your business allows you to create and share content that grabs attention, keeps your prospects interested, and converts them into long-term buyers.

You'll discover how to demonstrate results in advance for your products and services. There is risk in any transaction. Either clients are accepting the risk or you're accepting the risk. Most companies offer guarantees, but that is only one form of risk reversal. In today's world, you can go further and help your clients achieve results before they've even purchased from you. This creates a bond with your prospects and builds loyalty that turns them into a long-term client.

You'll discover how to strategically create content that turns prospects into clients. It's not about the quantity of content. It's about calling out to your ideal client, providing them value in advance, and transitioning them into buying products and services that improve their lives. You'll see how to quickly create this content, multipurpose it into several different forms, and publish it for maximum impact. You'll connect with influencers who can multiply your reach and provide you with a steady stream of highly qualified clients.

Paid advertising has also changed. Just a few years ago you may have run ads directly for your products and services. Because the overabundance of advertising has turned off your prospects, many of them are almost completely blind to your advertising. Today there is a better route. Instead of immediately asking for the sale, you can provide value to your prospects upfront. When you provide this value strategically, you can quickly transition it into the sale. In addition, online advertising allows us to pixel our visitors and follow up on them across a wide range of websites and social media venues. This creates opportunities for advanced remarketing campaigns that have never been available before.

Who Is This Book For?

This book is for anyone who serious about generating results from their business. You're frustrated with sales techniques that belong in the dustbin of history. It doesn't matter if you're just getting started in business or you've been in business all your life. It doesn't matter if you have a brick-and-mortar retail store, a professional service, or an online only business. These techniques have been proven to work for hundreds of my clients in wildly different markets.

This isn't for everyone though. If your goal is to simply make money and you don't care about the end results for your clients, this isn't for you. This is for entrepreneurs who are on a mission. It pains you to see your client struggling and facing challenges alone. You're not satisfied with the status quo. And you're willing to go a little bit deeper than the competition.

As you go through the steps in this book, you might get a little uncomfortable. That's a good thing! When you stay in your comfort zone, you never experience growth. Your business stays at the same level or even begins to move backward. If you want to achieve new heights, you have to take new steps you've never taken before. Change is never easy. I can't promise you everything in this book will be easy. You're going to have to be strategic. You will develop new skills. You will test new approaches. You're going to stand-out as different from all the other competitors in your market.

What Will This Method Do For Me?

This is the pathway to accomplishing your mission. You can have a business that changes the lives of your clients. You can provide more value than everyone else in your industry. And you can attract clients that add energy to your life instead of taking away from it. Have you ever had a client that seemed to drain you? You felt like all the energy drained from your body when you met with them or called them on the phone. You saw their name on your schedule and you wished you were doing something else.

What if there was an easy way to sort and sift those clients out of your life? This is just one of the additional benefits of the methods I'm going to share with you. The strategic content you share not only attracts your ideal clients, but at the same time it repels those who shouldn't do business with you anyway. Think about a couple of your favorite clients. What if your entire practice was full of ideal clients that made you feel good about yourself? How would that make a difference in your life? How would you feel about each day when you arrive at work? Would it inspire you? Would you be ready and willing to grow your business even faster?

This could soon be a reality in your life. I've seen the dramatic transformation that occurs when an entrepreneur fills their business with ideal clients. They might've been discouraged, worn out, and completely burned out on their business. We underestimate the importance of attracting the right clients. Your business is either adding to or taking away from your clients lives. And your clients are either adding to or taking away from your life. When you don't have enough clients coming through your door, you suffer with whatever scraps you end up with. When you have an over-abundance of new clients, you're able to pick and choose the ones who are the best fit for what you do.

These methods may allow you to raise your prices. I love the Internet, but one of the negatives of the digital age is that anything and everyone is being turned into a commodity. Whatever you do, there's someone out there in the world today willing to do it for less. Your competition is only a few clicks away . It's easy to price shop. Building a business based on the lowest prices is a recipe for failure. Only the largest businesses can pull it off because of their large infrastructure and huge buying power. You have to find another way to serve your clients other than the lowest prices.

Brand loyalty is nowhere near as powerful as it used to be. You have to go beyond the brand by tapping into a story and creating a community your clients identify with. Everyone wants to be a part of something larger than themselves. You can create that purpose. You might say, *"Well, I'm just a CPA, I do taxes."*

Change that point of view. Taxes are simply a way to get the client through the door. It's an immediate desperate problem that has to be solved now. But it's only the beginning of the services you can offer to your client. What other needs do they have? If they're a business owner, they need bookkeeping. They need to keep a close eye on their finances. They need an advisor who can look at the numbers in the business and how they apply to everything else. What other services could you provide in addition to taxes?

Why is the Strategy Behind Free Content So Important?

You may have produced a ton of content online without success. Many of my clients have come to me in that situation. They created hundreds of emails and blog posts. They published videos and they wasted months on social media without results. Some of them even built a large email list of tens of thousands of subscribers. Yet that large list wasn't working for them. Very few sales were coming through. Others told them they needed to produce even more content, but that just made the problem worse. They sent out offers to their list, but they got more complaints than sales. Some of these entrepreneurs were ready to throw the towel in. Maybe the Internet is just packed with freebie seekers.

The problem isn't the Internet. It was the kind of subscribers they were attracting. In addition, they were sending out the wrong kind of content. You can't just create content full of tips or even step-by-step guidance. There has to be something more. You have to make a personal connection with your audience. That means integrating in your own personal stories or even case studies from other clients. Think about a professional speaker or an author you admire. You've probably gained a lot of value from them, but I bet you it's not the step-by-step systems you remember most. It's the stories they tell. Every professional speaker knows the audience will forget their five tips before they even walk off the stage, but they remember the stories for years to come.

Your Strategic Myth includes your origin story, but it goes beyond this. It's a story about a dream. It's about overcoming challenges. It's about a hero who wouldn't take NO for an answer. There is a story inside you that you have to share with the world. And you're inviting them in along on your journey. You're inviting them to take part in your story and your mission.

There is already too much content online. You're not going to cut through all the noise online by publishing just another series of boring articles. You have to grab your prospects by the lapels and give them a story that will stick with them. It has to be memorable. It has to be entertaining. And it has to be something they want to share with others. What story are you telling? Is it a story about just another business that wants a share of their hard-earned cash? Or is it an exciting story that inspires them?

By the end of this book you will know who your ideal clients are. You will have a story to tell that they identify with. And you will know how to get your message out there using simple step-by-step methods that are proven to work in virtually every market.

Bonus Gift:

Visit **www.MyMarketingCoach.com/free** for your Free Email Conversion Kit including 64 story shortcuts to create personalized feel to your emails, 5 subject line templates, a 27 word email template for increasing engagement, and Terry's special report, *"7 Unique Ways to Create Profitable Emails...Even If You're Not a Writer."*

My 20+ Year Journey

I first started online in 1996. I had already tried multiple businesses and failed. I tried network marketing. I tried direct sales. At one point I even had a job working selling satellite dishes door-to-door. Over a two-week period I sold a grand total of zero. Sales, at least the old method of generating sales, just wasn't for me. There had to be a better way.

I stumbled from one dead-end job to another. My last job, the last job I will ever have, was delivering pizzas for Little Caesars for $8 an hour. Back then, they paid me minimum wage plus tips, or $8 an hour if you didn't get enough tips. I always got paid the $8. My wife and I were deep in debt. Creditors were calling all hours of the day and night. It looked like there was no way out of that nightmare.

Even back in 1996, I heard rumors about people who were making a living online. That inspired me. If others could make money sitting behind their computer screen, then maybe it could work for me too. It wouldn't require me to get in front of someone and make a sales presentation. I'm shy. I'm an introvert. But neither of those would hold me back online. Sitting for hours alone behind a computer wasn't a negative to me. I relished the opportunity.

The Internet is the great equalizer. It doesn't matter if you're an introvert or extrovert. Your sex, race, and nationality don't matter. And instead of being held back by weaknesses, you can focus on your strengths as your advantage. For example, one of the skills I focused on in the beginning was writing. I'm comfortable writing. I enjoy it.

Maybe you're not a writer? Perhaps you enjoy speaking with others. Where I might produce written content, you could do interviews. Someone else may love producing videos. Another might love the live interaction of webinars. You can create strategic content using whatever method works best for you, and you can expand that type of content into other forms of media.

It wasn't quite as easy as I hoped it to be. During the first few months, I spent most of my time trying to figure out how in the world to use that old computer. I went online and investigated what others were doing. I put up a couple of websites. I'd be embarrassed if you dug one of them out today. They were ugly. They had big flashing images all over the page. The font styles didn't match. And the color schemes looked like they came out of a designer's worst nightmare. But as amazing as it sounds, those ugly websites started generating a few sales.

I made a few deals with some self-help video producers. I licensed a few of their VHS videos to sell on my websites. A small trickle of traffic started coming in. It was just a few dollars at a time in the beginning, but that was enough to motivate me to keep going forward.

That's when I made one of the best decisions of my life. I started a once-a-week email newsletter. When people came to my website, they were given the opportunity to subscribe to my email newsletter. Each week I would send them an article about something related to one of the videos I was selling. My whole purpose was simply to give them value in advance. I started giving them 'free samples' of the kind of information they would learn on the videos selling on my site. Visitors started subscribing, and those subscribers started buying.

Where was I getting these subscribers and buyers from in the beginning? They came from those old CompuServe message boards. If you're under 40 you probably don't even know what CompuServe is. They were one of those early Internet service providers in the days before AOL started sending out those disks to everyone in the US. CompuServe had a series of discussion forums on just about every subject you could imagine. I became a regular participant in those forums. It wasn't about running ads. It was about being a resource to others who had questions. I would answer those questions and add a little link to my website in the resource box. People clicked the link, joined my list, and got my weekly emails.

Each month my list grew along with my income. It wasn't long before my online income replaced my pizza delivery income. As I started generating income online, I spent a portion of that on advertising. It seemed next to impossible to make a sale directly from an ad. People just weren't comfortable buying online at the time. So I adapted my strategy. Instead of selling directly from the ads, I took visitors to a landing page where they could subscribe to my email list. Once they were on my list, they would receive my weekly emails and hopefully gain value from them. Each week I'd also make an offer in the email for one of my products.

At first, there was only a small trickle of sales, but I kept experimenting with the emails. Would people be most responsive to receiving highly detailed step-by-step guides or short personal notes and tips? The answer may surprise you. While subscribers said they appreciated the guides, they were much more likely to click on emails with short stories in them. Sometimes you have to pay more attention to what people DO than what they say.

Since I didn't have any previous writing training, I naturally wrote in an informal style. I write exactly as I talk. This appealed to readers. I was somebody they could relate to. I was an "Every Man" who was similar to them. I faced the same struggles they did. And I was taking them on a journey alongside me as my business faced and overcame one challenge after another.

When people met me at conferences a few years down the road, they told me they could hear me speaking to them directly in those early emails. Many of those subscribers even mentioned printing out my emails and taking them over to the park during their lunch break. Some kept the emails and filed them in a 3-ring binder. I was shocked the first few times people brought me a binder like that and asked me to sign it for them! I had become a mini-celebrity no one ever heard of outside of this little group of followers.

It's amazing what you can accomplish by simply being yourself and sharing your own journey with your audience. If you have professional writing training, take advantage of it. Use correct grammar and spelling, most of the time. But you can also create your own phraseology. What phrases or words are unique to your writing? What words could you invent that would immediately identify you to the audience? All movements, religions, and professions have their own jargon. You can create your own community with jargon unique to your market. We'll talk more about this in a later chapter.

I experimented with multiple techniques back then. Most of them were a waste of time. No matter what I did, at least 80% of my online income could be traced directly to the emails I sent to my list. Emails drove the business forward. The more personable they were, the better they connected with the readers. Authenticity may be a word people talk about today, but it was a key success secret all the way back in the beginning.

Sales came in every time an email went out. You would have thought I'd at least test out emails more than once a week, but I heard too many people talking about how you could burn-out your list with too many emails. So I kept sending one email consistently week-after-week. It worked, but I could have been even more profitable if I upped the frequency. I had no idea at the time just how frequently your subscribers want to hear from you when you're sending the right kind of emails!

This was when I stumbled upon another big online marketing secret. I decided to go shopping on Black Friday morning. This was before a large portion of buyers started shopping online, so it was crazy out there.

People were shoving each other. Walmart ran out of stock on certain items, and customers threw fits right there in the aisles. Limited discount specials caused buyers to go bonkers. The 'mob' got caught up in a buying frenzy.

Could the same emotions take over online? I tested this theory initially by simply putting one of my products on sale for a limited period of time. The sales were 4 times the normal rate that weekend. There must be something to this. The experiments continued. People responded whenever they were given a reason to act now. The reason itself almost didn't even matter. The deadline for the discount could be a specific day such as Sunday at midnight or it could be a limited opportunity such as only 100 copies of this free bonus CD available for the first 100 orders.

There needed to be a reason why behind the special. I've used the 1 year anniversary of my business, my birthday, my wife's birthday, my wedding anniversary, tax time, end of the year special, and pretty much any major holiday. If you're like me, you may feel a little uncomfortable 'pressuring' people to act now, but it's part of human nature. The easiest decision to make is no decision at all. A large portion of your future clients will never take action unless you motivate them to get off their duffs and take action now. If you're not using ethical and authentic scarcity, you're sacrificing a large portion of your sales and you'll letting your audience down. They could have received the benefits you had for them, but they never decided to act now and get them.

How I Earned $96,250 in Sales From One Email In Front of a Live Audience

Eventually others started to take notice of what I was doing online. I was invited to speak at some of the early internet marketing conferences. At one of these events, we issued a challenge to demonstrate the power behind these methods. We guaranteed attendees would see me earn at least $10,000 in sales from my list during the 3 day event.

Frankly, that promise terrified me. I'd hit that number multiple times, but you never know what kind of problems can come up. Your email might not go out. Your offer may not be exciting enough. Or the order form might not work. One time I did a special where I sent people the WRONG website link, and didn't realize it until I checked my email around noon and saw dozens of people complaining about not being able to access the special.

Could you imagine how it would have looked if I made that big promise and missed the goal? I'd be left standing there with egg on my face as the story got around of what a fraud I was. I planned an insane special of 50% Off for that weekend only. And I wrote a very authentic email about why I was making such an incredible deal. You could get 50% off this weekend only, because I was standing in front of an audience of over 100 people and told them they would see at least $10,000 come in before Sunday. I didn't want to look like an idiot in front of the entire audience! That's a believable reason why! No one wants to be embarrassed in front of a crowd, especially an introvert like me. The audience even mentioned later they saw my hands visibly shaking as I spoke to them and sent out the email live on Friday morning in front of them.

I finished my presentation that morning nervous about the results, but I hit over $10,000 before the end of that first day. By Sunday I had sold over $33,000 in products to my list with one email. The challenge was soundly beaten. It was so life changing for the audience that we scheduled future events to feature a similar challenge.

Each time, significantly more than $10,000 came in during the challenge. As I kept running these specials I continued to discover more and more about what caused people to respond during them. One of the variables that caused the most dramatic difference in profits was the price point of the offer made during the special. Higher ticket offers consistently produced a higher return. You can build a close relationship with your audience through the methods you'll discover throughout this book, and that also means releasing products at different price points to fulfill on their desires.

My highest total was $96,250 in sales in a weekend from one email in front of a live audience. It drove the audience wild. And this demonstrates the importance of sticking to your guns with your specials. We hit the 'limit' of what I promised to sell at around 3 PM on Sunday. People encouraged me to leave it open and see if I could break $100,000, BUT You have to be honest with your deadlines. I closed down the special and put a notice up on my website that it was sold out. Too many people try to fudge the dates or move the numbers. They're always trying to pull a fast one. Telling the truth builds loyalty, and it's the right thing to do anyway. I've had subscribers who missed out on a special email me and tell me they'll respond faster the next time!

Not bad for a solopreneur working from my home office! Here's a testimonial from Steve Duce, Internet marketing manager at the event...

"Terry, what you did at the Internet seminar in Jacksonville was incredible. Twice now I've seen you make an offer to your newsletter subscribers and each time you made over $30,000. This last time, $96,250! I see many people who claim to make a lot of money online. It's a whole different ball game to be able to go before a crowd, send an offer, and actually "show" everyone. You told your subscribers you were only taking a limited number of orders. No matter how much the crowd wanted you to keep going and break that $100,000 mark, you did what you said you would do and stopped the sales. Terry, watching you generate $96,250 in person from one email was something I'll never forget."

Who's-Who of Internet Marketing Experts

New breakthroughs kept coming. A free list is valuable, but buyers are even more valuable. What happens when you turn buyers into ongoing members of your community? I created one of the first membership sites designed to help small and home based business owners market online. It was called Netbreakthroughs and it had a pretty simple concept behind it.

Each week I'd share results from one of my personal ad experiments. Members would see which forms of advertising were working, which landing pages got the best results, and how to maximize the dollars they invest in their marketing. It was basically 'live lab' into my back office of what was working and what wasn't. Close to 50% of the experiments didn't work out. Again, authenticity was key. I wasn't a miracle worker where everything I touched turned to gold. Instead, I was just like them and learning along the way. They could come alongside me for support.

In addition to my weekly ad diary, they also had access to a members-only forum where they could ask questions, get reviews of their website, and communicate with each other. A community atmosphere is king for membership sites. The initial launch was to my own list, but the members themselves quickly spread the word. Over 63% of members were referred by one of my affiliates. And while there were 5,000+ affiliates in the program, 15 of them were generating the vast majority of the sales.

I'm sure you can guess pretty quickly what those 15 super-affiliates had in common. That's right. They had their own email lists which they were communicating with on a regular basis. They were a member of my program and they personally endorsed it to their lists. The most effective affiliates were those who used something from inside the program and then reported the results they received. They shared a personal case study for the value they received from the membership. You just got a major success tip for increasing your results as an affiliate for any product or service.

There was a surprising side effect to the membership site. It multiplied the sales for all of my other products and services. Members felt like they were a part of something greater than themselves. Finally they found a community of people who understood them. It was a place they could plug into. All I did was put links in the sidebar or at the bottom of the page to my other products or related resources, and people purchased. No selling necessary. They bought because of the low-key recommendation inside their community. When you build a community around your message, you've tapped into one of the strongest emotional bonds with your audience.

Disaster Strikes And a New Beginning

Business was booming, but disaster was in the wings. I made a major mistake. While my wife helped me with some of the customer support and product fulfillment, I continued to do the vast majority of the work myself. I refused to hire anyone else and didn't outsource even when it was obviously needed. Soon I was spending over 4 hours a day, every day, just answering email. I spent hours every day managing the discussion area inside the membership. And I continued to produce the content, create new products, and speak at events. I couldn't sleep. I was thinking about the business 24 hours a day. I didn't take vacations. Soon I hit the wall.

I burned out. The joy was gone. I debated shutting the entire site down, but instead sold it to a business associate who had worked with me on a number of projects. But the overwhelm didn't disappear. Just a few months later I sold my primary website and my entire email list to this same associate. I couldn't take it anymore. I went into 'retirement' for the next 18 months to refresh and recharge…to just take time for my wife and I alone.

I've noticed something about entrepreneurs I've worked over the years, and it was true of me as well. We have a fire inside of us to create. During that time off I relaxed, but I also wrote. The desire to get back online was strong, but this time it would be different. Besides the overwhelm, there was another issue I continually struggled with. I was bored working on just my own projects. When I came back into business, I would focus not just on my business, but I'd also coach a small group of dedicated entrepreneurs one-on-one. This would allow me to have my hands in dozens of different markets at once and see even more live test results....without having to be responsible for all of these businesses. I get to be the person behind-the-scenes.

I created MyMarketingCoach, LLC in 2006 and focused on helping entrepreneurs Earn More, Work Less, and Enjoy Life. I took several speaking engagements. What amazed me most at these events was how attendees often repeated stories I told in my emails from 2 to 6 years previously. That's how much my email stories stuck with them. They talked about my living out in the country, the horse farm next door, the Cow named Oscar, and my dogs. They remembered the stories I shared even after they forgot the lessons in the emails themselves.

I started coaching entrepreneurs one-on-one and then launched the Monthly Mentor Club in 2007. My clients sell anything from chiropractic marketing to online tennis instruction to baby diapers to paleo meals from a local restaurant owner. Whatever market you're in, it's likely either one of my private clients or one of the members in my Club is already profiting from it. My experience helping clients in a multitude of industries has shown me how to apply the same "Sell Without Selling" techniques that work in email and membership sites to other forms of online media. This includes blogging, Youtube videos, Facebook, Linkedin, Pinterest, Google Hangouts, and dozens of other ways to communicate with your audience.

Entrepreneurs are making the same mistakes with all these mediums that we made in the early days with email. I know, because my clients have now tested multiple approaches in all these markets. Each site has a few unique variations based on its culture and why people use it. For example, Youtube users are often either looking for specific how-to information or they're looking to be entertained. When marketing to them, we have to tap into these desires. People go to Facebook for the socialization aspect, and your message needs to be adjusted to appeal to this audience. We discovered these secrets by trial and error until we created a system that consistently attracts high quality leads and converts them into clients.

Clients often come to me because they're struggling to gain a foothold in their market. Or they've been making sales, but they can't seem to get that breakthrough that allows them to fully roll-out their marketing to larger audiences. The solution is often the same. They're trying to sell using old techniques that aren't optimized for online audiences. You need to sell without selling online. You'll soon see how this subtle difference in what you share and how you share it completely transforms your online results no matter what market or media you're using.

Action Steps

- Focus first on growing your list. Your relationship with your list determines your income.
- Send a mixture of stories, content, and offers to your audience. Be authentic and real.
- Make an irresistible offer to your list with a specific deadline for taking action now.

YES, This Will Work For You

Your business is different. I understand that. That's what makes the strategies I'm sharing with you so powerful. Your business is different, and we have to demonstrate that difference to your future clients. You're being turned into a commodity because everyone looks the same. The Internet has not only opened the doors for clients to be exposed to your local competitors, but now you're dealing with competition from around the world.

To the average prospect, most businesses look alike. The prospect doesn't know what they don't know. They don't even know the right questions to ask. That's why you have to position yourself as their consultant, their trusted adviser. They don't understand the root cause behind the problem they're experiencing. And they're being tossed back and forth, not knowing who to believe.

All your competitors are making similar promises. They're telling clients all about their features and benefits, but the client doesn't even know where to start. That's where you can come in as their knight in shining armor. Not only will you help them expose the true root cause of the problems they're facing, but you'll help guide them to the right solution for them personally.

Just like your business is different, your prospect sees their problem as unique. And it truly is unique in their view. Even if you've seen and helped thousands of people solve the problem before, this client is a unique individual who needs your help. They have a lifetime of experiences which has created preconceived notions about what you offer already. That's why just screaming about your benefits can't cut through the noise. They can't hear you. The words don't even mean the same thing to them. Often entrepreneurs and clients are talking right past each other because they're not even speaking the same language. This is where your Strategic Myth comes in. It becomes a story they can connect with and understand no matter their background.

But before we get to that, I want to cut through a few of the barriers which could stop you from coming on this journey with me before we even get started. I didn't write this book just to add another file to your marketing knowledge. If all I do is entertain you for a couple of hours, then I've failed in my mission. While it would be nice to entertain you, that's not my purpose.

This message is all about implementation. By the end of this book you will have identified your Ideal Client, created your Strategic Myth, outlined your content calendar, made a list of Influencers, and started reaching out to your audience. You will be attracting higher quality clients for immediate returns and long-term profits.

Nothing happens if all you do is add another file to your marketing knowledge. I've been there. My business and marketing library is extensive, and I haven't implemented even a fraction of what is contained in those books. Often it's because I had objections going into the material. I wasn't quite sure whether it would work for me and my business. I'm unique just like you are.

That's why I keep mentioning my work with clients in all different markets. Sometimes you have to dig to find the golden thread that runs through your message. It's not always easy. I'm going to ask you to think. You're going to have to investigate your business. You're going to have to ask yourself some tough questions. If you're struggling, you can ask another entrepreneur to go through this book and participate in it together. It's tough to see the forest for the trees when you're knee deep in the daily running of the business.

Of course, I also offer both private and group based coaching to help you identify and act on all the steps in this book. Visit my website, **www.MyMarketingCoach.com,** today to grab the free gifts I've reserved to help you get started.

Here are a few of the questions you may be asking yourself right now…

Isn't There Already Too Much Online Content in My Market?

Probably. But that's why you're not going to share "content" in the way most people think about it. More facts and figures aren't going to change anyone's mind. For example, if logic and numbers could do the job, there wouldn't be such division in politics. We'd all believe the same thing. But we come from varying backgrounds which causes us to look at the world with different eyes. Your unique upbringing and life experiences have created the person you are today. You are who you are based on the story of your life up till this point.

There are people out there in your market right now searching for a community they can plug into. They're looking for someone who 'gets' them. They want to connect with someone who understands what they've went through and what they're going through. They want someone who can tell them everything is going to be OK. Or they're looking for someone who can challenge them and inspire them for what's possible. Will you be that person for them?

Today is the day of the specialist. If you're in an over-competitive market, one of the secrets to growing your audience is niching down. It's counter-intuitive, but you can grow your reach by narrowing your audience. Media was dominated by a few large TV stations a few decades ago. Now there are hundreds of channels on TV, and the Internet has exponentially expanded on this growth.

There are millions of Youtube channels about everything from dog training to children opening Disney toy boxes! Yes, 'unboxing' videos of popular products in all different markets is a very profitable niche for some Youtube channel creators. People have made millions of dollars just buying stuff, opening the box, and showing you what's inside!

One of my clients, Edmund Woo, has branded himself as The Cave Gourmet. You can check him out at **saskatoonrestaurant.com/low-carb-paleo/**. He owns a fine dining restaurant that also has a paleo meal plan which has helped thousands of clients lose weight and keep it off.

Restaurant owners are busy. It's tough to eat healthy when you're on your feet all day and surrounded by gourmet food. It's easy to just grab something and munch on it. How will you get time to exercise? He bucked the trends and focused on losing weight and getting himself back into the level of fitness he had when he was young.

From there he expanded into offering paleo low carb meals to his clients. Busy professionals don't have time to cook and most restaurant meals are loaded with calories and unhealthy ingredients. He gave his clients a way to lose weight while eating meals prepared by 5 star chefs at one of the finest restaurants in town.

Weight loss is super-competitive, yet he has a unique hook of offering these ready-to-eat low carb paleo meals in his local area. It's next to impossible to get weight loss meals of this gourmet quality anywhere else.

Not only has this added an additional stream of income for his restaurant, but it has dramatically increased the local exposure of his restaurant overall.

Edmund is passionate about the healthy lifestyle and also publishes a podcast with interviews from leading experts throughout the paleo and health communities. He is just one example of how a small business owner can go past the normal strategies for growing their business, and create a unique offer that multiplies their income and their overall reach...even in super-competitive markets.

It doesn't matter how competitive your market is. You can set yourself apart by thinking strategically about your business, what you do, and who your ideal client is. It comes from finding the story behind what you do and how you do it. You're a unique individual and soon you'll be sharing a message that demonstrates what you can do for your clients.

What If You Just Don't Have the Time?

You have to invest a little time into this, but it may surprise you just how little time is actually required. One of the secrets to producing a ton of content on a limited time frame is through interviews. Write down the questions your clients regularly ask you. And write down the questions they should be asking you! Have someone interview you on audio for 20 to 30 minutes each month. Those audio interviews can be turned into multiple shorter 3 to 5 minute videos (one for each question). They can be transcribed and turned into written content. You're the expert who produces the content, but the distribution can be handed off to others for minimal fees.

If you can't invest this small amount of time, then I have to question whether you're serious about your success. Too many entrepreneurs are satisfied with feast and famine cycles. When they have too much business, they complain about not having the time to market. Inevitably this lack of marketing eventually leads them into a famine situation. And they can't understand why all their leads dried up! Sharing your message consistently smooths out these curves and keeps the lead flow turned on.

Of course, if you have more time, you can experience even greater results. Once you get into the groove and know what to write, most people can write profitable emails in 15 to 30 minutes each. You're not producing an encyclopedia or even a feature article for a magazine. You're sharing a tip or a few steps along with a portion of your story in each email. It's like a little, running commentary on how your products and services can help your clients.

What If You Don't Have the Money for Marketing Online?

That's what's beautiful about online marketing. You can start campaigns with a tiny daily budget. I've had clients who started Facebook and/or Youtube advertising with a budget of $5 to $10 per day! And even with that tiny of a budget, they can see signs of life in the campaign in just a few days. Compare that to virtually any other form of advertising. You might spend thousands on a newspaper ad or billboard. And you have no clue just how productive it will be. With online advertising, you get to see the exact results from each ad individually.

John Wanamaker would have LOVED the Internet. He is credited with the quote, *"Half my advertising is wasted. I just don't know which half."* With the tracking available to us online, not only can you see which ads are working and which ones aren't, but you can identify down to the exact keywords that are producing leads and clients for you. Turn off the losers and ramp up the budget on the winners. Out of several $5 daily campaigns, we might turn off 2 of them. The third one does well and we bump it to $10 a day…then $20, $40, $80, $160, and on up. We keep an eye on the numbers and raise the budget every few days only when it continues to generate profits.

Investing is a shortcut to results online, but you don't have to spend any money on advertising if you don't want. You can rely on the relationships you build with influencers. You can produce additional content that attracts organic searches. You can invest time in Facebook groups or Linkedin groups to help your ideal clients directly. Attracting leads requires an investment of either time or money, but the beauty is you can choose the right balance and mix for where you are right now.

What If You Don't Have Any Ideas For Content To Create?

First apply the 'Question' trick. Write down all the questions clients are already asking you. Once you finish, take a short break for a few minutes. Then come back and write down all the questions clients should be asking you. Just going through this exercise should give you enough material for the next few months or even the next year. Once you get started putting yourself out there, your audience will ask you additional questions. You can keep the system rolling by answering questions that come in.

If you feel you're not able to come up with enough questions initially, go over to Amazon and search for books about your subject. You can generate ideas for 'questions' to answer by going through the table of contents of bestselling books or reading the reviews of those books. You can access Amazon's Search Inside feature by clicking the image of the book itself. Scan through the table of contents. The chapter titles reveal many of the topics you want to cover. The value you share will be different from these books because it's coming from your viewpoint and experience. But the overall 'questions' being answered will be the same.

You can also get ideas for what to create by reading through the reviews. What do they like about the book? What did they learn in it? They're telling you exactly what is most important to them. What don't they like about the book? What is missing from the book? Both the good reviews and the bad reviews will leave you clues about the type of content the audience wants. As we get deeper into the research chapter, you'll discover even more ways to find ideas just sitting out there for you in cyberspace.

What If There Isn't Anything Truly Unique About You and Your Business?

I've heard this one many times from clients. It's never been true. Not once. There is always a unique story you can tap into about your business. There's a reason why you got into this business. Something motivated you to choose this path. It wasn't just about the money. It may have been to solve a problem you personally had. For example, I went to a chiropractor for years who became a chiropractor because he had suffered from TMJ.

He was going to medical school and was injured by an elbow to the face during a basketball game. He suffered with this pain for months and his doctors weren't able to help. He went to a chiropractor and was shocked by the results. This experience changed his path in life and he choose to become a chiropractor instead. I know this story because he shared it across his advertising. It was part of why he does what he does. Even though other chiropractors may offer the exact same type of treatments, he shares a personal story that attracts his ideal clients.

You may respond that you don't have an interesting story to tell, but in 20 years of working with clients I've never found that to be true. There is always an interesting story hidden in what you do. It may take some soul searching to find it. You might need to have a friend or coach interview you to pull it out. You've lived with your story every single day, so it often doesn't jump out at you personally. But someone else, especially someone experienced at interviewing, will be immediately curious to know more when they stumble upon the '*hook*.'

What makes you unique may come so naturally to you that it doesn't look special at all. Ask friends, family, and co-workers what they rely on you for. Send them an email about this. What do they see as coming naturally to you? What do you seem to do better or easier than others? You're going to be tempted to be humble and not accept their answers. You may think your results come from hard work. I'm sure that's true, but don't discount the possibility you have something extra special that gives you an advantage. Everyone has it. We just need to find yours and share it with the world.

What If You've Already Tried This and It Didn't Work For You?

You may have tried "*content marketing*" because everyone is talking about it today. Or you may have set up a blog and participated on social media sites, but we're not talking about getting likes, shares, or comments. What you're learning in this book is about attracting more paying clients for whatever you offer. And not just any clients, you're after high quality clients. These are clients who will pay your premium fees because they care about the end results.

Most content marketing is simply shotgun marketing. You're putting content out onto the Internet. That doesn't work. At least it doesn't work anymore. In the early days of the Internet, it was so new that 'good enough' content could get attention. Today even great content won't grab attention unless it has the extra special sauce behind it. If the content is not mixed in with a bulls-eye strategy and connected to your ongoing story, it won't attract and hold the attention of your ideal client.

Take the time to go through this book. Follow the exercises in the Strategic Myth chapter. If you're going to do this at all, take the time to do it right. The Strategic Myth is the foundation behind everything else you do. If you try to move forward with just the tactical elements without getting the strategy right, it simply won't click for you. It's like trying to build a home without laying the proper foundation first. Sure, you may save money while you're putting it up, but I don't want to be the one living in it!

What If You Already Have All the Clients You Can Handle?

This question goes beyond the scope of this book. It's something I help both my one-on-one clients and my group coaching clients with at **www.mymarketingcoach.com**. My first question would be whether you're happy with your current client base? If you were to grade your clients on a scale of A-B-C-D-F, how many of them would you qualify as A and B clients? This means they're enjoyable to work with. They're not demanding. They're happy with the results from your products and services. They pay on time. They refer others to you.

If the majority of your clients fall into this category, you deserve congratulations. You're already ahead of 99%+ of the businesses out there. But if they don't, if you have F, D, or even C clients that don't meet the above qualifications, you can use this system to attract higher quality clients to your business. Often you may accept working with low quality clients because you feel trapped. You don't have enough high quality clients coming through your door. You're stuck with clients that drain your energy instead of filling you with energy.

Your energy levels themselves are often one of the greatest gauges of how well you're flowing inside your mission. When you're passionate about your mission and message, you attract clients who want to be a part something bigger than themselves. These clients add to your life in more ways than just money. I love the clients I work with. My systems sort and sift leads. By the time a client ascends through my different products and services and works with me personally, they're often a perfect fit. They're the kind of person I enjoy working with and they add energy to my life.

Examine your energy levels. How do you feel after you interact with each client? Are you better off after each one? Sure, you may get physically tired and a little drained, but there's a feeling of joy and satisfaction deep down inside you because of who you're helping and what you've done for them. If you're not feeling that for each client, ask yourself why. Something needs to change. Fire some of those 'low energy' clients. Replace them by generating more, higher quality leads and clients.

By the end of this book, you will know how to generate more leads. You will know how to generate higher quality leads. And you will know how to 'sell' to them without selling. They'll sell themselves on what you offer as you simply share your message and the story behind your message. You're adding value to their life instead of taking away from their life. And they walk away better off for having met you whether they ever chose to purchase from you or not.

Action Steps

- No matter what type of business you're in, you can apply these principles to attract high quality clients who are willing to pay premium prices for the results you deliver.
- One of the quickest ways to come up with content ideas is to make a list of questions your audience is asking. Take a short break and then write down all the questions they should be asking.
- Give those questions to a partner and have them interview you on audio to create the initial content for your website.
- Take honest stock of your current client base. How many of them fit into the A and B categories, and which ones are C level or below?

Proven 5 Step Persuasion Formula

There is a simple 5 step formula at work behind every transaction where money changes hands. Gaining a basic understanding of this formula and how to use it can boost the results you're getting from everything you do in your business, both on and off the Internet.

Customers will buy from your website. Subscribers will open, read, and click the links in your emails. Influencers will be more likely to share your content with their audience. And this formula even influences persuasion outside the business world. You'll find your persuasion skills increasing in your daily life, such as trying to convince your children to make the right choices.

Dr. Glenn Livingston and I first shared this formula in our high-end Total Conversion Code training course. It came from going back over years of reviewing websites and other forms of advertising to find the most important persuasion elements. Why does one website convert visitors into buyers and another one doesn't? What pieces of the puzzle do all the winning ads have in common?

The understanding behind this system came from years of reviewing websites for clients and doing 'hot seats' at workshops. I've been asked to review hundreds of websites by attendees at workshops. When you're reviewing a website and need to improve the results in 15 minutes or less in front of a live audience, you need a way to spot the conversion cracks that are sabotaging their results quickly. This 5 step formula is the outgrowth of all those reviews along with testing hundreds of variables online to find out exactly what works and what doesn't.

The beauty of this system is in its simplicity. Dr. Glenn Livingston and I call it the Golden Glove. It's based on the five fingers of your hand. That way you always have a reminder with you of the 5 steps as you count them off. If your website, emails, webinars, videos, blog posts, speeches, letters, or any other form of marketing is missing one or more of these elements, you're sacrificing your persuasion power.

You have to be careful you don't gloss over these points because they're so simple and easy to use. As I share each step, you'll be tempted to say, "*I already knew that.*" Intellectually I'm sure you've encountered and likely understand each of these points. The question is whether you're making sure to include them every time? There is a pattern behind the choices people make and products they purchase. It's not random even though it seems like it at times.

People don't buy based purely on logical reasons. In fact, they buy based off emotion first. In the end, when you cut through all the noise, you'll find people buy because of how it makes them feel about themselves. One of the biggest markets in the world now is anti-aging. Feel young again. Remove the wrinkles. Sixty is the new forty. They want that feeling of vibrancy and youth. They're nostalgic for the past.

Let's transition to one of the hardest transactions to make. In a business, you're providing an exchange of value. A CPA does your taxes, handles bookkeeping, or helps you understand the numbers in your business. They're paid for the value they provide. It's the same whether you're a real estate agent helping a customer sell their home or a bakery selling wedding cakes, clients pay you for the value you provide. But what about a charity? They're asking for their donors to give money without any value exchange. They're giving out of the goodness of their heart. Perhaps there is a token gift provided to donors or they honor their name somewhere for the donation, but the no real value is being exchanged.

Why does someone give to charity? They give because of how it makes them feel about themselves. They feel good providing for the needs of others. It's an investment based on emotion. There is no 'logical' exchange of value here.

I brought up donations to charity to demonstrate two factors. First of all, when we talk about the emotional component behind persuasion, this is neither good or evil on its own. It can be used for good when value is provided to client or when the money goes to good use helping others. It would be evil if those same emotions were used to manipulate a client to act against their own interest. It's all based on the motives behind your persuasion.

The second reason I bring in donations to charity is to demonstrate how persuasion can work even in the most difficult transactions. What could be more difficult than asking people to give their hard earned money in exchange for 'nothing' in return? They do it because they care and the transaction makes them feel good about themselves and their place in the world.

In 2015, an estimated \$373 billion was given to charity in the USA (source: Giving USA: The Annual Report on Philanthropy). You will see all of the 5 fingers of the Golden Glove at work in these appeals by charities around the world, just like they're in action for business transactions and even day-to-day persuasion with those around you.

Here are the five fingers of the Golden Glove:

- Desperate Problem
- Unique Promise
- Overwhelming Proof
- Irresistible Offer
- Reason to Act Now

You can follow along with me as I go through each of these points. Pull up one of your websites, emails, or ads. Or if you're going to be producing a new ad for your business soon, you can create an initial outline of what you must include as we go through these steps. Every effective presentation will integrate in these points, and they all fit together like fingers in a glove.

Desperate Problem

The first finger of the Golden Glove serves two critical functions and sets the tone for everything else. The first step is to define the audience you're addressing. Who are you speaking to? If you try to reach everyone, you'll end up speaking to no one in particular. You need to clearly define the audience and how they already feel about this situation.

I don't do a lot of public speaking outside of online webinars because I'm not big on travel. But when I've done presentations I always ask the host to tell me as much as they can about the audience. In addition, I'll show up early if possible so I can mingle with the attendees and ask them why they came to this event. What specifically did they desire to learn and accomplish? The insights you can gain from speaking to multiple attendees for a few minutes each will allow you to customize your presentation to speak directly to them.

The better you define your audience, the easier it is to speak to them. For example, I've worked with multiple clients who sell health and weight loss products, both courses and supplements. We'll often advertise to male and female audiences separately (*this is easy to do with ads on Google, Youtube, and Facebook*). These audiences have different motivations and we can better serve our clients by focusing on separate messages. At times, we'll even create two separate email lists for these audiences so our messages can be custom tailored for them.

An advanced marketing tactic you may consider as your business grows is introducing additional segments in your email follow-up and other sequences. For example, a CPA would want to break out their clients into personal tax clients and business tax clients. Marketing material that appeals to the business clients would be wasted if also delivered to the personal clients. They could further segment their audience into large businesses, medium businesses, and small businesses. Or they might separate them out into industry categories such as chiropractors. They could create marketing materials specifically to appeal to chiropractors in their area. They would end up generating a much higher conversion rate because they zeroed in on a specific market with similar problems and offered them a custom solution that was just right for them and their needs.

That brings us to the 2nd step of the Desperate Problem. Identify a pain point you can help your audience solve. Describe the problem and the repercussions of this problem in detail. How is this problem influencing the life of your potential client? What frustrations are they experiencing? What are they tolerating that could be fixed? What are they laying in bed at night worrying about? What are the end results of this problem if it's not fixed?

There are really only two motivations in life: pain or pleasure. Of these two, pain is a much stronger motivation. You can see this demonstrated with health issues. While everyone would like to be healthy and live to a ripe old age, it's difficult to motivate yourself into action on this goal. It's tough to sell people on prevention. But as soon as pain enters the picture, that's when people are motivated to take action. Go to the doctor. Take the medication. And if the problem is painful enough, perhaps even modify their nutrition.

It's hard to educate people and sell them on prevention of a future problem. Persuasion is much more effective when it taps into a current problem they're already experiencing. Eugene Schwartz said, "*Copy cannot create desire for a product. It can only take the hopes, dreams, fears, and desires that already exist in the hearts of millions of people, and focus those already-existing desires onto a particulate product.*"

Don't waste your time with anyone who talks about 'mind control' in relation to marketing. We can't control anyone's mind, nor would we want to. Instead all we do is tap into desires they already have and focus them on our solution. We zero in on a desperate problem they're already experiencing. We shine our light on that problem. We often define it in a new way and then as we move into the unique promise we'll share how to eliminate that problem.

How deep you go into the problem depends on what you're selling and how well your audience already understands the problem. You will often go into more detail about the problem when you're offering something like an information product or a done-for-you service compared to a physical product. An information product is a difficult purchase, because most people don't want to learn. The average person out on the street doesn't want to read a book to improve their business. They have to be reminded of just how bad the problem is to motivate them to not only purchase the book, but even more so to read it and apply it to their life.

A done-for-you service is often a higher ticket offer. Several of my clients offer pay-per-click management services on Facebook and Google. They will often demonstrate all the steps that go into setting up and optimizing an account. The 'desperate problem' is the client wants high quality traffic without spending a fortune for it. They could run ads themselves, but they'd have to follow all these steps which they simply don't have time for. My clients show the steps involved and how important they are as part of talking about the problem. It's NOT easy to generate high quality leads online.

Apple doesn't go into all the problems you may experience by not having a computer when they're demonstrating their Macbook Pro. Instead they focus on the problems in comparison to a PC you may already have or have been considering. They talk about how the PC software and hardware doesn't integrate well together. They might demonstrate how easy it is to use their tools in comparison to the difficulty on a PC. The consumers they're marketing to already know the importance of having a computer, so they focus their presentation on the pain points where PC's may be failing their customers.

You might argue that your offer doesn't solve a desperate problem at all. Maybe you provide guitar lessons or sell guitars. That's not a desperate problem, is it? It is for those who think about playing the guitar all the time. They're spending money on lessons and not getting anywhere. They think about playing the guitar while they're at work. They fiddle around it with when they get home. They're watching videos about playing the guitar on Youtube. They invest time in this dream, but they're not making the progress they want! It's a desperate problem because they need your help.

There is a popular formula used by copywriters called Problem-Agitate-Solve. You bring up the problem. You agitate the problem by looking at it from every possible direction. Once the reader understands the problem in detail and all the long-term effects of it, then you share your unique solution.

The basic question you ask yourself to uncover your Desperate Problem is, *"Who is this for and what problem are you solving for them?"*

Unique Promise

Next you make a unique promise that stands out from the competition. This is directly connected to your desperate problem. If you struggle to come up with a unique promise, often you haven't fully defined the Desperate Problem you solve. In fact, all three of the "P's" are connected to one another. You're making a unique promise to solve their desperate problem, and you back up that promise with overwhelming proof. Make the strongest promise you can prove!

There are two types of benefits in every market. "Price of Entry" benefits are promises that everyone in the industry has to make to even be considered an option by the client. For example, a plumber has to be able to fix leaks. If they can't fix your toilet, they're not even in the running. That is a price of entry benefit. What sets you apart in the market is a 'Point of Difference" benefit. That same plumber may promise to show up within 30 minutes of the agreed upon time or the job is free.

That would be a unique point of difference because not only does it stand out from what all the other plumbers offer, but it also pinpoints one of the frustrations clients have in that market. How many times have you heard people complain about plumbers being late? If your toilet is overflowing, you don't want to wait! This is a Unique Promise because it speaks directly to the Desperate Problem.

My client Edmund Woo who I introduced earlier offers a unique promise for his weight loss clients. In weight loss, everyone has to give you a system that helps you lose weight without being hungry. That's a price of entry benefit. For his local clients, his restaurant actually prepares the low carb paleo meals for them. All the meals are pre-cooked and ready to warm-up and eat. All his clients have to do is eat the chef prepared food and watch the pounds melt away. That's about as unique of a promise as possible. The work is already done for you.

Here are two of the tricks my clients and I have used to come up with our Unique Promise:

Method #1: Make a Strong Guarantee

What kind of guarantee could you offer? For example, Best Buy was getting crushed by showrooming (*where a customer picks out a product at a local store but then buys it online for the lower price*). They came out with their "Price Match Guarantee" which promises to match the price of any local competitor and even the large online retailers like Amazon.com. If a plumber guaranteed to be on-time, that would also be a guarantee example.

Method #2: Create a Comparison Chart

You've probably seen comparison charts before, especially when buying software. The chart lists the features and benefits along the left side of the chart. You compare your products with several of the other most popular options by check marking the features each of you have. The charts are designed to demonstrate how your product beats the competition. Most commonly we use the chart on our websites in software and done-for-you service sales.

Clients and I have put together a chart like this privately to help us find the Unique Promise we can offer, even if we never intend to show the chart to others. By going down the list of features and benefits, you can discover where you have the advantage over the competition. The best unique promises focus on something that matches up with the desperate problem your clients are trying to solve. For example, if your research, which we'll cover in the next chapter, reveals that customers are most upset about competitive solutions durability, you could focus on how you have the longest warranty in the industry.

Your Unique Promise question is, *"Why should they choose your solution compared to every other option in the market?"*

Overwhelming Proof

You've laid out the desperate problem in detail, and you've made a unique promise about how you have a better solution than any other option. Now you have to prove it! The amount of proof required depends on the relationship you have with the prospect up till now. If they were referred to you by one of their best friends, the burden of proof may be low. Their friend's referral is enough proof for them, if they trust their friend! But if they're a cold lead, that hurdle is going to be much higher.

The first form of proof everyone thinks about are testimonials. Have you produced similar results for others? That's another little tip for finding your unique promise. Look through all of your current testimonials. Why did they purchase from you? Why do they recommend others buy from you? If you tie your unique promise into your current testimonials, you already have the proof to back up the promise you make.

Testimonials are only one form of proof. Your personal story can be a form of proof also. For example, I'll often mention that I got started online in 1996. That's over 21 years of experience in online marketing. There aren't many other business coaches who can match that. In addition to personal experience, you may have spaghetti after your name that demonstrates your credibility. This includes your degrees, certifications, and past work experience.

Have you appeared on popular TV, radio programs, or podcasts? You've probably seen media logos on some of the websites you've visited. You use the text, "As seen on..." with the media where you've appeared. You're applying the 'halo' effect where you're tapping into their credibility. If you have endorsements or you've spoken alongside well-known names in your industry, you can use those as part of your proof also. For example, when sending out emails to 'influencers' which we'll do later in this book, you could mention other experts you've worked with in the past. Name dropping can get your foot in the door even though they've never heard of you personally.

Are there any scientific studies that either back-up the problem you identified as the real problem or back-up the promises you've made? I'll often look for quotes from expert resources such as government studies or high-level research conducted by Universities, Hospitals, or other credible institutions.

One of the most powerful forms of proof is a demonstration. Vendors give away free samples at the grocery store. They're giving a taste test of their product. The auto dealer lets you take a test drive. The retailer may demonstrate all the product features in store. An infomercial shows you the product in action multiple times during their program. We can model that process online also. If you have a physical product, use videos to show it in action. That's one of the most powerful uses of video online. My clients have used videos to show the food they prepare, how software works, and even a tour around the inside of a membership site.

Consultants and coaches often deliver a 'free demonstration' session. You get your first session for free to demonstrate the value they can deliver. I've trained dozens of business coaches and one of the methods I shared with them was the free discovery session. You invite your potential client on the call and you interview them. You ask them questions to determine the desperate problems they want solved. Then you go into questions about the available resources to solve those problems.

Together you come up with a step-by-step system for delivering the end results. At the end of the call, you share your rates and ask the potential client if they would like your help in implementing the advice. They could follow the system you shared on the call themselves if they choose, but it will be so much easier having you alongside to help them. The beauty of this type of 'selling system' is that you're not selling at all. You're simply delivering value in advance. You're selling without selling.

You can also use this demonstration model to build credibility with a mass audience. Several of the coaches I work with initially offered free sessions to their subscribers on the agreement they could record the session. They use those recorded coaching sessions as content they send out to their free email list. Each coaching session is another demonstration of their methods. After they recorded enough free sessions to prove the value to their audience, they started charging for their initial session. Their initial session which used to be free is now $50, $75, or $200. They have proof from all the recordings to back-up their value.

This is also where we create and distribute content to our list, on a blog, or through social media. You're demonstrating your proof by providing value in advance. There are some clients who purchase from me within minutes whenever I send out a new offer to my list. They don't take time to read my website or watch my video. They see the email, click the link, and purchase. They know from experience that I deliver value to their life. That long-term relationship is all the proof they need to make a purchase.

Higher ticket purchases require more proof than lower ticket ones. It doesn't require a lot of proof to get someone to give you their email address. If they think you may have the answer and that you'll protect their information, they give it a try. It's the same with a $20 book. There's not a lot of risk here. If you're asking them to invest $10,000 with you, now you're going to have to prove it. You might even need to stair step them up to this purchase. It's tough to make that kind of sale directly from a website. Instead, you generate leads you speak to over the phone or possibly even in person first. That ability to connect with you personally gets you over the hurdle of making the higher ticket sale.

The question you ask yourself about proof is, *"Why should they believe the solution is for real, you're a credible person to purchase from, and the solution will work for them personally?"*

31

Irresistible Offer

It doesn't matter whether you're selling a bargain basement appliance or a brand new Porsche. The client wants to feel they walked away with a great deal. You might do this by discounting your offer below the price of the competition, but that's only one possible method. When selling information products, we'll often add a "Bonus Overload." That's where you add in several bonuses worth more than the cost of the product itself.

For example, when someone joins my Monthly Mentor Club at **www.MonthlyMentorClub.com**, they receive multiple bonus gifts immediately. These include a video training on how to increase the sales of your website by spotting and fixing your conversion cracks, a special report on how brand new beginners can get started online without a product or service, and a guide to generating highly qualified traffic by buying banner ads at 'wholesale' prices. That's in addition to the monthly webinars and special issue I create each month. You're being 'overloaded' with bonuses just for giving the Club a try...and you're backed by a full 30 day money back guarantee.

A chiropractor I've worked with offered an initial visit for just $17. This included your examination, x-rays if needed, and your first adjustment. This was a discounted rate designed to get you through the door. At times he even offered this package totally free to get people through the door, especially for higher dollar conditions. The lifetime value of a client in his practice could easily equal $4,000 to $5,000 and up (*lifetime value of a client is the total billings you generate over the lifetime of doing business with a client*). Offering a reduced fee first session or even a free session was worth it as a loss leader to generate a new client.

Where does this offer fit in your overall funnel? You might create your own loss leader to get customers through the door. Retailers offer door busters during Black Friday sales to get you into their store. Consultants and coaches do their free discovery session. A dentist might offer a discount exam or teeth whitening. The restaurant might give you a free entrée on your birthday because they know you'll bring someone else with you.

At the other end of the offer spectrum, you may have your high value offers which have a much lower volume. For a dentist, this may include cosmetic surgery. For a coach, it could be the corporate package which they coach 10 executives in the company for $10,000 a month. For a real estate agent, it could be the five million dollar home. For a manufacturer, it could be getting your product into a major retailer such as

Walmart. For a website selling project management software, this could be a corporation purchasing a license for 1,000 of their employees.

Most businesses have the opportunity to have a Value Ladder with multiple offers and price points throughout their funnels. You have to get people through the door initially with an Irresistible Offer that's virtually risk-free to them. You continue to provide value at each step up the ladder, as they purchase additional products and services from you.

Here are a few of the ways you can make your offers stand out:

- **Soft Offer**: We'll bill you later. This is the ultimate risk-free offer, but can be tough to collect.
- **Low Cost Trial**: Pay $1, $4.95, or just shipping. Billed later. Often doubles or triples response.
- **FREE Shipping**: Improves the sales on any physical product. Better results than discounting.
- **Fast Delivery**: Amazon.com's bread-and-butter offer of 2 day shipping or even 1 hour shipping!
- **Base/Deluxe/Premium**: Offer 2 to 3 simple options. Increases sales and profits per sale.
- **Custom Offer**: Add a consultation. Engrave the product. Build the custom computer.
- **Online Demonstration**: Have them register for a free "tour" of your product or software.
- **Premiums**: In these cases, you sell your bonuses even greater than the product itself.
- **Payments**: Offer easy monthly payments where many people look at payment price only.
- **Outrageous Guarantees**: Double your money back. Performance guarantees.

Here's how to create your Irresistible Offer. First, describe your offer. What does the client get? What bonuses go along with the product? With information products, I'll often offer Cheat Sheets or templates because these are high-value items people often want more than the infoproduct itself. Set the price. This includes any payment plans or trial offers and free shipping. State your guarantee. How do you remove all the risk from the customer?

In every transaction, there is some risk. Your goal is to transfer as much of the risk as possible to yourself. Yes, some people might take advantage of your generous guarantees. They might even 'abuse' you. Think about how you could limit the abuse (for example even a generous retailer such as Zappos who offers free shipping both ways doesn't allow you to wear the shoes outside if you're going to return them).

You can offer conditional guarantees where the customer needs to use the product itself. My clients often do this with coaching groups. They require the client to show the steps they put into action before receiving a guarantee. In spite of this, you'll still have some refunds. Compute these in as a cost of doing business. A guarantee, especially if the competitors don't have one, is a powerful way to attract new customers into your business. You simply have to make sure the numbers work.

The question you ask with the Irresistible offer is, "*How can you make it more painful for them to walk away than to purchase your offer?*"

Reason to Act Now

What will a client lose out on if they don't act now? What's at stake here? This could be as simple as reminding them of the problem. What will happen if they allow the problem to continue? Will it get worse? If so, how will it get worse? The fear of loss is stronger than the desire for gain.

This is even more effective if there is a hard deadline coming soon or a limited number available. For example, I only accept a limited number of one-on-one coaching clients. This means my coaching program is often sold-out and prospects have to enter their name and email list on the waiting list for when slots become available. When I email this list and let them know about the availability, they almost always sell out within 24 hours. Sometimes they sell out in 15 minutes! This is real scarcity. There is only one of me! I can only handle a limited number of clients while living the Internet Lifestyle. I'm not going to give up my lifestyle just to take on a few additional clients.

A specific deadline for your offer can be just as effective. Retailers run limited time discount specials every major holiday (*and minor ones too*). They can create buying frenzies with a strong enough offer and limited availability. It seems like there is a 'hot' toy that's hard to find in stock every Christmas season. Black Friday has specials that only last till noon. Many of my clients run 3 to 7 day specials to their email lists. On a special like this, we'll generate around 1/3rd of the sales on the first day, 1/3rd to ½ of the sales on the last day, and a small percentage of the sales throughout the rest of the week. They jump on the offer when they first hear about it or they wait till close to the deadline.

I've had specials where the majority of clients waited till the last day to purchase. I call this the 'heart attack curve.' It seems like the offer bombed completely and nobody took advantage of it. Then a flood of orders come in on the last day. They were waiting until the deadline motivated them to take action.

Authentic scarcity is a powerful motivator to action. I'd never recommend making up fake scarcity. If you say the special lasts till Sunday at midnight, then program your shopping cart to end the special on Sunday at midnight. No moving the goal posts. Some clients even offer a new subscriber special. We make an Irresistible Offer to new subscribers and program the email list and cart to only offer the special for a limited number of days such as 7 to 10 days after each new subscriber joins.

If you offer coupons, put a deadline on them. You wouldn't want to redeem that coupon ten years from now when inflation has doubled your prices. So tell them when the special ends. And the closer the deadline, the more effective it is as a sales tool. Of course be careful if you're mailing out specials or coupons. Snail mail can be unreliable and you're not sure exactly when it will be delivered, so give clients a little more time with anything sent in the mail.

You might respond that you don't like setting deadlines because you don't want to be pushy. You don't want to be an aggressive sales person. I understand and agree. I wasn't comfortable setting deadlines on my offers initially either. I didn't change my tune until I saw just how effective they were at motivating people to take action. And it's not about being pushy. You've set the deadline based on the special you're offering. I can only take a limited number of clients. The scarcity is real. There is only one of me. When I offer a discount off one of my products, it is only available for that limited time frame.

Think back to your own purchases that were made on a deadline. Maybe you bought it during Black Friday. Or you purchased it on CyberMoney. I went to a Ford dealer where there was a $2,000 rebate which would expire at the end of the month. They weren't pushy at all. Surprising for a dealer! I didn't purchase on my first visit, but I used that rebate deadline as my incentive for when I had to make a decision. I went back to the dealership and purchased before the deadline.

I remember searching for new homes. There was one particular house I wish I would have made an offer on sooner. If my real estate agent would have been pushy, I would have complained about her being too salesy. But after missing out on this house (*someone else purchased it*), I wish we would have discussed more just how great of a deal it was at the time. Reiterating the reason to act now would have been a valuable service in that situation even if I, the client, wouldn't have realized it at the time. I missed out because I waited.

Are you failing your clients because you don't stress to them the importance of making a decision or acting decisively? Don't be pushy. Don't make up fake scarcity. Make sure they have all the facts to make a quality decision. And a deadline for that decision can be a key aspect here. If you're speaking to someone on the phone and they want to think about it, get a commitment from them about when you should call them back. So even if there isn't a 'deadline' for the offer, you're still motivating them to talk about when they'll make a decision. It's easy to put off a decision until another day…and it's possible they'll miss out on the benefits you offer forever.

The question to ask yourself about the Reason to Act Now is, "*Why must they take action today?*"

Putting It All Together

You now have the five fingers of the golden glove:

- Desperate Problem
- Unique Promise
- Overwhelming Proof
- Irresistible Offer
- Reason to Act Now

Now is the perfect time to put these 5 steps into action. If you own a website, review it using each of these five fingers. Is it obvious who you're speaking to and what problem you can help them solve? If not, what can you say to further identify your audience? Can you add additional details about the problem? For example, have you personally suffered with the problem and could mention your own experience?

Do you make a unique promise that stands out from the competition? Would a visitor land on your web page and say, "*I haven't heard that before…Tell me more?*" If you're saying the exact same thing as everyone else in your market, then it's easier to just click away than dig any deeper.

Do you back up your promises with proof? You could feature a few testimonials or share your experience in helping others get results. Or you could provide a video demonstration of your product or service in action. Or you can quote scientific studies that back up your claims. The stronger your promise, the stronger your proof needs to be to back it up.

What irresistible offer are you making? The offer depends on where someone is in your funnel. If they're brand new to your website, it could be an offer as simple as a free 10% off coupon for subscribing to your email list. Or it could be a free report or free white paper for subscription. Or you offer a discount on the first sale to get customers in the door. Maybe you offer FREE shipping if they purchase $25 worth of products. The goal of the first sale is simply to 'buy' a new client. It's not about maximum profits here. It's about starting a relationship that can expand into long-term profits from additional offers in the future.

Do you have a reason for them to act now? This can be more difficult to do on a website compared to an email. You can easily send out an email with a deadline for your special that ends in just a few days. You likely don't want to update your website that often. On a website you can point back to what they miss out on by not making a decision today. How will the situation get worse or what are they losing by putting off the decision?

You can review your website, emails, webinars, or any other marketing material for its Persuasion Power. You can also use the Golden Glove to create an outline for your message. As a quick example, I'm going to write a quick Golden Glove Outline for this book itself. This will be the initial rough draft version of my message which will be further optimized on my websites and other marketing materials. I want you to see what the initial brainstorming may look like when you put it together.

- **Desperate Problem**: Entrepreneurs struggling to generate leads, sales, and clients without being salesy. You may have tried worn-out sales approaches that simply don't work on today's better informed clients. Or you've tried content marketing only to find it takes too much time and money to cut through the noise in your over-competitive market.
- **Unique Promise:** Attract high quality clients with a simple step-by-step system to reach your ideal client, share a message they will passionately embrace, and earn more while working less in your business…all without compromising your values.

- **Overwhelming Proof**: I went from delivering pizzas for a living to creating my first online business in 1996. Over the past 20+ years, I've helped thousands of entrepreneurs just like you create "Lifestyle Businesses" in virtually every market. Show testimonials from my clients.
- **Irresistible Offer**: You get 20 years of my knowledge and systems condensed into one easy-to-read book with action steps at the end of every chapter. In addition, you can connect with me and get even more ways to improve your business at **www.MyMarketingCoach.com**.
- **Reason to Act Now**: The Internet is only going to get more competitive in the future. You're falling further behind each day you ignore these systems. In addition, I'll run a limited time special bonus package at launch and at other special intervals.

That is rough, but it was intended to be. It was the very first outline I created for the book marketing message. The key principle here is to think about each piece in the puzzle when you are creating your marketing. Have you identified your audience and are you speaking to a problem that's important to them? Is your promise unique in some way? Do you have the proof to back it up? What is your offer (*the higher priced your offer is, the stronger this has to be*)? And is there a reason for your clients to act now? The easiest response is to simply do nothing. If you care about their results and you have a product that can effectively solve their problem, you owe it to them to motivate them into action.

The Missing Link to Motivating Your Clients

The Golden Glove helps you spot the 5 most important elements of persuasion, but it's still possible to leave out one of the core components that motivate people to action. You and I, along with our audiences, are not primarily motivated by logic and reason. They definitely have a factor in our decision making process, but they're ineffective on their own. They speak to rational "left" side of our brain. Decisions are initially made by the "right" side of your brain, the creative side that controls your imagination. Influence is based first on emotion, and it's backed up by logic.

The secret to multiplying your persuasion powers tenfold is communicating through stories. People don't need more information today. They're overwhelmed by information. Facts don't influence someone to action until they change the story that's going on inside their heads. They'll simply take the facts you give them and try to twist those facts into their current story.

For example, if one of the stories inside you is that rich people all take advantage of people and successful salespeople always manipulate their customers, it doesn't really matter how much information I share with you. It can't be turned into action because what I'm sharing with you goes against your core beliefs. You likely wouldn't have picked up this book unless there was hope though. That's why I have and will continue to share stories throughout of those who care about their clients. They've found an audience they can help and they're sharing a message of hope with that audience.

If your internal story is that making sales requires manipulating people, you will struggle to put any of these techniques into action. We have to change that internal story first. Yes, some salespeople manipulate people and take advantage of them. But thankfully, that's becoming more and more difficult in our day. Authenticity gives you the advantage in a world surrounded by social media and clients who are better informed than any other time in history.

By understanding basic persuasion skills, you can share content and value that improves the lives of your audience even if they never purchased from you. You can not only make sales of your products and services, but you can do good in the world at the same time. That's a totally different story than you've likely heard in the past. Taking that new story to heart is key for achieving results. Otherwise, it's like trying to drive with the emergency brake on. You might get somewhere, but you have unnecessary resistance that's going to constantly hold you back and eventually cause mechanical failure.

Your clients also have a story they identify with about the problem and possibly why other solutions haven't worked for them. You have to give them a new story. It's a story about how you or your clients have faced similar situations and overcame. It's a story about conflict and challenges, but you overcame. You discovered a new and better way. And that solution is available to others today. If you want to motivate your client to action, you first have to change the story in their heart.

In the next chapter, we'll get to know your Ideal Client better. We'll discover the story that drives them currently. And we'll make sure our message matches where they currently are.

Action Steps

- Analyze one of your current websites or marketing pieces using the 5 fingers of the Golden Glove: Desperate Problem, Unique Promise, Overwhelming Proof, Irresistible Offer, and Reason to Act Now.
- The most common mistake is hiding your proof. How can you add additional proof and credibility to your website or marketing piece with your personal story, testimonials, or some kind of demonstration?
- Now create a quick Golden Glove outline for an offer you have coming up in the near future.

How to Fall In Love With Your Clients

One of the biggest mistakes you can make in business is falling in love with your product or service. I've seen would-be entrepreneurs beat their head against a brick wall for years. They were convinced everyone needed their product. It doesn't matter what you feel people 'need.' It only matters what they want to buy. As a small business, you can't afford to change your audiences' wants and desires. It's your job to identify what your audience already wants and help them get it.

One of my good friends and associates, Dr. Glenn Livingston, often says, "*You need to research your market until it changes you as a person.*"

This means immersing yourself in the market. Who is your ideal client? What desperate problems are plaguing them? What are they already buying? What do they like about the current solutions? What's lacking in the currently available options? What are your most successful competitors saying? What is the dominant story being told in the market?

Starting a dialogue with your ideal clients can change you as a person. Your heart goes out to them as you hear more about their current stories. You identify with their struggles. You hear the pain in their voice as they describe how they've previously tried to solve their problems.

You develop an essential ingredient for your marketing message: empathy. Marketing is a numbers game. You can look at the number of leads you're generating, what percentage of leads turn into clients, and the lifetime value of each client to your business. You make decisions based off these numbers, but never forget that every market is made of individuals with problems, hopes, dreams, and a story of their own to tell.

Clients can spot empathy. It's a cliché' but it's used for a reason, "*People don't care how much you know until they know how much you care.*" Demonstrate your empathy by telling stories they identify with. You're one of them. You're someone they'd want to be around, someone they'd want to hang out with for the day.

You can only create that experience by knowing your ideal client and speaking to them in their language. Luckily, the Internet provides us multiple ways to discover more about our clients and even tap into the unique language they personally use.

The most powerful form of research is talking to your current clients. That's one of the benefit of providing one-on-one consulting and coaching. They're sharing the obstacles they face with me every week. This personal contact filters out into my other products and services. The majority of my Monthly Mentor Club issues are written based on problems my clients and I have overcome together. Many of my members have commented how I seemed to 'read their mind' and talk about something they were thinking about that month. It's because my writing comes out of direct contact with my high-level clients.

You can gather a lot of information just in your day-to-day interaction with your best clients. Ask them how you can help them. What other problems are they facing? What other products or services would they like to see you offer in the future? If you're in an online business where you don't regularly interact with your clients, consider calling a few of them on the phone.

Don't tell them you're calling them to get to know them better. That sounds creepy. Instead, you're simply calling because you want to say THANK YOU. You appreciate their business and you wanted to know if there was anything else you could do for them. Is there anything you and your team could do even better in the future? Are there any other products and services they would like to see you offer in the future?

Never underestimate the power of direct contact. There are times where I've personally handled some of the live chat on my website, especially when I'm launching a new product. Visitors ask questions about the product or service and that feedback can help me refine the message in the future. I also handle a portion of my customer support at times. Even if you have a full team of customer support agents, consider handling support for a few hours once a month. Or at the bare minimum, review the chat logs and support tickets to see what questions or issues are coming up most often.

Send Out an Email Survey

The next step down from speaking to clients is running a survey to your email list. If you have a large responsive list (*5,000 subscribers or more is a decent number*), you can use online survey software such as SurveyMonkey, SurveyGizmo, or even Google Forms. Create a short survey of just a few questions and send your email subscribers over to the survey. The benefit of these programs is they will tabulate the results for easy review. If you receive hundreds of responses, you'll need this!

If you have a smaller list, you can often generate more responses by simply asking your subscribers to reply to your email with their answers. An additional benefit of this 'reply' method is you can start a dialogue with your subscribers which can turn into additional sales. Often they're surprised you responded personally to their email! If they ask a question, you can answer it. If they have a problem that can be solved by a product or service you already have, you can mention it. If there's nothing specific to respond to, you can just say THANK YOU. That's always a proper response.

Here's a sample email you could use (*which I first picked up from Dr. Glenn Livingston*):

> Subject: I need your help
>
> I'm putting together some cool new content for you right now.
>
> If you could just hit "reply" on this email and answer the questions below, I'd appreciate your feedback.
>
> 1. What is the single biggest problem I haven't yet helped you address about online marketing?
>
> 2. Specifically, why would it be helpful to you to solve this problem?
>
> 3. How difficult has it been for you to find a good answer to this problem?
>   (Not at All, Somewhat, Very Difficult)
>
> Just hit reply and answer those 3 questions. THANK YOU!
>
> Sincerely,
> Terry Dean
> The Internet Lifestyle Mentor
> Earn More, Work Less, Enjoy Life!

I've found you can use that subject line, "*I need your help*" about every 6 months. It's surprising how well it works as I've had clients use in all kinds of different markets effectively. You've built up a relationship with your list over time and they're willing to help you out also. You're doing the survey to come up with future content which tells them what's in it for them. They can get an answer to a question that's been bugging them.

Often I'll include a one question mini-survey as one of the first few emails in an autoresponder sequence (that's an email sequence that is programmed in advance and every new subscriber receives these emails in order). The above version of this email will work well for subscribers who have been on your list for a while. If you want to generate a response from brand new subscribers, here's the short version.

Subject: I need your help

Could you do one quick thing for me please?

Just hit reply to this email and let me know what you're currently struggling with?

I personally read every email sent to me.

Since I receive a lot of email, it could take me several days to get back with you.

Thank you,
Terry Dean

Your subscribers will tell you exactly what problems they're facing, no matter which of these two emails you send. The first email just picks up a little additional information such as what answering that question would do for them and their lives. I love that question! Some of your audience will tell you the exact language you should use when describing your unique promise. They essentially write your ads for you. With a brand new subscriber, they won't go into as much detail for you, so I'll often send this 2nd shorter version so I can get the answer to what they're struggling with.

These questions can become the foundation for the content you produce. Let's say you only receive 20 responses total. You analyze the questions and decide there are only 10 separate questions as many of them are asking very similar questions. You now have the subjects for your next 10 pieces of content. You could write an email where you mention that "Sue" sent in this question. You ask the question and then you answer in the rest of your email.

You could follow the same system for video. Get on the video. Thank your subscribers for the question. Ask it. And then answer the question. This is one of the quickest and easiest ways to create content you know your audience wants!

How to Find Out What Your Clients Want to Buy

Maybe you're just getting started and you don't have clients to call or subscribers to survey. You're in luck because I've used this next method dozens of times. The easiest way to find out what your audience will spend their money on is to look at what they're already buying. My website of choice for this is Amazon. Google and Bing are search engines. Users are often searching for information there. They want answers to their questions. Youtube is used in a similar way. You search for free videos related to a subject. You want to either learn something for free or be entertained.

Amazon is different. People only search Amazon when they're considering buying a product. Someone may search on Google when they're considering making a purchase, or they may just be looking for free information. The only reason to search Amazon is to find something to buy. And you can find out the best selling products in any category by going to their bestseller section: **www.amazon.com/Best-Sellers/zgbs**

Click on any of the categories on the left and search the best sellers for that category. If you're selling a physical product that may be sold on Amazon, navigate from here to that specific category. If you're an author or in any type of publishing or coaching business, you would go into the "Books" category. Let's say you're a marriage counselor. We'd choose "Books" and then "Parenting and Relationships" followed by "Marriage and Adult Relationships." Keep drilling down until you're in a category related to what you do. I can now see the most popular books in the marriage and adult relationships category.

At the time I'm doing this search, the most popular book in this category is, *"The 5 Love Languages: The Secret to Love That Lasts."* This book is often one of the top selling books. It has over 8,400 reviews right now and it probably has even more by the time you read this. I scan down the bestseller list and I find additional books such as "The Seven Principles for Making Marriage Work" and "The Meaning of Marriage." It will be interesting to see how this list has changed if you view it.

The first thing I do when researching a market is copy over the titles of some of the most popular books. They demonstrate some of the words and concepts that are already working. While you wouldn't copy any title directly, you could mix-and-match some of the words you see repeated multiple times. For example, I see the concept of making Love and Marriage Last is a key here.

Next I'll click on a few of the top books. One of the features that helps you when coming up with content ideas is using the "Search Inside" feature available on most books. Simply click the image of the book at the top left of the listing and you can often search inside it, including the table of contents. Copy over the table of contents from the most popular books. What subjects appear in most of the best selling books? You've just been given another set of content ideas. If everyone is talking about the same subjects, those are 'price of entry' benefits in the market. Those are the things you too need to be talking about.

Scroll down the listing and you'll find the review section and this is where it gets even more exciting. You'll see both good and bad reviews for any popular book and you can learn from both. First look at the most popular reviews. Viewers vote on the reviews. On the bottom of the first review, I see this, "791 *people found this helpful. Was this review helpful to you?*"

That means 791 people found this review helpful in making a buying decision. It included the language they needed to hear to either buy or not buy this book. In some cases you'll even see comments at the bottom left of the review. Those comments allow you to go even deeper in seeing WHY this review was so important to people or what they disagreed with in this review.

Make sure to visit **www.mymarketingcoach.com,** my website. I demonstrate this on video so you can better understand just how powerful this actually is to helping you understand your ideal client and come up with the exact language they need to hear.

In the first review I spotted this language, "*rekindle relationships where people don't even seem to like each other anymore.*" That's a pretty strong benefit, the ability to rekindle relationships where people don't even seem to like each other anymore. Is that something you can do in your marriage counseling practice? If so, then that's the kind of statement you might make somewhere on your website. That was a positive statement about the book.

Here's a negative one, "*My only critique is that they didn't focus more on understanding and discussing your emotions.*" Again, that could be turned into potential language you could use on your website or email, "*In addition, we'll focus on understanding and discussing your emotions with each other.*"

You would never use language that doesn't apply to your business or practice, but if it applies, this is a great way to tap into how your clients are already communicating with each other. This is the exact language they use to help make a buying decision. It's easy to fall into using industry jargon when you're the expert. You end up writing your website for your colleagues instead of your clients. Your goal shouldn't be to impress your colleagues. That doesn't benefit anyone. Instead, your goal is to communicate in language that speaks to those hurting in your market.

Continue going through the reviews. As you go through, you'll find which benefits are important to your audience. You'll find out what they're missing in other approaches. You'll have a large list of content your audience is interested in hearing. And as you scan through the reviews on multiple books in your industry, you'll begin getting an understanding of what causes someone to buy in the market.

While Amazon is one of my favorite methods of online research, we're still not done yet.

How to Eavesdrop On Your Ideal Client's Conversations

Your future clients are right now sharing valuable insights about what problems they're facing and the questions they need answers to, and you can find it all online for free. Just about every niche market has free discussion forums, Facebook groups, or Linkedin groups available. These types of sites helped me add some of my very first subscribers for free back in the Internet Stone Age.

We didn't have Facebook or Linkedin back in 1996, but we did have the Compuserve forums. I participated in those groups, listened to the questions people were asking, and provided helpful advice which helped me grow my initial list. You can do the same thing today!

Let's start out by searching Google. Type in "Keyword forum" or "Keword discussion board." If you're a weight loss coach, you might search for "weight loss forum" or weight loss discussion board." If you're a career coach, you might look for "career forum" or "career discussion board." You're looking for a large, active discussion board full of questions (and answers) from your target audience.

Sometimes you'll even see them discussing other products in the market! What does large and active mean? It's all relative. For example, in bodybuilding, you'll find huge forums such as **forum.bodybuilding.com/** where there are hundreds of new posts a day. In another market, you may only see a few new posts per week. You can pick up ideas from either one. Of course the more active it is, the better.

On some of these forums you can even organize the posts by their popularity. Often they'll display the number of views or replies to each post. See if you can click on one of those options and order the forum by how many views or replies each post has received.

First I'll scan through all the posts. Often you can 'swipe' the post titles for email subject lines, blog post titles, or even video ideas. If a post is getting a ton of views on a popular forum, you know it's a subject the audience is interested in. You don't have to reinvent the wheel. Instead do something that has already been proven to work.

Now click on a few of the popular posts. What questions are being asked? What information is being shared? Where does the conversation flow? What language do they use to describe the challenges they're facing? It's amazing what people will reveal online to an audience they don't even know. They're basically running around saying everything that pops into their head. It's both revealing and scary at the same time.

You could also save these discussion groups and revisit them. Join them and begin participating. Don't post ads. They'll get deleted and you'll get kicked off the group along with developing a reputation as a spammer. Instead, join the group with a desire to help. Answer questions. Share your personal story. Become a resource they can count on for good advice. Link to your website over in your personal profile instead of in your posts. Don't be 'that guy' who comes into the room and just talks about himself. Be the person that everyone listens to because the advice you give is so valuable.

In addition to Internet based discussion groups, you can also find groups on both Facebook and Linkedin. If you're in a consumer focused market, you can likely find additional groups on Facebook. If you're in B2B, Linkedin will usually have a few industry groups that match your theme. On Facebook, you can use the search function at the top left of Facebook. Then select "groups" to search. Some groups are public and you can join these immediately. Others are set to private and you have to apply to be a member. You'll find the ones that require you to wait till they approve you often have a lot less spam and are more valuable overall.

On Linkedin, search for a keyword phrase. Immediately after you search, you can select "Groups" just a little under and to the right of the search bar. If you're in sales, you can definitely find sales groups. If you market to chiropractors, you'll find groups that cater to your audience here also. You can find groups in pretty much any B2B subject on Linkedin.

Scan through the posts to gain insights on what your target audience is thinking. Make a list of topics you could cover in your content. If you decide to participate, become a resource instead of an advertiser. Help others out by answering their questions. Provide advice and tips. And make sure you've fully filled out your own profile and linked over to your website from there. Some people will see your advice, click on your name, and visit your profile. That's how you can turn these groups into leads and sales in your business.

But what's even more important than connecting with the target audience in these groups is connecting with other influencers. The manager of the group is likely a valuable connection for you. We'll get into contacting and building relationships with influencers later on in this book. That's one of the most valuable aspects of social media. It's not even the connections you make with clients. It's the relationships you build with other influencers. There are people out there who already have your future clients on their list. If you can find a way to provide them something they want (such as even offering to moderate their discussion group for them), you can often get what you want.

"You can have everything in life you want, if you will just help other people get what they want."

Zig Ziglar

Reverse Engineer Your Most Successful Competitors

Your most successful competitors in the market probably know a thing or two about what clients want. If they didn't, they wouldn't be so successful. Identify a couple of your competitors with large audiences. You may already know them because of their influence in your industry. Or you may have to look them up. When looking for top competitors, I like to look for 'definite' signs of their success. For example, have they run ads on Google and Bing on competitive keywords for the past year? If so, they're probably doing something right.

Buying advertising is expensive. You can use a tool such as **www.ispionage.com** to help you spot websites which have placed in the top few positions under competitive keyword searches. Sign-up for a free account and type in your keyword to look at the rankings. You're looking for a website which has consistently been in the top 3 or 4 positions for a long period of time. If no one has an average position of less than 4 or they've only been there for a month or two, then it's likely no one has figured out how to make Google pay-per-click work yet.

I'm specifically looking at PAID results when I do these searches. Someone could get a top position in the organic rankings simply because they're a big brand name already. Or they worked their butt off to generate a lot of links to their content. That's one of the most important search engine optimization tricks. If you can get 'authority' websites that rank well in Google to link to your site, you're going to get a big boost in your rankings. Basically Google looks to see if other influencers link to you as a gauge of whether your content is useful enough to share or not.

Having a top organic ranking doesn't mean a thing about converting leads into buyers. The traffic is 'free' and they might not have a clue about converting visitors into leads or sales. But if someone buys their way into a top pay-per-click position, and they keep that position for months or even years, they have to be doing something right. Eventually they'll run out of money if they're not generating a return on their investment. Visitors could be costing $2 to $3 apiece. In some markets, visitors could cost as much as $100 each (legal services for example).

A large business such as a pharmaceutical company or a company with a lot of venture capital behind them may be able to lose money on advertising over the long-term, but most small businesses simply can't afford that. Keeping a top position in the pay-per-click results over a long-term period points to them knowing how to convert those visitors into leads and sales.

Visit their site. Join their email list. Purchase a low cost product to get on their buyer list. Many times they won't show everything they offer on the website or even to their free email list. The real money is in the back-end and some of the best offers may only be sent out to the buyer list. Set-up a separate email address or create a folder in your email where you collect all the messages that come from these competitors. This way all those messages won't disturb you or distract you from what you're doing, and you can review them all at your convenience.

If you're a small brick-and-mortar business owner, it would make sense to look at top competitors in Google pay-per-click in a large competitive market. Look at the websites which are holding top positions in markets such as New York City, San Diego, Miami, and other 'expensive' markets.

You can use the Golden Glove to review your own websites, but you can also use it to reverse engineer the competition. Open up a Spreadsheet, a Word document, or even a piece of paper. On the left side, write: Desperate Problem, Unique Promise, Overwhelming Proof, Irresistible Offer, and Reason to Act Now. Look at the competitor's landing page. This is the first page you land on after clicking on their Google ad.

- **Desperate Problem**: Are they calling out to a specific audience? Or are they calling out to a specific problem they can help solve? Scan the full page. Copy down any statements that refer to the audience or the problem they're solving.

- **Unique Promise**: What promise are they making? What benefits are they offering? When I'm researching a competitor, I don't 'require' the promise to be fully unique. I'll make note of any promises or benefits they focus on. The main headline and smaller subheadlines and/or bullet sections are where I focus most of my attention.

- **Overwhelming Proof**: How do you know they're credible? What proof do they offer for their promises? Here you're looking for things such as media logos or even safe shopping logos. Do they have testimonials or case studies? What about photos of the company or the team? On this one, I'll often dig deeper into the site. A lot of business owners have 'Proof Hiding Disease' where they hide their strongest proof deeper in the site. They might have a separate testimonial page or talk more about the team on the About page. Perhaps you find out that they funded a research study with 1,284 participants on page 3 of the site. Look for any proof they have to back up their main promises.

- **Irresistible Offer**: What is their main call-to-action on the landing page? Do they want me to opt-in as a lead? Are they holding a 30% OFF sale with a link to where I can search specific categories? Do they mention things such as Free shipping or extra bonuses on the page. What is the core offer they're making to a new visitor?

- **Reason to Act Now**: Is there anything available for a limited time? This is something you might not find on the top ranking Google ads, since you're only considering winners who have kept that position over the long-term. They may or may not mention why someone should take action now. So this one is forgivable on the landing page just like with your own website. A lot of the 'scarcity' comes from individual emails and limited time specials which you will see by getting on their list or purchasing one of their products, not necessarily on the landing page.

Why reverse engineer the top performers in your industry? Since they're at the top of the rankings and continue to do so month-after-month, they're doing something right. They're attracting the right audience. And while you wouldn't copy any of them individually, you might gain additional ideas on problems to cover, promises to make, and proof that could be demonstrated. And you'll get an idea of what kind of offers clients are interested in.

Use the Golden Glove to make notes across several sites, and you have a basic foundation for putting together your own marketing message. We'll innovate by coming up with a Unique Promise that helps you stand out from the competition, but you can always gain ideas from what's already working in the market.

In the next chapter we're going to take the knowledge we've gained from our research and put together our Ideal Client Avatar.

Action Steps

- The only way to write in an authentic and engaging way is to feel real empathy for your client's problems and frustrations. Fall in Love with your Ideal Clients.
- Speak to clients in-person or over the phone. Interview them to find out what problems they were facing and why they choose you.
- Email your list and run a simple survey to find out more about your client's situation.
- Research Amazon and discussion groups to find the language your clients are using.
- Reverse engineer your most successful competitors' websites using the Golden Glove.

Ideal Client Avatar

You're not writing to 'everyone.' As I mentioned previously, when you try to speak to everyone, you end up writing to no one in particular. The better you understand your Ideal Client, the easier it is to write to them personally. It becomes easier to identify the elements of your story which resonate with them. Out of the millions of websites online, you're the one who understands them. You 'get' them. And that's what your prospects are searching for. They're looking for somewhere they can plug into. They're looking for a community of people like them. That's what you're going to create for them.

You're going to create an Ideal Client Avatar. That is one person who becomes the representation of your market. That's who you're writing to in your emails. That's who you're speaking to in your videos and audios. They're your client. Think of them as a collection of the most common traits among your Ideal Clients. If you already have clients like this, what do they have in common?

For example, your best clients may be in their 40's and 50's. The baby boomer effect is big online. Many of my clients have been surprised at how their best clients trend older than they expected. A slightly older audience is more established. They have more discretionary income to spend. They have more overall wealth. Even the 'entrepreneur' audience trends older than many assume. The Kauffman Foundation reported that 25.8% percent of new entrepreneurs were 55 to 64 in 2015. And that's just the new entrepreneurs, not counting those who have been entrepreneurs for decades.

There were more people in the 55 to 64 range becoming new entrepreneurs than the 20 to 34 year old range. The media presents an image of entrepreneurs as young people wanting to change the world. There are more grey hairs than you'd expect in the new entrepreneur ranks. And yes, they too want to change the world. They just have a little bit more life experience. They're going into business as a second career. They're moving out of the corporate workplace to take control of something they personally own.

Age is just one element of your avatar. What else do your Ideal Clients have in common? Are they male or female? Are they married or single? Do they have children? What is their income? If you have Ideal Clients already, write down what you know about them. For example, a majority of my clients are married although some are now divorced. Almost all of them have been married at some point.

If you're not sure of the demographics, Facebook has a useful tool, **www.facebook.com/ads/audience_insights**. You can search out interests which would be similar to your audience. For example, of those competitors you researched, do any of them have Facebook pages with large audiences? Check to see if you can type in the business name or their Facebook page name as an interest and find out more about this audience. Or you can look for a well-known expert, speaker, or author in your industry. Can you list them as an interest in Facebook Audience Insights?

Once you find at least one big related interest or several smaller ones that add up, Facebook can give you all kinds of information about this audience. Facebook will tell you how old the audience is compared to the average user on Facebook. They'll give you some Lifestyle Descriptions. Mouse over each of these and they'll tell you what each one means. They'll list the percentage who are married and have kids. You can even see the other pages this audience likes to gain even more intelligence about them. You'll know what they read and where they shop online.

You can find similar insights by researching mailing lists in an industry or contacting an industry journal/magazine which sells advertising. They'll have a detailed description of the demographics they target so you can better understand your customer. I generally use Facebook Insights just because it's free and quick to access. And I can research multiple different interests to make sure the trends stay true across the market.

Organize All Your Research

It's easy to get lost in never ending research. You could spend months or even years doing research and you never move past this. That's why I recommend giving yourself a deadline on the research. Spend 2 to 4 hours reviewing Amazon one day. Investigate the discussion groups another day. And then invest the time to research the competition on the third day. Now you're going to review all your notes, organize them into the core problems, and create your target avatar.

This early version of your avatar is just a starting point. You will update what you know about them...likely before the end of the next 30 days. Getting to know your customer isn't a one-time event. Instead it's a knowledge that grows over time as you see how they respond to your marketing and the conversations you have with them.

Go back through all your research. You may have half a dozen pages of notes. Start off by slowly reading through your notes. Your first goal is to categorize everything you know about your Ideal Client. Create no more than 6 categories total. You might find that you can get by with 3 to 4 categories, but you want no more than 6 categories to keep it manageable. You'll come up with these categories by thinking about the problems/obstacles that each note represents.

Perhaps they say something about how difficult it is to generate new patients. Or they talk about a new technique they discovered for attracting new patients. Both of these notes would go into the category, "How to Generate New Higher Quality Patients." Everything about newspaper advertising, Adwords, Facebook, Yellow Pages, referrals, and websites would be put into this category.

Classify every comment, bullet, problem, benefit, or promise into no more than these 6 categories total. As you're going through your notes and organizing them, it's likely you'll combine a few categories, rename them, or expand them out. When you're finished, you might come up with 6 categories that look something like this for your audience of dentists.

- How to generate new higher quality patients.
- Finding, training, and retaining good staff.
- Long-term patient retention and selling more to current clients.
- Dealing with insurance hassles and getting paid for work.
- Creating systems to save time and provide consistent results for each step in the practice.
- Managing cashflow, finances, and saving for retirement.

Once you've classified all the comments into your chosen categories, decide which categories are the most important to your ideal client. This is what you'll focus on first in your headlines and your offers. The other elements will be introduced and included in your stories and content, but there is always a starting point. If you don't grab the attention of your prospect immediately, you can lose them forever. So the hook has to be focused on one of their most important interests.

I have many clients in B2B industries, and "How to generate new higher quality clients" is often the hook we focus on. It's the biggest drawing card. Even when there are other problems in the practice, the customer will still often point to not enough new patients coming through the door as the problem they want to solve first. They may think, *"Sure, the staff is overwhelmed and turns over every 6 months, but if only there was more money coming in, everything would be better."*

You may know from your own experience what your client NEEDS even better than they do. Remember , they don't necessarily buy what they need. They buy what they want. Your marketing needs to focus on what they perceive to be their biggest problem first. Sell what they want and sneak in what they need. It doesn't matter how experienced you are as a marketer. I've let this mistake sabotage me several times. It's not about what you know. It's about connecting with the conversation that is already going in the head of your Ideal Client.

For example, I have a couple of clients who offer website design, PPC management, and search engine optimization services for niche industries. Even though they know the majority of new clients are generated through the PPC campaigns, they generate more customers when they also offer social media updates on services such as Facebook and Twitter. They have all the stats in place and know the vast majority of customers are generated through PPC, but they have to include the social media focus heavily in their presentations. That's what the customer BELIEVES should be important!

Answer a Few Questions About Your Ideal Clients

Let's write down some of the things we know about your Ideal Clients based off of direct experience with clients and/or the research you've done up till now. Below I'm going to give you multiple questions in two primary categories.

First, we'll talk about Client Desires. What are the problems your clients are worried about? And what do they currently think about these problems and the possible solutions? This is where they are right now. Next, you'll write out some of the demographic information you have for the clients.

You don't have to answer all the questions below. They've just been provided to you to get a better fix on your clients. The better you understand them and where they're coming from, the easier it is it to create websites and marketing materials that speak directly to their hearts.

What are the 3 biggest problems your customers are facing right now?

1.

2.

3.

What does the client believe is currently causing each of these problems?

1.

2.

3.

What are these problems COSTING your clients (financially, emotionally, relationships, etc.)? The more specific you are here, the better.

1.

2.

3.

What are 3 ways a client could try to solve these problems (other than buying from you)?

1.

2.

3.

What are the 3 most common objections they'll bring up to buying your product or service?

1.

2.

3.

Who or what does your buyer HATE? This could be a person (their butt-kissing coworker), a subject (low carb dieting), or an organization (the government).

1.

2.

3.

Describe your Ideal Client. How old are they? Are they male or female? How much money do they earn yearly? Do they have a spouse or kids?

1.

2.

3.

What separates an Ideal Client for you from the Average Client in the market? What is different about them that qualifies them to be an Ideal Client? Describe 3 characteristics of them.

1.

2.

3.

You can't help everyone. What kind of person can you NOT help? What does someone believe or do that would make them unqualified to be your Client?

1.

2.

3.

What do you personally or professionally have in common with these Ideal Clients (your backstory, hobbies, interests, passions, and desires)?

1.

2.

3.

What are the biggest myths, misconceptions, and mistakes being made in the market that are keeping your Ideal Clients from solving their problems or achieving their desires?

1.

2.

3.

Select a Photo to Represent Your Ideal Client Avatar

This exercise will be easier if you have a photo in front of you to represent your Ideal Client. You're speaking to a specific individual. If you already have a client like this, you could use their photo. But most of the time you'll want to search for a photo to represent your client. Pull up Google and search for a keyword phrase that identifies your client. In this example, I'll search for a "dentist."

You can use Google Images because we're never going to publish this photo anywhere. It's simply a visual image for you to focus on as your Ideal Client. This is the individual you're helping. You're not speaking to a group. You're speaking to this one person.

Click on "Images" just under the search bar. Now you're looking at photos of dentists. These dentists look way too happy to me. I want someone over 45 who looks a little stressed out. So I change my search to "dentist stressed." Now we're talking. I scan through the photos and look for several photos that could be a stressed out dentist who is over 45.

If I'm not positive about the age of my customer, I'll generally skew a little older. For example, if I sell golf products, then my customer could be anywhere from 25 to 90 (or older). BUT people in the older demographic on average will have more money and more free time. So I'd likely choose someone in the 50+ range as my target bulls-eye. Those clients are more likely to have a higher lifetime value to me.

I suggest choosing a total of 3 separate images. If you write up a quick 'story' for each of them, you'll have a higher chance of hitting the right hot buttons on one of them. Also choosing 3 images and writing 3 quick stories allows you to get out of the perfectionist mindset which can hold you back. You don't have to get it perfect. You won't get it perfect. You might even decide that your Ideal Avatar is a little bit of a mixture of your stories and you combine them into one when you're done.

If a majority of your Ideal Clients are male, then choose male images. If the majority of your Ideal Clients are female, choose female images. If the audience is almost dead even, choose at least one of each. Pay attention to the face of the person you choose, their background, and especially their facial expression. Does this look like someone who has the 'pain point' or desire you're focusing on?

Make your choices fairly quickly. Don't waste a lot of time here. You're not going to get it perfect and you don't have to. Make some choices based on what you know about your clients and then move to the next step. Give each of your photos a name. "Tim" is the name of my new dentist friend.

Write Out Your Avatar's Story

Now you're going to do a fun free-writing exercise. You're going to 'tell' your avatar's story. In this story, you're going to write about their home life. You're going write about their frustrations and desperate problems. And you're going to write about their biggest ambitions and goals. You can go back and review any research up till this point before you start writing. Once you start writing, let it flow. That's one of the keys to this exercise. Don't sit there and second guess what you write. Instead, write as your ideas come to mind. You're just describing what life is like for your Ideal Avatar.

Let's start writing about Tim, the dentist, and let's see what comes out...

> *"Tim is a 45 year old dentist, married, with 2 kids at home. Outwardly he has all the trappings of success including a nice house, car, and a boat his family sometimes takes out on the weekend. But he is stressed out of his mind. Each year he has seen the net profits decline to the point that he isn't sure he can make payroll or how next month's house payment will be made. Patients aren't coming in like they used to. There are too many dentists in the area now, and customers aren't loyal like they used to be. He doesn't have time to do all that internet stuff and he has hired 4 webmasters in the past 3 years...and none of them produced any results."*

OK, let's take a timeout here. How do I know Tim is married and has 2 kids? I don't. At least I don't know it for sure. All I know is that it seems likely based on the research I've done including the lifestyle information I found on Facebook. I may have noticed how some of the competitors had an origin story which talked about their devotion to their spouse and family. They were specifically trying to identify with that audience. They were talking about how their family motivated them to succeed. So I bring in that basic story into my avatar.

Other elements in my story may have come from Amazon reviews or hanging out in the forums and groups. If you joined a Facebook group that was designed for your target audience, did you click on the profile photos of some of the participants to find out more about them? You're not trying to get it perfect. You're simply trying to write a 'likely' story for the audience. You'll often hear movies are 'based on a true story.' Your Ideal Avatar is based on the true stories and information you find out about your audience. You're just expanding out on those stories and combining them into one Avatar.

Take some liberties when writing your avatar. You're limited in your knowledge of your customer and simply have to do your best. You'll come back to this later on once you've spoken to more customers and know how they're responding to different messages. There is no right and wrong answer here. And yes, writing this is likely to be a little uncomfortable. You're never 100% sure you're doing it perfectly. Get it done anyway. The actual writing of your avatar shouldn't take longer than 10 to 15 minutes. You invested a lot of time in doing the research. Free writing should be done quickly.

Here are some of the questions you may answer in your free writing exercise:

- Are they married or single?
- Do they have kids?
- What is their family life like?
- What do they do for a living?
- What are their ambitions and dreams?
- What do they lie awake at night worrying about?
- What frustrates them the most?
- What do they do during their free time?
- What hobbies do they have?
- Imagine spending an entire day with them. What obstacles do they face?
- How have they tried to solve their problems previously?
- What do they believe about the problems or the current solutions?

You don't have to answer all these questions. They're simply idea starters to get you writing. Be willing to go off course and write whatever comes to mind. That's what makes free writing valuable. If you've done your research, you can write about your avatar. Of course, if you haven't done your research first, you'll simply be writing what you "think" about the audience instead of what you've seen in the research.

Keep writing until you run out of ideas. My previous example was a very short Avatar. It was just the beginning. You could continue on where I left off by describing what an average day is like in the life of your client. What challenges do they face today? What are they worried about? What do they celebrate? See the world through their eyes as you write.

It should take you 10 to 15 minutes at most. Often you'll be done in less time. Take a break. Get up. Walk around. Come back in 5 to 10 minutes. You're now going to do the same exercise again using a different photo. You might name this Avatar, "Joe." Write his story. Perhaps you came up with some additional ideas when you were on break. Enter those on this version. You might have been divided about exactly how Tim's day went. Use one of the other options you were considering now. There will still be similarities between your Avatars because they're from the same audience.

Keep writing for another 10 to 15 minutes. You're going to follow this process one more time. Take a 5 to 10 minute break. Choose a different photo and write one more avatar for it over the next 10 to 15 minutes. If you're not 100% confident about the age or home life (Facebook might have showed you several different lifestyle possibilities), make sure to vary this avatar's home life. This time your story comes out with a little different twist. For example, this version of my dentist could overwork himself, have trouble collecting on billings, and experience marital problems from all the time he spends at the office.

This may sound a little difficult when you first hear it, but it is actually easier than it seems. The key principle is there are no wrong answers. As long as you did your research coming into this, each of these will become a decent story. It's impossible to get it perfect when you're just starting out. You simply don't have enough personal experience with the market. You haven't spoken to enough of your clients. And anything you write simply comes down to educated guesses.

The good news is that educated guesses based on research will usually be good enough...

Multiple Segments In Your Market

You now have 3 photos and 3 Avatar stories. Review your research, especially your top 3 categories. Which one of these 3 Avatars best matches up with the top category in your list? That's your objective basis, but there is also a subjective component. Which one of these 3 Avatars feels right? If you need to, read through all your research again. Then read the 3 Avatars out-loud. Which one is the best match for your Ideal Client? Which one will you have the easiest time speaking to?

Choose your Avatar. This is who you'll be writing to starting out. This is your Ideal Client. In the next chapter, we'll start writing out your story. You've written a short version of your Client's story. The next step is writing out your own personal story that appeals to this Client.

In some cases, you might have more than one Avatar in your market. That usually happens when your top categories are completely different in nature. For example, as an online business coach, I deal with 3 distinctly different types of clients. These include brick-and-mortar local business owners, experienced coaches and infoproduct creators, and those starting their first online businesses.

Brick-and-mortar business owners may be restauranteurs, CPAs, chiropractors, real estate agents, etc. This client already has a business in place, but is almost always struggling to generate enough high quality clients of their own. They're confused and overwhelmed by all the online marketing techniques. And they simply don't have enough time to put what they do learn into practice. They've often been taken advantage of by webmasters and marketing services that simply don't deliver real results. They don't need likes or visitors to their website. They need real leads and quality buyers. That's what I specialize in, generating higher quality leads for less money.

The 2nd type of client is a consultant, coach, or infoproduct marketer (such as an author). They already have a successful business online, but they're often working too many hours for too little income. They come to me to help them optimize their marketing strategies so they can generate more clients for less money and in less time. After we put traffic and conversion systems in place, we transition into putting systems in place to get more done in less time. I help them focus on their vital activities while eliminating, automating, or delegating the less important elements of their business.

The 3rd type of client that comes to me is the person starting their online business from scratch. Often they haven't selected their market niche, and they need help choosing where and how to get started. We examine their skillset, past work experiences, and their hobbies to find where we can give them an advantage online. If you don't know what your advantage is, you're doing business at a disadvantage. You can't just "follow your passion." Instead you want to find the intersection of a hungry buying audience, passion you have for the market, and value you can share. Having a story you can tell can also give you an immediate advantage.

Those are 3 distinct markets with totally different Avatars. If I tried to mix them in with each other, I'd just end up confused. Instead, I think of them as 3 different types of clients. When I run advertising, I'm speaking to one of these audiences at a time. I have several separate email lists for these audiences even though many of my email broadcasts go out to all of these lists.

Choose the largest and most profitable segment to get started with. You're not going to be able to 'divide' your time initially to multiple possibilities. You'll just slow yourself down and get overwhelmed. Instead, focus on the segment which will be most profitable initially. After you've put these systems in this book in place for the first segment, then expand out to the others.

Some of the ways you can segment your audience is by installing a "traffic light' on your website where you ask new subscribers to select another box in addition to their email address. For example, I could ask subscribers which of these 3 options best describes them. You can then have them added to different lists based on their response. Write to the largest list first and then modify your other emails to appeal to the other audiences.

Here's a little trick for simplifying this process. The first 2 to 4 weeks are the most important emails. Instead of writing multiple email sequences forever, just edit those first few weeks. You'll have established your brand positioning, built your relationship, and made your initial sales. We'll go deeper into writing effective emails in a later chapter.

If the last few paragraphs confused you, don't worry about it. I recommend choosing just one Ideal Client Avatar and focusing on speaking to that Avatar. Segmenting your audience is an advanced tactic which we don't need to get into right now. It's just a way to further optimize your marketing and produce an ever greater number of leads for low cost. It's NOT for everyone, and it's especially not for those who are just starting with online marketing.

How Can You Reach This Audience Online?

You may be asking why coming up with an Ideal Client Avatar is so important? It sets the tone for your marketing. If you try to speak with everyone, you end up writing to no one in particular. That's why presidential candidates struggle. They're trying to gain votes from large groups of people who have almost nothing in common. Republicans and Democrats often have almost totally different ways of looking at the world. But it gets even more refined than this. A liberal Democrat from California may have a completely different viewpoint from a moderate Democrat in Ohio.

These differences often lead presidential candidates to make promises in one area of the country they backtrack on while in another. They're trying to communicate with too many people at once. It's close to impossible, and it's become even more difficult today since the Internet allows us to segment ourselves into our little groups. Instead of the Internet bringing us closer together, it has actually driven us further apart. You can cluster in with those who think similar to you, and you can block out voices that don't align with your beliefs.

Mass marketing is available in today's world, but niche marketing is much more efficient and profitable. That's why you create your Ideal Client Avatar. That's your niche. That's who you're communicating with. And the Internet makes it easy to identify and market to just about any audience.

Facebook alone allows you to target by demographic information and tens of thousands of possible interests. If you want to target 35 year old men who listen to country music and like Joel Osteen, you can do that. If you want to target married parents age 45 to 65 who like online brokerages, have a net worth of over one million dollars, and earn $200,000 or more per year, you can do that too. It is crazy what Facebook knows about us and the options they give us for advertising our business.

Having your Avatar in front of you allows you to start making some of these connections. Instead of writing a 'mass ad' that needs to appeal to everyone, you can narrow down your audience to your Ideal Client and create something that appeals to only them. If you were running an ad to 45 to 65 year old chiropractors, you might include industry jargon that only they understand. If you're writing to entrepreneurs who also read Brian Tracy's books, you might include a phrase or concept they will understand (make sure not to use anything in your ads that is trademarked to someone else).

You might even come up with some seemingly unrelated concepts to combine in your advertising. For example, I could target entrepreneurs who also like dogs. Then I run an ad about how to increase the number of leads coming through and I use a photo of me alongside my dog. Or I write a business lesson that involves my dog, knowing I'm speaking to an audience which will appreciate this message. It's amazing what you can do when you start thinking laterally like this.

We could also use Google or Youtube advertising. On Youtube, you can advertise under specific keywords or you can advertise to people who are watching specific videos. That's right! As long as a video has monetization turned on, you could choose to run your video ad ONLY to people watching that video. You can also select hundreds or even thousands of videos you want to advertise on. One of the biggest mistakes I see people making in their online marketing campaigns is using old mass advertising principles from decades ago. Instead, you can laser target your audience and deliver a message that appeals directly to them.

Action Steps

- Create Your initial Ideal Client Avatar. This single avatar represents your best clients in the market. Your marketing, websites, emails, and videos are all produced for this Avatar.
- Organize all of your research from the previous chapter into no more than 6 total categories. These categories usually correspond to desperate problems/challenges your audience is facing.
- Answer the questions about your Ideal Client throughout the chapter.
- Select a photo to represent your Ideal Client.
- Write out a quick story about your Avatar. Have fun with this.

How to Eliminate Sales Resistance By NOT Selling

Our defenses naturally go up whenever we're confronted by a sales person. No matter how kind they appear, you know in their heart they're out for the sale. They can tell you how important you are to them, how they're not 'paid on commission,' or how they only want the best for you, but none of that matters. The traditional sales process is a confrontational experience. That's likely why you picked up this book on how to sell without selling. You don't want to be another sales person. And I can't blame you! Most sales people suck!

Traditional sales training has focused on 'always closing' and 'closing tricks.' These types of sales classes will teach you to assume right through the sale. Instead of asking them to buy, you ask them whether they want option A or option B. If the customer has objections, you try to get them all out in the open. You ask questions like, "Is there any reason you can't buy today?" They give you an answer, potentially an objection. You note it in your mind and you ask, "Is there anything else?" Eventually you have your list and you go through each of these objections, knocking them down one after another.

This is an aggressive confrontational style to selling. You're overwhelming the prospect with the force of your personality and your arguments. While some people are very successful with this (cough...cough...car dealers), it's not comfortable. It doesn't bond you with the prospect. It's you versus them. Not the type of approach I want to use with my clients. Our goal is to make the world a better place, and that won't be accomplished by abusing your clients.

Another common technique you will commonly hear about is called consultative sales. Instead of knocking down objections by brute force and applying multiple closing techniques, you act as a consultant with your client. This approach has a lot more value to it. You're asking them questions that reveal what the problem is they need solved, what the ramifications of the problem are, and you're deciding together whether your solution is a good fit for them.

I have used and taught this to my clients. It's effective especially when you're dealing in person or over the phone with a client. But it has one major weakness. People don't trust you when they see you as a salesperson. And make no mistake about it, they expect you to sell them. That's why you're there. That's how you make money. If you want to produce the best results even with a consultative sales approach, you first have to turn the selling system on its head.

Remember this rule. You cannot change someone else's beliefs. While you could potentially debate someone into a purchase by the strength of your personality and arguments, this will not result in a happy customer. Instead it will create buyer remorse. They'll feel manipulated. You sold them on something even though it didn't match their personal beliefs about the subject.

The secret to sales without selling is to eliminate the sales resistance by connecting indirectly to their beliefs. That's why it's so important to understand your customer. You need to know where they are right now, what problems they've experiencing, what they believe about those problems, and what they believe about the current solutions.

All good marketing starts first with an understanding of the audience you're speaking to. While traveling is not something I do often, I have spoken at multiple events. One of the secrets to delivering value to an audience is getting to know that audience. You can speak to the event organizers to find out as much as you can about the attendees in advance, but I often find it even more valuable to show up early to mix and mingle with the attendees. I'll straight out ask them why they came to this event and what they want to get out of it. That way I can customize my presentation to help them solve the problems that are most important to them.

You Will Never Change Someone's Core Beliefs By Arguing With Them

Have you ever spoke to someone and you just couldn't come to agreement? Your viewpoints were totally different and it seemed like there was little or no common ground. That's common in politics especially. You both may watch the same presidential speech, but you've heard two totally different things. You may have heard the same words, but you interpreted them in completely different ways.

This all comes back to your own personal story. I'm a believer in a limited federal government that is for the people. This means that anytime I hear about bigger federal programs, that connects with my internal 'story' about government and I see it as a corrupt organization taking even more power from the people and eliminating more of our rights. You may have a completely different story inside you, and you see increased government programs as the government doing more for the disadvantaged.

Neither of us would be able to 'debate' the other one into changing our beliefs. It just won't happen. The core foundation of the two beliefs are diametrically opposed. That's why you see many politicians who appear to be talking right past each other, and why it seems almost impossible to understand the viewpoints of the other side.

When I hear about the expansion of virtually any government program, what I personally hear is that politicians want the government to become even more corrupt (and be even further above the law) while stealing the rights of private citizens. How could you persuade me to agree with the growth of any government program when the very thought of that is equal to increasing the corruption that already plagues us?

Hopefully that's not your mission. Politics is not something I enjoy talking about. I only brought it in here as a powerful example. And if your political views disagree with me, the example should be even more powerful since the 'story' your mind hears is completely different from the story I hear from the exact same news report.

Let's turn this around and think about your customers. Since you did your research, you now know some of your audience's core beliefs. You could come in and slam head-first into those like a sledgehammer. But you will come off like another pushy salesperson, and it's not likely to be effective anyway.

Instead, start thinking about the narrative that's going on in the heads of your clients. What is the story they have about this problem? Perhaps it's been with them for years. They have deep-set beliefs about the problem. What are they? Instead of trying to 'sell' them into believing something different, you can help them replace their old story with a new story.

"People don't buy a product, service, or idea; they buy the story that's attached to it."

Michael Margolis

Stories Are the Language Of Your Clients' Subconscious

I mentioned the power of charities to 'sell' their mission in the earlier chapter about the Golden Glove. People give to a charity because it makes them feel good to know they're making a difference in the world. They're helping others less fortunate. Have you ever paid attention to how effective charities advertise? They focus on the stories of those they help. Sure, they may mention some facts and figures, but that is NOT where they focus first. For example, check out Make-A-Wish America at **wish.org**.

Their website is full of stories about the children they've helped. They share their origin story, stories of those they've helped, and their big hairy audacious goals at **wish.org/about-us/our-story.** Their vision is to grant the wish of every child diagnosed with a life-threatening medical condition. Their origin story is about a little child with leukemia named Chris which you can see here: **wish.org/about-us/our-story/how-it-started**

When you give to them, you're not just helping children with medical conditions. You're helping other children exactly like Chris. You can read the stories and feel good about the difference you made. You can't save everyone, but you can make a difference in the life of someone. Their website has names, photos, and stories you can carry around in your heart for the rest of your life.

Every successful product, service, and company has a story behind it. It starts with your origin story and what influenced you to start this business. But it continues past this and also details what gives you purpose today. It ties into a mission that's greater than you alone and forces you to build a community that's connected to a higher purpose. You're on a mission to CHANGE something about your industry, improve the lives of your clients, and even extend your message outside your personal influence.

I'm NOT just a business coach. I'm on a mission to help other entrepreneurs Earn More, Work Less, and Enjoy Life Without Compromising Your Values. I accomplish this mission through individual one-on-one coaching and group based programs designed to help you identify your audience, attract highly qualified clients, tell your story, and put systems in place that grow your business. And you can do all this without being salesy. In fact, the best way to attract hungry buyers is by delivering value mixed with personality using the methods I'm sharing with you here.

This mission is based off my background story. When I first discovered the Internet, I was a dead broke pizza delivery driver with over $50,000 in debt, mostly on credit cards. Discovering the power of how to sell without selling is what delivered me from that existence and allowed me to run a highly successful online business for over 20 years now. In the early days, it was all about email marketing.

Lately it has become even more obvious how important this method is on Facebook, Twitter, Pinterest, Youtube, and other social media sites. You'll get completely shut down if you go in as a sales person. What gets liked and shared on social media? Feel good stories. Very few people want to hear your 'sales message.' But they'd love to hear an underdog story.

They want to hear a story that helps them feel good about themselves. That's what they'll share with others. In fact, even advertising will do poorly if they're all about you, your product, or your business. Facebook has a metric called Relevance. This compares how often your ad gets liked, shared, and commented on to how often viewers hide or call it spam. If you want to generate low cost leads, you need a high Relevance score. That means you need people liking and sharing your advertising. People share your ads when you give something of value upfront, especially an attention grabbing story (*we'll talk more about Facebook and Youtube advertising in a later chapter*).

The Hero's Journey

We're going to bypass the sales resistance of your clients by positioning you as an authority in the marketplace. And the first step is to tell your Hero's Journey. Joseph Campbell created The Hero's Journey after studying the myths and legends of many cultures. It is a metaphor for the inner transformation that every heroic character goes through. This includes you. You need to demonstrate the journey you went through that took you from being a mild mannered average Joe into a super hero that is able to help free them from the challenges they're facing today.

- **The Ordinary World**: You identify with the hero and their background. What problems and challenges are they facing? What are their motivations? What characteristics and flaws do they have?
- **The Call to Adventure**: The hero's ordinary world is knocked off course. A major problem occurs that needs a resolution or

they're presented with a quest. The stakes are HIGH if they choose not to take action. The higher the stakes, the more drama and interest generated.

- **Refusal of the Call**: The hero doesn't accept the initial call-to-action because of fears and insecurities. They prefer keeping it 'safe' instead of facing the risks of moving forward.
- **Meeting the Mentor**: The hero seeks wisdom or guidance from someone who has gone before them OR they receive guidance in the form of a gift, book, tool, solution, etc.
- **Crossing the Threshold**: They commit to the journey and there is no turning back. Bridges may be burned behind them. There is no other choice than to commit fully.
- **Tests, Allies, Enemies**: Challenges are faced. New friends may join the journey. And additional complications occur. The hero's commitment is tested, but they're committed to the journey.
- **Approach**: Preparations are made for the big ordeal that is soon to come. Often there is a time-out in the action as the calm before the storm.
- **The Ordeal**: The hero confronts his/her greatest fear, a life-or-death crisis, and the entire journey could fail. The hero may confront the villain and lose (or lose something precious).
- **The Reward**: The hero has survived death or conquered his/her fear. There is a short time for celebration before the situation becomes even worse.
- **The Road Back**: The hero recommits to completing the journey. The stakes increase again as the tension increases in preparation for the final challenge.
- **The Resurrection**: This is the most dangerous life-and-death ordeal that can only be defeated because of the growth of the hero. The stakes are the highest now.
- **Return With the Elixir**: The hero has been transformed and brings home a treasure that benefits others as well (or the entire world).

George Lucas has mentioned how much the Hero's Journey influenced him in the writing of Star Wars. When we look at the original movie, it's pretty easy to spot each of the steps along the journey (*serious spoiler alert if you've lived in a cave your whole life and haven't seen Star Wars*):

- **The Ordinary World**: Luke Skywalker at his uncle's moisture farm on Tatooine.
- **The Call to Adventure**: He receives Leia's message through R2-D2.
- **Refusal of the Call**: Luke can't go on an adventure because he has to help with the harvest.
- **Meeting the Mentor**: Obi-wan saves Luke from the sand people.
- **Crossing the Threshold**: Luke's family are killed and he escapes from Tatooine with Obi-wan.
- **Tests, Allies, Enemies**: He befriends Han/Chewie, practices his lightsaber, and Alderaan is gone.
- **Approach**: The Millennium Falcon moves toward the Death Star. Oh noes, they're trapped.
- **The Ordeal**: They fight their way through the Death Star and save the Princess. Obi-wan dies.
- **The Reward**: They escape with the plans to the Death Star.
- **The Road Back**: The Death Star will soon be in range of the Rebel base.
- **The Resurrection**: Luke destroys the Death Star with help from Han against Vader.
- **Return With the Elixir**: Luke and other heroes are rewarded with medals at the end of story.

Star Wars is an easy example to apply the Hero's Journey, but you can apply the Hero's Journey to most literature and movies. You'll start seeing this everywhere now. Action movies are often the most obvious, but you can also see when the internal conflict in other types of movies follow this same structure or at least major elements of this structure.

Your Strategic Myth

Why does your business exist? Why did you choose to do what you do? What or who influenced you? Why did you decide to add yet another option to an already overcrowded marketplace? What happened that caused you to have to take action? You just couldn't sit on the sidelines any longer. There is a background origin story behind the creation of your business, product, or service. What was your Hero's Journey to get from where you were to where you are today?

We're going to use the Hero's Journey to help create our "**Strategic Myth.**" We've already established that every brand has a story behind it. Your Strategic Myth is a message that encapsulates your unique promises into a story you share over and over again. It takes center stage as part of your message. It's the reason you do what you do. It's the why that influences you. And it also gives a story that others can tell when they recommend you.

While you could go through all 12 points in the Hero's Journey, we're going to trim it down for ease of use. The Hero's Journey was designed to tell the whole story, but your story isn't complete yet. Your business will continue growing into the future. You'll add new benefits. You'll have new experiences and case studies to share. Your story continues along the same theme, but it is always growing and expanding. Your customers and clients will be the next step in your Journey. You've already walked this path before, and you can help free them from the ordeals they're facing today.

To simplify, we're going to focus on these 8 Components:

- **The Ordinary World**: Who are you and what was life like? Were you satisfied, frustrated, etc.? How were you an ordinary Joe just like anyone else? This is the 'back story.'
- **The Call**: What is the Inciting Incident? What crisis or opportunity occurs that starts the story?
- **Refusal**: How did you struggle? What stopped you from success? Or how did you refuse the call to adventure and change? What objections did you have to moving forward?
- **Mentor**: Who or what comes to your aid? What solution presents itself?
- **Cross the Threshold**: How do you launch out and put it to the test? The higher the stakes, the more powerful the story.
- **Ordeal**: You confront the challenges and/or the villain and you conquer them.
- **Reward**: You've gained insights into how it really works. You've developed something unique.

- **Return With the Elixir:** What is your mission and purpose? What will you share with the world?

You have value to share with the world. How did you get to where you are today? What struggles have you faced? What have you discovered that will help others in their journey? That's the point of your own Hero's Journey. You faced the challenges to become the Hero so that you can lift others up to where you are today. They see their own journey in your story. It gives them hope. Maybe they too can overcome the challenges in their life.

Telling Your Full Story

I dropped Tests, Allies, Enemies, The Approach, The Reward, and The Resurrection because these would require an even longer story. If you're been in business for quite a while or you've experienced a lot of ups and downs in your road to success, you could extend out your story to include all these components. When you analyze the full 12 component Hero's Journey, you'll see that it basically has a series of ups and downs.

You go through tests and challenges while recruiting new friends. You get a little break in the action. Then you hit an even bigger challenge in the Ordeal. Then there is another break in the action with the reward. Finally you hit the biggest challenge of all in The Resurrection. You come back with the elixir...the final reward that can help the world.

I don't know your story or all the twists and turns which might be in it. I'm giving you a model to follow that can be used by virtually anyone to create their own Hero's Journey. If you have the additional details to fill in, you can create an even more powerful story.

A lot of times you can extend the story out AFTER you're in business. You faced struggles and challenges. You overcame each one. You faced an even bigger challenge...that almost knocked you flat on your back. You'll hear a lot of business gurus talk about how they built a successful or semi-successful business and then went bankrupt. It could be a partner embezzling the funds from their company, a marriage break-up, or a disaster such as 9/11 wiping out their travel business. This is their 'bigger ordeal'.

The Resurrection is often their greatest challenge of all. It is often a story of moving to a new level in their business. In the above story, Joe could have already been receiving good results from clients one-on-one but he wanted to expand his business. He creates an online membership site, but without his personal help, he finds clients are getting little or no results. He comes up with a new delivery system that allows them to get personal help from him, an accountability buddy, and more to make sure they can generate real results. Here are all his case studies to prove why this works better than any other option.

From now on, you're going to start recognizing these components in the origin stories other entrepreneurs use about their business. You'll start identifying the ordeals and the rewards. You'll see where the stakes become even higher and how they return with an elixir to benefit the world. Each step in their Hero's Journey leads to greater challenges and even bigger rewards. A good storyteller can hold the audience on the edge of their seats as they share on a webinar, in a live presentation, or on an interview. But more than that, they can get the audience to take action and follow them on the journey.

Note: These techniques can be used for good or evil. I'm recommending you go through your journey to get to where you are today and look for each of these crossroads. You might not have all 12 components. That's why we're focusing on the 8 most important pieces. You will find entrepreneurs out there who don't have any qualms about making up the missing pieces. Don't do that. Be authentic. You have a story to tell. Tell that story. There is a reason you are who you are today.

Step 1: The Ordinary World

This is your back story. What was your ordinary world like before the adventure started? If you teach people how to lose weight, this would likely be back when you were overweight. What pain points did you experience back then? You might have had health problems related to this. Maybe you had a lack of self-confidence. You want to really describe it. Think about specific instances where you could describe someone being mean to you or perhaps you feel you were even skipped over for promotion because of your weight even though you can't prove it.

When I talk about my ordinary world, this includes being a college drop-out. It includes the $50,000 in debt and all the dead-end jobs I worked including selling satellite dishes door-to-door, signing people up for credit cards in front of Sears, and delivering pizzas for Little Caesars for $8 an hour. I can go into even deeper detail and talk about digging for change in the couch to get enough money to go out to eat at McDonalds or how the little house we rented had a leak in the kitchen ceiling that the landlord never fixed. We were borrowing from one credit card to pay the others, and I didn't see any way out.

Your ordinary world speaks directly to the Desperate Problems you help your customers solve. If you're a consultant to dentists, then it could be about all the struggles and obstacles you faced in your own dental practice. What if you never owned your own dental practice? Then we need to move back to how you choose to work with dentists. If you ran a business in another field, we'd talk about struggles that dentists could also identify with. What if you didn't run your own business? You could talk about the first client you helped generate results in their practice...and the problems they faced. How and why did you choose to start working with them in the first place?

Step 2: The Call to Adventure

What was the Inciting Incident that called you to action? For the weight loss expert, it could be the doctor giving them the Type 2 Diabetes Diagnosis. It could be an emotional situation where someone they cared about hurt them and they went crying to their room. For the dental consultant, it could be not being able to make payroll. Their wife/husband leaves them. It could be a big tax bill coming up they couldn't pay. Perhaps they have a chat with a 60 year old dentist buddy who talks about how burned out he is and how he wants to end it all.

It could also be a positive story such as me stumbling upon rumors that some people were creating home businesses on the Internet. That was a real turning point for me. I had failed at business opportunities including direct mail and multiple network marketing companies. I simply wasn't good at person-to-person direct selling, but the Internet sounded like something I could do. Those rumors were my call to adventure in the early days.

I had to do something. Creditors were calling me both day and night. We had been borrowing from credit cards and we were almost at the limit across all of them. But I took our last credit card which was from Best Buy and maxed it out to purchase my first PC. That was one of the best decisions I ever made, even though it meant we went even deeper into debt. But we were already at the point where we pretty much didn't have any other option!

Your Call to Adventure is an opportunity to leave the Ordinary World behind and do something greater. The mass of men lead lives of quiet desperation. They are looking for a light, a hope that there is something better than what they're experiencing right now. Your Call is that hope. It's the door to a new beginning. They suspect that they're missing out on something, and you're confirming that belief. There is something better for them if they only reach out and take it.

Step 3: Refusal of the Call

Your customers and clients will be tempted to say, "*No.*"

They'll have reservations and fears. They'll consider taking a different road or making no decision at all. What types of fears did you face? Did you say "No" at first? Voice some of the same objections your customers and clients will feel. What eventually caused you to overcome your fears and move forward in spite of them?

Perhaps you had a false start and you didn't succeed. Maybe you 'dabbled' in the subject without going all the way. Possibly you gave up several times along the way. You were skeptical. There were barriers standing in the way that kept you from moving forward. These could be external barriers such as a spouse who doesn't support you, a job that consumes all your time, or a complete lack of money. They could also be internal barriers such as that voice in your head saying why you can't do it or the cravings that keep you from staying on the diet. It could even be objections of why this won't work for you.

I haven't done a good enough job of integrating this into my own story until now. Since I was at the end of my rope when I discovered the Internet, I really did dive into it headfirst with no other option. It was sink or swim for me. But that doesn't for a minute mean I didn't face my own opportunities to give up. I had never used a PC before which meant spending every minute of my spare time just trying to figure out how to use the thing.

At first I ran some ads online and they generated zero sales. I lost money I didn't have. We couldn't pay our bills. My mind told me over-and-over again how I'd fail at this just like I had failed at everything else. I faced the same doubts and fears everyone else faces, but there simply was no other option. I had to make this work or else it was all over…

Did anything hold you back when you first heard about the Call to Adventure? You'd share what that is here. If you jumped in headfirst like I did, then this would be based on your internal feelings and doubts. Your customers and clients likely feel they're alone in their fears. They're not.

You're comforting them and letting them know you faced the same doubts. The story becomes even stronger if you turned your back on the Call initially or had a false start where you got started, but gave up because it was simply too difficult.

Step 4: The Mentor

You didn't go it alone. You had a mentor who came alongside to help. This could be a literal person who comes along and gives you advice at the right time, or it could be books, resources, videos, or even just stumbling upon a secret on your own. There is something that changed your failure into success. They gave you inspiration and guidance at just the right time. This is important in your Hero's Journey because you're serving as a mentor to your customers and clients. You gained wisdom from someone else. Now you're passing on wisdom to them.

In my situation, that mentoring came in the form of books and courses by Jay Abraham and Gary Halbert. I studied what they taught and tested each of their techniques to see which methods applied to the Internet and which ones didn't. The most important lesson I learned was the importance of building your own audience and list. That's the secret that set me free in my online business.

You may have me as one of your mentors in this book, but you also have mentors in your field of expertise. For example, one of my clients who teaches tennis talks about how he discovered the secret to massive power on the serve from traveling to take part in a golf instructors bootcamp. That's a mentor story that jumps out at you because it's totally unexpected. It makes you curious. How could you add power to your serve by learning from a golf instructor? Golf was more advanced in the efficiency of movement, and he pulled those lessons over to the tennis world.

We found that 'Mentor' story while I was interviewing my client over the phone to find a hook for that product. There are a ton of products on adding power to your serve, so what made his different? That's when you start asking questions such as *"Where did this idea originally come from?"* You look for a hook behind the story. That's interesting. It sounds like news someone would want to read. And it stands out from what the other tennis instructors are saying. It's an emotional story first that can also be backed up by logic (*golf really was more advanced in their methods*).

Step 5: Cross the Threshold

How did you make your decision to go forward in spite of the risks? The higher the risks, the more interest you build into the story. In the case of the fitness expert, it could be a medical condition that would end their life early. Perhaps they threw out all the junk food and even lost some relationships. For someone going into business for themselves, it might be quitting their job. They're terrified they're not going to make enough to survive, but they need that extra time in their business.

For the dentist who consults other dentists, it could be using their mortgage money to finance their big ad campaign. The guitar instructor might play their first live gig, with all the fear that comes along with it. The dog trainer might be faced with the most aggressive dog they've ever trained. Perhaps you invested more than you could afford in learning more about the subject. Or the speaker talks about getting up in front of a hostile audience. You're turning your back on the past and you've decided to move forward in spite of the risks.

This is another point that my story has been a little weak. Yes, I maxed out my final credit card to get moving online. But in the past I haven't really talked much about the dangers involved. I was so miserable BEFORE I started online that the difficulties and trials online didn't feel like that big of a deal at the time. Yes, my internal voice kept telling me about the possible failure, but I kept moving forward anyway. I quit my job after earning some money online and dedicated myself to making it work. That was my crossing the threshold. Everything I did was focused on making this work since there was no other option left.

Step 6: Ordeal

What challenges did you face AFTER you said "Yes"? You've made the decision and you may have burned the bridges behind you. There's no going back now. In weight loss, you now have to face those cravings. You have to exercise even when it's uncomfortable. Your co-workers tempt you with cake and cookies. You might even get so busy that it's tough to stay on track. You get knocked off track from time-to-time. It's not an easy process as you reach for success.

Your customers may have tried to succeed before, and they know it's not easy. They struggled and failed for some reason. You're facing some of those same struggles and you even fail, possibly multiple times, as you're going forward. But there is some discovery, product, or service that makes the difference. When you feel like giving up, there is some breakthrough that turns it all around.

This is the point where you could continue out the story with multiple challenges and multiple breakthroughs. That's what the full Hero's Journey is all about. It's one wave after another that comes crashing into you, each one larger than the last. Then at the final moment, the greatest darkness, that's when the dawn comes through. You've seen that story told hundreds of times in movies and books.

The number of challenges faced may vary along the way, but it always leads to a final confrontation. That's the climax of the movie. In American cinema, it will almost always be a victory...as people love the underdog story. That's not necessarily the case across other literature, but YOUR story will be a story of VICTORY. You conquered the villain (*challenges*) and now you can set others free.

Learning how to use a PC was only the beginning of the challenges I faced. I participated in those old Compuserve forums. I ran ads. I bought products. I created websites that didn't generate any sales. Back when I started in 1996, we didn't have all these easy to use email services like Aweber, Getresponse, or Zaxaa. Instead I had to use software that ran on my own computer to manage an email list. My ISP, Earthlink, even canceled me for spamming even though my list was totally opt-in.

The email list was the secret to success. My creditors kept hounding me in the early days...giving me an urgency that I had to make it happen. But money started coming in, first in a little trickle, but it quickly grew after discovering the importance of the email list.

Step 7: The Reward

What new insights came out of your ordeals? What you teach or share was forged in the fires of the ordeals you faced. If you're an information publisher, consultant, or coach, the techniques you share were proven during tough times. The hardest sale to make isn't that you or others have succeeded. It's persuading someone that your techniques will work for them. Your audience will always have objections about why their situation is different. It's more difficult. That's why you often see some of the most successful leaders talk about very humble beginnings and trying times. They're identifying with their audience (*and hopefully their story is true*).

If you sell a product or service, you may talk about the difficulties in getting the product to where it is today. What challenges did you face in creating something that's so effective? How did you prove its effectiveness in action? You could consider this the raspberry stain test. What is the worst situation your product has been tested in and what were the results?

You may share your message in a 6-week group coaching program where you teach your clients step-by-step how to move forward and defeat each of the challenges that come their way. It could be the new software you developed that shortcuts the entire process and solves the problem. This is what you wish you had available when you started as you could have avoided most of the ordeals!

If you sell a physical product such as a supplement, this is the secret formula your scientists created to solve the limitations of other products on the market. If you sell video equipment, it could be package deals you put together to eliminate all those frustrations you experienced along the way.

When I analyzed what was making money in my early days, it all came back to the email list. But it wasn't just any emails. It was sending out the right kind of emails which are a mixture of personality, content, and pitch. Content alone doesn't work. Pitch alone only works in the short-term until you burn out the list. Mix in your own personality, and more importantly YOUR STORY, and that is the breakthrough that propelled my business forward from then until now. Today we have additional tools to tell your story including video, social media, and more, but email is still the foundation of what works.

Step 8: Return With the Elixir

We're now skipping over the other trial and challenges stages. If you have the additional up and down stories, you can include those. If you've been in business for a long time, you might have your original Ordeal story, but then you faced something even greater that gave you additional insights for your Strategic Myth. But this is about MORE than your product or service. It's about your mission. It's about more than money. It's your PURPOSE!

You're sharing your magical elixir with others to FREE them from their Ordinary World. They're trapped by the old ways of doing things and you're showing them the light. For example, one of my clients teaches a totally new way to speak Spanish. Textbooks and classes teach the 'hard' way of doing things. People can spend years trying to learn all the grammar rules and get no closer to speaking Spanish. My client is passionate about helping others speak Spanish instead of just trying to learn it. And his system works for customers of any age. That's a mission for him based in his Strategic Myth of how he struggled for over 18 months to learn Spanish while living in a Spanish speaking country.

My Elixir is about how you can use proven systems like this one to Earn More, Work Less, and Enjoy Life. Instead of following random business opportunities, my systems include finding a hungry buying audience, positioning yourself as an authority, and bringing real value to your customers. They're long-term strategies for an ever-growing income even in the most competitive markets. These systems have been developed not just through my own 20 years of experience, but optimized through helping thousands of clients create their own Internet Lifestyles. Your Elixir is about changing the world around you. I want to see more people FREE to do business on their own terms!

How to Use Your Strategic Myth

Get started by writing out your Strategic Myth. After you've written each of the pieces, combine them together so they flow. Read it out loud and edit it down. This is your story. When someone reads it, they should understand the desperate problems you went through. They should see what makes you different from the competition. Your story should inspire them and get them excited about your subject. The correct response is they want to know more!

You can put the full story (*often a couple of pages*) on the About page of your website. You can break it up into several emails in the beginning of your email sequence. After someone has been on your list for a week, they should know why you do what you do…and why it's so important to you. If you didn't want to write out the story in your emails, you could at least link over to the full story on your About page in the PS of several of your initial emails.

On a webinar or in a live presentation, you will want to include the story. Whenever I've tried to leave out my story, it has cost me leads and sales. You may get tired of telling your story, but there will be people who haven't heard it before. You can include insights and value throughout the story itself. How did you defeat the challenges that came against you? How does your story integrate into your message and your mission?

Find a way to integrate your story when others interview you. Interviewers almost always ask for a list of questions. Your goal isn't just to share information. That's boring. Instead you want to organize the questions and the answers to integrate in your story. A common question is, *"How did you get started at X?"* Answer it with your story. Find ways to include your story and get people fired up about your mission. Content is NOT king. Connections are king.

Stories are how we communicate. Others will invite you inside their belief system through a good story. You will never change anyone's mind with an argument or a debate. But you can change their beliefs by changing the story they have inside them.

When telling your story, don't just say what happened. Also share the emotions you felt during the story. For example, you wouldn't say you were 'nervous' when you were speaking in front of a room. You'd talk about how your hands were shaking and your heart was pounding. You're making the story real to those listening to you. You're inviting them into your world to experience it alongside you.

Action Steps

- Remember this rule. You cannot debate someone into changing their personal beliefs, because those beliefs are rooted in their story. If you want to change someone's viewpoint, you first have to change their story.
- The strongest marketing campaigns grow from an attention grabbing story.
- Go through each of the 8 steps from the Hero's Journey to create your Strategic Myth.
- If you're struggling with this, ask someone to interview you about how you first started your business, came up with your ideas, or what motivated you to help this audience.
- Integrate your Strategic Myth into your initial email follow-up sequence and on the About Us page of your website.

How to Attract High Quality Pre-Qualified Clients With the Authority Architecture™

How do you create a loyal client base that buys from you not just today, but for decades into the future? That's the holy grail of business. Once you find this recipe, you can virtually write your own ticket no matter what business you're in.

Most people underestimate just how much it costs to generate a new client in their business. If you can generate new subscribers and customers at breakeven or better, you have the foundation for an incredible business. Whether it takes you 1 month, 3 months, or even 12 months to break even on bringing a new client through the door, everything after it is pure profit.

I've recently worked with a client who sold a yearly membership as their primary offer. While they had individual purchases here and there, the majority of clients purchased their 'yearly plan'. In that business, we consider any advertising which generates new clients at break-even or better as profitable. We've seen the stats and know that 70%+ of his new clients will renew next year. Each new client through the door equals ongoing yearly income. In the case of a future buy-out offer, those yearly clients will be seen as the most valuable asset in the company. They're a future income stream other companies would love to tap into.

In your business, you're also building up assets that create long-term passive income. Your hyper-responsive buyers are at the top of that list. Those are the clients who join your loyalty programs and any ongoing billing programs you have in place. They buy higher-ticket offers from you. They buy from you more often. They're first in line for new product and service offers.

The 80/20 rule affects everything in your life and business. The top 20% of your clients will usually create 80% of your income. When you take it even further out, you'll find 5% of your customers generate 50% of your income. I have clients who have been worth considerably more than $100,000 to me over the years. I have many customers who have been worth $20,000 or more. There are customers on my lists who first purchased from me way back in the 1990's. And they're still buying today.

That's customer loyalty. It doesn't take many customers like this to change the math behind your business. If 95% of your clients are only worth $100, and 5% of them are worth $10,000 or more, your overall lifetime value per client jumps from $100 to $595 each. That dramatically changes how much you can afford to pay for each customer coming into your system.

By now you've probably realized the new model of sales and marketing involves delivering content and value before the sale. You hear this from virtually every book, magazine, and business publication. You hear constantly that "Content is King." Yes, content is valuable. You're not going to build a loyal client base if you don't provide value and content online.

But content alone is not enough. As we discussed in the last chapter, you need to connect any content you share with a Strategic Myth. This is the story of why you do what you do. It's an emotional hook that attracts the attention of your target audience and explains why you're different from the competition. This is about more than just money to you. You're on a mission because of the experiences you've had in the past.

In this chapter, we're continuing this theme and I'll show you how it's about more than just your story. There are so many options available in the market today, and people are also looking for a community they can plug-into. They buy from those they Know, Like, and Trust. While this may be more obvious for some professions such as a real estate agent, business consultant, or even an accountant, it is still true even for less 'expert' focused business models.

For example, Steve Jobs was the face of Apple for decades. Dave Thomas was the face of Wendy's. These are huge corporations who tapped into the story of their founder. But they went beyond just the story. They tapped into them as an individual. They were the face of the company. In other companies, a paid spokesperson may become the face of the company. The "Old Spice Guy" had a series of very successful online video ads for Old Spice. And the "Most Interesting Man In the World" was the spokesperson for Dos Equis beer. They created a story and a character to be the face of their company.

An Inspirational & Entertaining Leader

Let's change direction and look at talk radio. Two very popular hosts are Rush Limbaugh & Howard Stern. They're about as different as they could be, yet they each keep audiences entertained for hours every day. Callers to Rush's show even came up with a unique title for themselves: "Ditto Heads." His listeners call into the show and praise Rush. They completely agree with everything he just said. Since he has so many callers do this, he had them just start saying "ditto" to say they approved the message unquestionably.

Rush's rants are so in tune with his audience that they want to call in just to tell everyone how much they agree with him. And they're fine with being called a Ditto Head. He taps into their frustration and anger. He channels it back to them on his show. Of course, when you become a bold voice you also attract those who disagree with you. No, it's more than that. They are outright angry with you for expressing that opinion. Some people listen to Rush just to get riled up against him!

In marketing, you want your audience to love you or hate you. Both show you have their attention. When they're apathetic, they're simply not paying attention anymore. Any successful radio show host has attracted an audience who agree with them almost without question. For example, Dave Ramsey teaches people the basics of getting out of debt with his **7 Baby Steps** (*notice how he is making it simple*). His message is so popular he has a whole network of consultants and his materials are even taught in many churches.

I could continue sharing other examples of radio show hosts, but all of them have these traits in common. They tell emotional stories that relate with their audience. They take calls and interact with their audience. If they teach a specific subject (*like Dave Ramsey or Suze Orman*) other experts will say what they teach is too simple. Some people love them. Others hate them.

You too can tap into these secrets to attract your hungry buying audience. Even if you don't have a radio or TV show, you can still become a mini-celebrity in your niche market. That's the best type of celebrity. You can become a famous person no one has ever heard of. You get all the benefits of fortune without the paparazzi hounding you.

Your email list, your Facebook page, or your Youtube channel can be your "Radio Show." You don't cultivate your fan base by just publishing content. YES, you need content. But they connect with you because of the stories you tell. They nod their head alongside you as you rant about the problems in the market. They identify with you as you tell your origin story. You invite them to reply to you, and you open a dialogue with them. Maybe you feature their question in your next email.

You can use any online medium to grow your authority. Do you produce a weekly video tip for Youtube? Or you run a weekly podcast on iTunes. Maybe you run monthly webinars. You could publish a monthly newsletter that you mail to your list. The medium isn't what matters. What matters is attracting a hungry buying audience and creating a connection with them.

Become a leader. You're going to give your audience a story they can hold onto. You're going to take them on an adventure. As Thoreau said, *"The mass of men lead lives of quiet desperation."* They're suffering through the dullness of their daily lives. The desperation is the lack of hope for a better day. They're so focused on getting through the day that they never let their voice shine through. You can become a lightning rod of HOPE they hold onto. You can give voice to their fears and their dreams.

Inspire your audience. Give them hope of a brighter future. Break free from the expectations of others. Quit playing it so safe all the time. What could you write in your email that would not only give value to your reader, but could also be a bright point of their day? Could you make them laugh…or make them cry? What could you rant about that would get them nodding their head in agreement and send you an email that simply says, *"Ditto"*?

You have to take some risks. Some readers may get upset. Others may even unsubscribe and stop listening to you. That's why it's so important to KNOW your addicted buying audience. You want to be in unison with their thinking and their actions. You want to voice the frustrations they can't quite express themselves. You want them to take courage in your story and desire to make it their own.

Some of the strongest brands in the world help their customers see themselves in a new light. They give them a new identity. Harley Davidson is an example of this. A Harley owner might be a mild mannered, middle age accountant by day, but they're FREE when they start up their bike. Maybe they don't get time to ride because of all their work and family responsibilities. But they smile a little each time they look at their Harley. Just owning it makes them feel better about themselves.

The Authority Architecture™

Many professional speakers are actually introverts. They recharge by being alone. It's show time the moment they step on stage. They're still themselves, but they're a more outgoing, animated version of themselves.

I get this way during interviews. I get excited about marketing techniques. Recently someone emailed me and told me I should do even more audios because they could hear the passion in my voice. They were inspired by my enthusiasm. But I'm as introverted as they come. I'd rather go for a hike in the woods than attend a party any day. My wife would literally have to drag me to a party. There are times where I have two webinars on the same day. When that happens I'm worn out and want to go hide somewhere to vegetate afterwards. Being in a group tires me out.

At home you might be a mild mannered Clark Kent, but when it's time to help your audience breakthrough all the barriers holding them back, you're Superman or Superwoman. What is your Authority Persona? Who are you to your audience?

What personality traits will your audience identify with and respond to? The beauty of the Internet is you can reveal your true self. But often it's an amplified version of you. Do you share your sense of humor with the audience? Do you share stories from your personal life? Are you willing to laugh at yourself? It's tough to use humor when writing sales copy, but humor is a basis of public speaking. And it's extremely useful in emails, webinars, podcasts, and videos. Can you come up with some unique words of your own?

When many people write an email, they get into their 'professional voice.' They try to become super-serious. That may be required in some markets. If you serve family members who suffered a recent family suicide, humor would be totally out of place. You'd need a voice that's sensitive and caring. It needs to identify and share their pain. Your origin story would likely be suffering through similar trauma yourself.

The voice you use must connect with your market. You might write in a kick-butt, take no prisoners attitude type of voice to young copywriters chomping at the bit to take the world by storm. But you'd want a totally different voice when writing to expectant mothers. Phrases such as 'killer copy' and 'financial bloodbath' may be part of your language when speaking to an audience full of copywriters or financial investors, but female audiences are often turned off by violent language.

What if I could wave a magic wand and you were suddenly a more outgoing, bolder version of yourself? You still have the same emotions, desires, and goals. But you are now truly willing to share from the heart with your audience.

What would you say if you had no FEAR? What if we hit the OFF button on your inner censor? It may take some time before you can fully move into that freedom, and you may want to experiment with what your audience responds to best. But what I've seen from over a decade of working with clients is we're overly cautious and it's holding back our success.

Below are the 10 foundations of the Authority Architecture™. Think about who you are to your audience. This is about presenting them with an authentic Public Persona who is bold about your message and your mission. Write out a couple of bullet points on each of these key principles.

As you go through each of these, pay attention to how many of them also line up with super heroes. Superman was created in 1933 and sold to DC Comics in 1938. That means he has been around for OVER 80 years. How many Superman comics have there been? How many movies? How many times have they rebooted the franchise and came out with a new version of the character? How many action figures and licensed products have had his name and likeness on them?

He will still be earning money for DC decades into the future. And he is just one of thousands of super hero characters. What creates such enduring franchises? They tell the same stories over-and-over again. How many times have we heard Superman's origin story? And I'm sure we're not done yet.

Heroes inspire us with courage. They overcome challenges and defeat villains (*just like in the Hero's Journey that we covered in the last chapter*). We identify with them and their struggles. We envy their capabilities and their integrity in the face of opposition. As you go through the Authority Architecture, you may even want to imagine yourself as a hero of your own franchise. You're a larger than life character. Your day-to-day life is your secret identify. But when you're helping your clients, you suit up and become their hero.

This doesn't mean you need to make anything up. Instead you're just looking at who you already are to your best clients, and you're focusing on those key principles. You could even say your business persona becomes a little bit of a caricature of you. When someone draws a caricature, they choose to focus on a dominant feature or two. You're doing the same thing here. You're focusing on something in your nature and you're amplifying it. You're focusing the light on it.

#1 - Origin Story (Strategic Myth)

Every super hero has an origin story, and your business does also. We covered this in in-depth in the previous chapter and hopefully you realized that this goes beyond just an "origin story." It also shapes the rest of the narrative behind your business and why you do what you do. It's one of the first and most important elements of your Authority Architecture, but we're not going to go into it in depth here since we covered it in detail in the previous chapter.

Every authority has a story they tell. My friend Dr. Glenn Livingston tells about his big two-million-dollar mistake with a conference center in New York. He invested everything he had into this conference center without doing his research first. It struggled and eventually went under. This huge failure made him realize just how important research is to your success. When he came online he applied his research skills in one market after another...succeeding in 18+ unique niche markets in a row. He became a client with me back in 2006 and he started sharing his message in the internet marketing world about how his research systems could give you an unfair advantage in any market you choose.

Salim Omar over at **www.cpamarketinggenius.com** was dissatisfied as a CPA working for others. He started his own firm and went into over $100,000 in debt while working 60 and 70 hours a week with clients who didn't appreciate him. They teach you how to be a good practitioner in CPA classes, but they don't teach you anything about how to market a practice. His origin story includes how he started breaking free from this and eventually got to the place where his staff works with premium clients while Salim works a couple of days a week and even takes vacations right in the middle of tax season.

#2 - Vision For Your World

Super heroes always have a dream for the world that's driving them to do what they do. Your Strategic Myth is more than just an origin story because it also points to your vision for the world. There may already be 100's of competitors in a market. Customers are overwhelmed with options. Why do they need yet another option? How does your product or service stand out or fill a gap in the marketplace that isn't currently being filled? Perhaps you solve a different problem than the others. Or maybe you appeal to a specific audience. There's a reason you do what you do…that goes beyond just giving people yet another option.

But your overall vision for your world goes beyond any individual product or service. It's your overriding purpose for doing what you do. And this vision is also often bigger than yourself. Maybe you want to help 1,000,000 people reach their perfect weight. To do this means you're going to release training products and coaching programs, but you need to go even further. You're going to certify coaches to use your methods. You're going to build up a network of trainers around the world. What is your "BIG" vision of what you want to accomplish?

My vision is to help entrepreneurs Earn More, Work Less, and Enjoy Life Without Compromising Their Values. That's why I talk about the Internet Lifestyle. While the clients I attract are willing to work hard, they're not tied down, spending every moment growing their business. They have lives. They have families. They have freedom to take vacations and have interests outside of work.

While many of my clients have seen big financial breakthroughs, I prefer featuring the ones who talk about their freedom since it matches up with my vision. Sure, you can give your whole life to your business if you want, but you don't have to. You can put systems and team members (employees or outsourced workers from around the world) that grow your business for you.

For example, here's the testimonial Florian Meier from OnlineTennisInstruction.com recently sent me (this is a transcript of his video): *"We started working together approximately 12 months and the results have been phenomenal. We've* **more than doubled revenues** *and the team has grown from 2 to 5 people. At the same time I've been able to reduce the amount of hours I work. I used to work 70 hours per week. I* **now work about 35 to 40. And I can take vacations whenever I want!***"*

You're going to show people a BETTER way. You're going to bring them HOPE and inspire them to reach their goals. Hope can keep people moving toward that brighter day they see in the future even if they're suffering right now. The entire weight loss and fitness industry is based off of it. If you sell anything to do with health/fitness, your customers have likely already tried other solutions. They lost weight and gained it back multiple times. They don't know if anything will work for them. One of your jobs is to encourage them and lift them up. You show before/after results from others to show them that, *"Yes, they can do it."*

A chiropractor isn't about doing adjustments. Those are simply a means to the end of natural health. Your vision of the world could be about helping 10,000 people live pain-free and active lives. You might even tie in photos of you enjoying the outdoors because it's part of your vision. Perhaps you partner with 5k races, bike shops, or wilderness adventures. It all depends on what your vision is, but a good vision of the world will be about a lot more than just visiting your office. It's about what you're enabling people to do outside of your office.

What is your Big Hairy Audacious Goal? Just helping clients save on taxes isn't enough to grab attention and inspire your audience. Instead, you want to help 1,000 entrepreneurs make a difference in the world today by managing their business well and keeping more of their own money. When I give a number like that, your first temptation may be to freak out, but that's what makes it a BHAG. You want a vision that's too big to accomplish on your own. You need to influence others, build a team, and possibly get other practitioners participating alongside you. That's how you inspire your audience!

#3 –Villain and a Polarizing Point of View

What is your VILLAIN? Every super hero has an arch enemy, their nemesis. In business, this is rarely a specific individual or group. Instead, it's about the DESPERATE PROBLEM you're helping your audience solve. One of the things I rail against is the business opportunity mindset online. Those are the "experts" who tell you to give your money to join some 'pre-packaged' online business opportunity that doesn't require any effort or work on your part. These scams never work. Any real business requires both thinking and action on your part. Those scams tell you everything is ready to go and doesn't require you to do anything.

Some of my worst hate mail comes when I expose those scams. Of course the promoters of these 'opportunities' are angry, but often times buyers can be also. They don't want anyone to burst their bubble. They've been taken advantage of, but if they ignore it, maybe it will go away. When I talk about this issue, some people are set free while others take it as an attack on the illusion they so desperately want to believe.

You can expect the same whenever you boldly proclaim the truth about your subject. What mistakes, myths, and misconceptions are there in your market? What are the big mistakes you've made, myths in your industry, and misconceptions the average person has about your subject? The paleo "believer" would tell you that grains are destroying your body. The vegan would tell you meat is the problem. Neither group would say their method is just a good way to eat. It's the right way. If you don't agree, then you're not a part of their group.

If we jumped over to the investment field, you'll find index investors who tell you that mutual funds are ripping you off with high fees and that you can't beat the market by buying individual stocks. You'll also find investment teachers who each have their own view: dividend paying stocks, small value companies, tech giants, FOREX trading, options, trend trading, etc. Each one teaches a method they use to 'beat' the market and promise higher returns. While they may agree there are other investment methods that work, here is why their method is the best way.

The message becomes a part of their identity. They become a paleo believer. They're an options trader. They do Crossfit. They're in an Internet Lifestyle business. They're a business coach. You're a leader who is attracting followers to your message. And that message becomes a part of them.

What are you dogmatic about? Ben Settle is an incredible email marketer. He teaches that everyone needs to email daily. While I don't feel it fits every single niche and business owner, following the strategy for 30 days would improve almost anyone's marketing. If you don't agree with his message and email style, then you don't belong on his list. And he's happy to tell you about it.

Be willing to drive away the wrong customers. As a small business, you don't need everyone as your customer. Write down the traits of your ideal customer. Now think about the customers you don't want to attract. What can you say that would attract your ideal customers while driving away those you don't want to do business with? That's why I often make fun of BSOs (*Bright Shiny Objects*) and the business opportunity, get rich quick mentality. Those are not the customers I want to attract.

Those who succeed online are those who are willing to position themselves as an authority in their market. They're willing to position themselves as a voice. The Internet is too competitive to just be another parrot in a sea of mediocrity. That's why I'm helping you find your message and your voice.

There are myths in your industry. People believe a lie. What are the lies you want to confront in your industry? What is the truth? What does someone have to believe or do to reach the results they're looking for? If you had to create the 10 commandments for your industry, what would they be? What are the core messages and belief systems you want to share with people in your market?

Salim Omar teaches his CPA students that they can put a team in place so they're not overwhelmed during tax season. He makes it a point to tell his audience about his 'light' schedule while they're busting their butts right now. And he also teaches how they can attract customers all year long with premium services including proactive quarterly strategy meetings with their clients. That's a radically different message than you'd expect in his market. What messages are you sharing that will attract your audience while repelling those who don't fit your ideal client profile?

#4 – Be a Likeable Person With Common Experiences

Yes, you should be a likeable person. Have you ever noticed how many super heroes and other mythical heroes are painted as orphans? They're an outsider, and everyone feels like an outsider at times. They're an underdog you want to root for. You could be an absolute expert at what you do, but if no one likes you, you're not going to do that well in business. One of the ways you can establish rapport is through shared interests. That's one of the reasons so many people in business play golf.

What 'common experiences' do you share with your audience? Many of my B2B clients come from the same background as their customers. Paul Wright is a physiotherapist who helps health business owners. Salim Omar is a CPA helping other CPAs. Michael Beck is a chiropractor helping chiropractors. They know the trials and frustrations of their audience. They can talk about how their university didn't prepare them for marketing their practice. And they can connect with their audience on a professional level. There are many business coaches and consultants who don't come from the same field they coach in, but they have to a find a different way to personally connect with their audience.

What common experiences can you share from your personal life? For example, maybe you have childhood experiences that have a lesson you want to share with others today. Perhaps it's a lesson taught to you by your mother or your grandfather. Maybe you had a pet when you were young. Or there are stories from school you can tell. Were you on a sports team growing up? In high school, did you have a desire to fit in (who didn't)? These are all little personal tidbits that could find their way into any presentations, emails, blog posts, podcasts, and any other content you share.

Invite your audience into your life. Mention your spouse or children. Share a story about your pets. Tell them about what happened on your adventure to Thailand. You can even tell them about daily adventures such as something that happened at the gym, restaurant, or store this week. Are there any movies or TV shows you love? Those are perfect fodder for emails or blog posts.

Perhaps you're on vacation to a tropical island. You could tell your audience all about the experiences in a blog post loaded with photos. Perhaps you relate it back to the peace and relaxation you felt. Or you could use it like some of my B2B clients do as an example of how the systems they've put in place in their business allow them to take breaks from the business while their business continues to profit. They're truly living the Lifestyle others want to experience.

#5- Personal Parables

A personal parable is a story that contains a profound lesson or illustration of your message. Your audience may not remember your 5 tips, all your facts, or the features behind what you offer. But they'll remember a good story. We first make buying decisions based on emotion, and back up those decisions with logic. A story is a carrier of emotion. They bypass the brain and go directly into our hearts.

Your Strategic Myth is your biggest and most important story, but there could be other little stories from your life or business that you share. Professional speakers would call this signature stories. Every speaker has a few stories they constantly tell.

Back when I lived in Hagerstown, Indiana, my nearest neighbor was the cow named Oscar. My wife and I lived right next to a horse farm and they had one cow in the field which always came right up to the fence next to our yard. We'd always talk to the cow and even our dogs got used to it.

Many of the horses also liked to stick their heads sideways through the fence to eat the grass on our side. Yes, the grass really is greener on the other side. I've used that quick little story to illustrate the Internet Lifestyle. You can do this business from ANYWHERE in the world. It's about your choices of where you want to live, what you want to do, and who you want to work with.

I've told that story at many presentations. People have come up to me years later and asked me how the cow was doing. I honestly don't know because we've moved since then. I'll bet they don't remember virtually anything from the presentation I gave at the event, but they remember the cow.

Hopefully they remember the core lesson of the cow also. That's also why I used to do email promotions to my list in front of conferences. It would demonstrate the power of email stronger than simply teaching people how to write their own emails. They remember the demonstration of seeing how much money showed up in my shopping cart. And hopefully that reminder forced them to think about growing their own list and relationship with their list.

What types of signature stories/parables should you be looking for and telling?

1. **Adversity**: You had a major challenge in your life. Maybe you survived cancer or your doctor told you that you'd never walk again. You lost a family member you were close to. Maybe you went bankrupt. These are stories of incredible pain or loss. You discovered a life lesson in the middle of the storm that you have to share with others. These stories are often the most powerful, but they can be the most difficult to tell because you reveal your vulnerabilities.

2. **Mentor**: You met someone who changed your life. They imparted wisdom to you. The "Rich Dad – Poor Dad" series of books is a mentor story. He talks about his Rich Dad who revealed these life lessons to him over time. The mentor story works well because you may be positioning yourself to be a mentor to others. For example, since Dan Kennedy sells conferences, he has often told a story about how he paid thousands of dollars, sat on a plane for hours, and rented a car just to see a 45 minute presentation from an expert. He is 'selling you' on the value of what you could learn at an event.

3. **Embarrassing**: This is a situation that might have been mortifying to you at the time, but you can laugh about it today. Maybe it's a family vacation gone bad or a time you were in a 'brain fog' and couldn't make the right decision for the life of you. This is where comedians shine, but anyone can use an embarrassing story as a way to make your audience laugh. And it also shows you're a human who makes mistakes just like them (you don't take yourself too seriously).

4. **Discovery**: How did you learn what you're sharing now? What experience did you go through to learn it? Perhaps you stumbled

upon this secret while you were doing something else. Or you may have put in years to discover this lesson. What has your experience taught you? For example I discovered the Golden Glove method as a quick way to improve any type of advertising after years of reviewing websites for attendees at conferences.

5. **Ancient Wisdom**: This could be a story from the Bible or other religious text. Or it could be something from Roman or Greek mythology. You tell a story you heard when you were a child from someone else. It might not be your own personal story, but it's a story that people can relate to that illustrates the principle you want to share.

These stories can be used over and over again. They get used in your autoresponder sequences, told on your webinars, and shared in your videos. How do you find these stories? You have to test them. Write an email about the story and see how readers respond. Do you generate sales? Do you get responses? Do people email you about a similar experience (*you've definitely connected with them when they want to share their story with you*)?

You may also have little stories about your daily life. What did the waiter do at the restaurant that you can transition into a lesson? What did your child say to you that got you thinking about your customers? Anything and everything that happens to you can become fodder for content in your business. You're the star of your own reality show. Use stories to demonstrate and share content. You never know which ones will become 'personal parables' until you try them out.

You could even tell a story you've heard from someone else. Client case studies are some of the most powerful stories you can share. Talk to some of your customers and clients. Find out their story. Ask for permission to share it with your audience. A case study by its very nature includes proof. It also has value in it as you hear what they did to achieve the results. And you can tap into the emotions of the market through the problems your customer experienced along with cheering their triumph.

#6 – Simple Principles Of Life

"Life is like a box of chocolates. You never know what you're going to get!"

Forest Gump

Use simple, easy-to-explain principles. Comics aren't deep literature. They're driven by simple principles. Celebrity authorities also simplify their message. It doesn't matter the subject. Dr. Oz, Dr. Phil, Oprah, Dr. Drew all focus on making their message simple to understand and follow. It doesn't matter how much you know. It only matters how much you implement. Is your core message simple enough that someone could repeat it to others?

That's why I use the "Golden Glove" so often. It's simple at its core: Desperate Problem, Unique Promise, Overwhelming Proof, Irresistible Offer, Reason to Act Now. Is your sales message hitting each of the 5 fingers on your hand? If you're missing one of these elements, then it's not nearly as forceful as it could be. But while it's simple, it's also a deep message at the same time. I can apply it to any type of persuasion from websites to emails to presentations. You can even use it to persuade your spouse. And we can dig into each of the 5 components. A desperate problem could be as simple as calling out to your audience and the problem you solve. In other situations, you might tell your complete 'before' story including all the pain and anguish you went through.

Right now I'm breaking down the "Authority Architecture" you can see in any celebrity authority's business. Take your pick of an authority you admire. You will find each of these aspects. While you could spend years discovering these on your own (*it's taken me two decades now*), you can go through this issue and have them all right in front of you. Of course, you need to have deep knowledge about your subject. Those who truly understand the subject and how to create results are the ones who can best boil it down to simple steps anyone can follow.

As you create these simplified systems, also create the terminology to go along with it. That way you can speak in code to your audience. It's shorthand for training they've already went through. It also helps identify those who are in your tribe. They know the secret handshake and your code words.

#7 – Unique Language

Heroes have catch phrases they constantly use. Spiderman's uncle Ben said, "With great power comes great responsibility." You'll hear that multiple times in his comics and movies. Authorities also have their unique language, catchphrases, and even titles for the products and services.

You've already seen the Golden Glove, Strategic Myth, and Authority Architecture. I'll use a phrase like "Magic Tipping Point" to refer to how long it takes you to reach break-even on advertising. If you spend $300 to generate 100 new subscribers, and over the next 30 days 5 of them buy your $60 product, you've now broken even. Your Magic Tipping Point is 30 days. Everything you earn after that point is pure profit. We may add more emails earlier in the sequence to earn money faster or we may add an upsell to increase the average transaction value.

We have numerous terms we talk about simply because we're in internet marketing that would sound like gooblygook to someone on the outside looking in: autoresponders, conversion, lead magnet, backend, lifetime customer value, break-even, affiliates, upsells, average transaction value, etc.

I mentioned Ben Settle and his email powers of persuasion earlier. One of his unique words is gooroos. When he uses that, he isn't referring to an expert. He's referring to someone who plays the role of a guru. They might have just read a few ebooks or possibly even had a success or two, but they're giving advice that will lead you down the wrong track. It's a play on words that again starts carrying the emotion he wants it to have with his audience. What words do you use, and what emotions are you connecting to those words?

#8 – Inner Circle Exclusivity

Every story has an inner circle cast of characters. It isn't made up of just the leader. In business, you want to make your clients feel like VIPs who get the royal treatment. And one of the best ways to do that is to have levels of access or even an element of exclusivity. You don't work with everyone.

The American Express Black card was a rumor long before American Express decided to get in on the game and create the card everyone was already talking about. It is by invitation only for those who spend at least $250,000 per year on their card. In addition, last time I checked it was $2,500 per year plus a $7,500 first year initiation fee to own the Black card. Of course this comes with additional benefits including a 24/7 concierge service for reserving restaurants, hotels, flights, etc. But more than anything else, it's a status symbol for a select group of clients.

Exclusivity raises your value considerably. For example, several clients sell "area exclusivity" with their service plans. If they're running a PPC campaign for a client in Ocala, they won't accept another competitive client in the service area. The size of the exclusive area varies depending on the industry and city size, but usually we base it on overall population. So the area in square miles is much larger in a rural area compared to the center of New York City. You also may only accept a limited number of clients such as how I only work with 20 one-on-one clients at any time. Or you set-up 'levels of access' such as group coaching vs one-on-one coaching or a Silver, Gold, Platinum type of access to you (*perhaps group, email, & phone options*).

How can you add exclusivity to your business or to specific higher levels in your business? For example, an ecommerce website could have a VIP membership only for those who spend a certain amount. Or it could simply be a membership fee such as Amazon charges for their Prime membership. Sam's Club and Costco work on a similar principle of member's only. In a publishing business, you could add coaching or done-for-you services as part of your high ticket backend. But you don't want to accept just anyone as a client.

If you've done any consulting or coaching, you know it only takes one bad client to make you miserable. Write down everything you know about your Ideal Client. This person is easy to work with, implements your advice, gets results, and gives you a testimonial. At the same time, write down a description of a poor quality client for you. Have you had any clients that drove you crazy? If so, why? What could you have spotted to disqualify them before they ever became a client?

I've used a pre-qualification discovery call process before for my high level programs. First, applicants paid a $100 refundable deposit. I've also done a free application process which generates more leads. Requiring a fee upfront will limit the number of leads that come through to only the most qualified (*you generate less leads but get a higher closing rate*).

After this, potential prospects filled out an application online that asked them their goals, previous experience, and why they would make a good member of the program. They need to sell me on becoming a member. After the application I did a short 25 minute call to make sure they're a good fit for the program and will be able to add value to the overall group. If they don't qualify or decide not to join, their $100 is refunded. If they decide to join the program, the $100 is applied to the full fee.

This type of application process flips selling on its head. Instead of chasing after a prospect, you're asking them to sell you on why you should accept them as a client. It's about them qualifying to work with you instead of you qualifying yourself to work with them. If I chase after my dog, he runs from me. But if I turn around and run the other way, he'll chase me. It's a game to him. And you can turn client qualification into a game instead of using a 'hard sales' approach.

#9 – Super Powers

What amazing abilities do you use to help your clients? If we look at fictional characters, they all have some type of superpower. You have comic book characters like Superman, but you also have characters such as Sherlock Holmes who can use his deductive reasoning to solve any mystery. All of our heroes have amazing abilities that make them stand out from the common person. This is true of celebrity authorities also. It could simply be how insightful they are or their ability to use humor in any situation. Or it could be their amazing ability to make a guest feel comfortable and share with them during an interview. There is always a reason they attract an audience.

What do your customers 'envy' about you or your lifestyle? Remember *"The mass of men lead lives of quiet desperation."* And social media makes this to be even more true today. The day-to-day humdrum seems so boring after you see all the exciting vacations and purchases being made by those on your Facebook feed. You're being exposed to all the highlights, and it makes people feel their own life just isn't that interesting. Psychologists even talk about 'social media depression' today.

One of the abilities I've focused on for years is pinpointing and improving the conversion of websites for my clients. That's why I've often said, *"I can increase the profits of any website in 15 minute or less with the Golden Glove."* It's my X-Ray superpower. This is part of what sets you apart. If you're not sure what your unique abilities are, ask your friends and family, *"What do they rely on you for? What seems to come naturally to you?"* A lot of times you don't spot what comes natural to you. It's invisible to you. It's normal for you to be good at this even though everyone else around you may struggle with it.

You can also look at what your customers and clients say about you. Milana Leshinky from JVInsiderCircle.com said this about me, *"I've been in business for 14 years, Terry Dean was one of my first online marketing mentors. Today I run two online companies generating $1.2 million a year, and it's amazing that I still continue to learn from Terry. He has a **unique ability to hone in on the most critical issues that can impact your income, then dissects the strategy behind it."***

She is an awesome businessperson, so when she calls out that I have a unique ability to hone in on the critical issues and strategy that impact your income, I listen. You can often use your customers' exact language to describe yourself and your offers. Review your testimonials. Send a survey out to your subscribers and buyers asking them what they rely on you for. Let them guide you!

#10 - Personal Flaws

Superman has his kryptonite. Achilles had his heel. Greek mythology tells a story about how it was foretold that Achilles would die young. So his mother dipped him in the river Styx which was said to make someone invulnerable. She held him by his heel as she was dipping him. The legend continues on to say that he died after receiving a wound from an arrow to his heel. He was invulnerable except for one area. You'll find any good character has weaknesses. If Superman was invincible, it wouldn't make for very good stories. He shows up and just automatically wins every time without any danger. Sherlock Holmes had a drinking problem. Popular TV characters often have compulsive behaviors.

When selling a product, you can add credibility to the offer by sharing a damaging admission. For example, several years ago I sold a series of audios which Glenn Livingston and I recorded casually at his house. I shared on the website that there were times you could even hear Glenn's dog pick up a squeaky toy in the background, and if that disturbed someone, then this wasn't the course for them. Not only does revealing a flaw increase your credibility, it also sets appropriate expectations for the product. If someone purchased that course expecting perfect audio, they would have been disappointed. By sharing that potential issue upfront, I already set the expectations appropriately.

Here's the key. While the audio quality is important, it's not nearly as important as the information contained on those audios. Any personal flaws you reveal are similar. For example, let's say you went bankrupt in the past. You'd want to reveal that information because it could be damaging if someone brought it up and you never talked about it. But this was in the past and doesn't affect the results you deliver for clients today. At the same time, you could use this as a way to identify with your audience and their struggles. You understand going through financial problems.

I've made a LOT of mistakes with money. Besides getting myself in ridiculous debt with all those failed business opportunities before coming online, I also found a way to spend virtually every penny I made online for years. I couldn't even tell you where it all went. Eventually I did start tracking and investing, but that doesn't discount just how irresponsible I was with money for years.

In addition, I often feel out of place with other entrepreneurs. Many entrepreneurs are workaholics, whether they admit to it or not. I'm personally a little bit of a slacker. While I could scale up to a large online organization like many other internet marketers, I have absolutely no desire to do so. Instead I focus on the freedom of an Internet Lifestyle! Most of my client's businesses are growing much faster than my own, and I take pleasure in this fact.

What personal flaws could you mention? Maybe you've been divorced 3 times…or you can't hold onto money…or you have no talent with sports whatsoever. Personally I have zero musical talent and I mention that fact at times also. Any faults you have that don't reduce the results your customers or clients can receive from you can become fodder you use to demonstrate you're a real person just like them. You have strengths and you have weaknesses. You're someone they can know, like, and trust.

Integrate All These Components

Remember all of this goes back to your audience first. It's about knowing and connecting with them. What are their desperate problems? What are their hopes and dreams? What or who do they envy? Look through your back story and who you are personally for places you can connect with them. Be authentic, but at the same time be a larger, more inspiring version of yourself.

If you're a consultant, coach, or author, you are your brand. If you're running a larger company or an ecommerce company, you're the spokesperson for your brand. Either way, you're still a character they can follow and relate to. They want to go on adventures with you. Give them a vision they can get behind. Show them a common enemy. Yes, you want to provide content and value, but that can't hold their attention or create loyalty for years or even decades to come. If you want to generate loyalty and long-term profits, you have to go beyond this and become someone who inspires them. You help them become who they aspire to be.

The 10 components in your Authority Architecture will be used in your emails, blog posts, interviews, and any other content you create. For example, your Strategic Myth should almost always appear within the first week of an email sequence. Insert your vision. Sprinkle everything you do with some of your signature stories and other common experiences. Come up with contrarian content that polarizes your audience. At the same time you want to simplify anything you teach while creating your own unique language. What words and phrases do you use that aren't commonly used outside your group?

Action Steps

- Tapping into your unique Authority Architecture can brand you as a celebrity in your market, enable you to raise your rates, and create long-term client loyalty.
- Become an inspirational Hero to your audience. Become that voice who speaks exactly what they're thinking...even if they're not able to say it themselves.
- Write down the 10 components of the Authority Architecture on a piece of paper and make a few notes about how each one applies to you personally.
- Become a bolder, more outgoing version of yourself. It's similar to a caricature. Enhance a few of your strongest traits that will attract premium clients to you.
- Sprinkle everything you do with little tidbits from your Authority Architecture. This includes your website, emails, interviews, and even advertising.

How to Use a FREE Preview to Sell Without Selling

How can you demonstrate results in advance? That's the key question to ask yourself to sell without selling. Your prospects have a lot of potential choices in front of them. Why should they choose you over every other available option? Of course you have your story, your Strategic Myth, to share with them. You can position yourself with Authority through the Authority Architecture. And you can make offers that sell using the Golden Glove.

But you're often dealing with a prospect who is suspicious and jaded. It's HARD to trust people today. All of us have been ripped off at some point. And especially now with so much business being done online, it seems like we often lose that personal connection. One of the best ways to cut through the sales barriers your prospects have erected is through giving value in advance. You give them a preview of the types of results they can expect.

The question is how can you best demonstrate results in advance? This depends on what industry you're in, who your Ideal Client is, and what you offer to them. For example, here are a few ways I share free previews as a business coach:

- Free videos on Youtube that share short tips and answers to common questions.
- Free Lead Magnet PDF guide to improve your email marketing when people join my list.
- Frequent Emails & Blog Posts to share stories, content, and my personality.
- Free webinars to introduce my methods and offer my courses.

In the past I have offered free discovery consultations and paid discovery calls which could be credited towards ongoing coaching with me. In addition to the free preview methods, I have additional paid methods which become a free preview for additional services I offer. For example:

- This book is essentially a Preview of my group coaching and one-on-one coaching.
- My monthly group program is often a first step for my one-on-one private clients.
- I offer several products priced $10 to $1,000 that are a first step into one of my groups or private coaching.

These steps are what we often call a Value Ladder. A client comes into your funnel by purchasing something low cost such as a book. And they upgrade through the levels to training courses, group coaching, mastermind groups, or one-on-one coaching.

A heating/air conditioning company may have a Value Ladder that looks like this: free or discounted AC service, ongoing service fees, yearly service plans, repairs, and replacement air conditioners. That free or low cost initial service is the doorway into additional services. They may be offering it as a 'loss leader' which means they actually lose money once you count the cost of advertising and the service technician's travel and time. But it becomes a demonstration for additional products and services in the future. It's a first step into their funnel.

Everyone thinks about their accountant during tax time, but profitable CPAs also have additional ongoing services such as quarterly meetings for business owners, book keeping services, and set-up services for Quickbooks. A dentist will have cleanings, yearly check-ups, filings, and teeth whitening services along with higher dollar services such as crowns, braces, and implants. They may use teeth whitening, a routine cleaning, or even a check-up as a low cost offer to get new patients through the door.

There are ways to integrate in a Value Ladder into virtually any type of business, but in this chapter I want to focus primarily on the FREE Preview method. That means we're demonstrating value in advance before a client ever hands us any money.

How to Share Strategic Content That Guides People Toward the Sale

You've already discovered in previous chapters that we don't just want to distribute content for content's sake. Content is not King. Yes, you want to give value in advance, but there are several key aspects to what we're giving away for free.

First of all, the content should strategically guide people toward what you're offering. For example, I created and shared a Youtube video that shows how to install Facebook retargeting codes on your Wordpress blog. This is great content and something people are looking for, but it isn't that effective for me because it isn't directly leading into my products and services. I primarily created this content piece because I needed it to share with clients who struggled with adding the codes. Creating a video I could point them to was quicker than going through and explaining it one-on-one each time.

A more effective piece of 'selling' content would be sharing a case study of how one of my clients produced low cost leads and sales through Facebook retargeting. That could then lead into a free opt-in gift about effective Facebook ad strategies and promote my coaching service. A case study would demonstrate the end results they could expect and provide value in advance of being my client.

How are you demonstrating results in advance? One of my friends who is a personal coach did a series of free sessions with clients with the agreement that he could distribute the recordings of these sessions online. He has more than 2 dozen of these recorded sessions and he sends these out as free mp3 audios to his email list. He is providing content while demonstrating his coaching. Anyone who listens to those recordings will get value out of them, but at the same time they're being introduced to exactly how he would work with them as a client. He is demonstrating what it is like to work with him.

Here's another example. I sell an email marketing course that includes 80 of my proven email templates. Buyers can model the emails and use them to create their own successful emails in virtually any market. As you can imagine, the primary way I sell my email marketing course is through getting people on my email list and sending them regular emails. Kind of obvious, right? My free gift to get people to join my list at **www.MyMarketingCoach.com** is an "Email Conversion Kit" that includes subject line templates, introduction sentences, and story starters. I'm giving a free demonstration of the paid product. If you like these templates that help you create emails, you'll love the full course that gives you the rest of the emails for you to model.

It's similar to the ice cream shop. You go in and ask for a sample. They give you a small taste of the ice cream you want to try. It's not enough to fill you up. They don't give you a full cup. Instead, it's just enough to know whether you like the flavor and want more. Any freebie you give shouldn't 'solve' the problem completely. Instead, it's there to get them started. You're giving them step one. You're guiding them in the right direction and leading them step-by-step toward your product.

Let's say you're going to be offering a marketing course for chiropractors on a free webinar. There are a lot of things you could teach in the webinar, but we want to organize the information to sell your course without selling. So you come up with 3 primary pieces of content. First, you teach your attendees the importance of choosing specific conditions to target in your advertising instead of just advertising for those who have general back pain. Next you teach an overview of how to create effective advertising. And finally you teach them where to run those ads. Throughout the webinar you would be sharing your own story and several case studies from your current clients. At the end of the webinar you sell your marketing course that INCLUDES the exact ads they can use.

They could follow the system you taught them on the webinar themselves, but the reality is most of them don't want to create their own ads. Most of them will never do it! That's the hard way. The easy way is to purchase your course which comes with the ads already done. That allows them to get started with what you teach immediately!

This works great for selling services, software, or products that make the process easier. You teach the 'hard way' of doing things, and your product/service is the easy way. For example, if you run a Facebook advertising service, you could teach your attendees how to you target audiences, show a few sample ads, and even talk about your step-by-step optimization process. Again, the biggest selling points would come from sharing case studies along the way. What kinds of results are you generating for your other clients? The majority of your attendees will want you to do it for them instead of doing it themselves.

Another approach is where you share information that's 'useful but incomplete.' This means you give them the first step to solving their problem, but you make contacting you or buying your product the next step in the process. Let's say you're a personal injury attorney. Obviously you can't give specific legal advice in free videos, but you could find out the questions people are asking during your research and prepare a series of short videos about how to understand the problem and what to do first. You'd end every video with a call-to-action to contact you for a free consultation. You're providing the initial advice to get them over their fears and to make sure they don't do anything that hurts their case and then you're immediately telling them to follow up directly with you for personal help.

A third strategy is to redefine the root problem. Everyone else may think the problem is X, but you know from experience that the real problem is Y. This is easy to demonstrate with weight loss programs because there are so many options available here. For example, if you were selling fitness or weight loss to women, you could redefine the problem by talking about how women's metabolism is different than men. What works for men doesn't work for women or has to be modified for women. By redefining the problem in this way, you've just disqualified any program that focuses on both men and women.

Another weight loss program may redefine the problem by talking about how the real issue is with your liver. It's the toxins in your food and your daily life. By defining the problem this way, they can help their clients understand why other diets and plans haven't worked for them. They haven't dealt with the core problem.

We could continue looking at different ways to define the problem. The purpose here is to disqualify other methods your clients may be considering or have already used. You're not like the other guys. While they may have failed to solve the problem previously, they haven't tried this yet. And not only are you selling without selling, you're also giving your clients hope. Nothing is accomplished without hope, and 'tough' problems drain hope, especially if someone has been living under the weight of them for years.

What if you're a consultant who helps tech companies improve the production of their staff? Your prospect think the problem is the people they hire, but you may redefine the problem as not providing the right expectations and training for new staff hires. Your free preview talks about the importance of this and what a good system looks like when it's in place. You share a detailed case study from one of your clients that demonstrates this step-by-step process in action. If readers want your help putting a similar system in place, they can get started with a free or low cost discovery call.

What Does Your Client Need to Understand To Make an Intelligent Buying Decision?

The 'root problem' method is just one of the ways you can set the buying criteria for your audience. Another strategy is to reset the buying criteria. What should a client look for to make a good buying decision? They don't

113

know what they don't know. You're the expert on the topic. What should they be looking for?

For example, since I sell business coaching, I talk about the importance of working with an expert who helps you directly. As an entrepreneur, you'd never want to work with an organization where the coaching is provided to you by a paid employee. Employees and entrepreneurs think differently. They have different instincts and fears. The entrepreneur needs to work with someone who is on the same wavelength with them.

It's shocking how many high ticket coaching programs assign you to an under-coach. That's the 2nd aspect. You need to work with someone who has experience in what you want to do. While a business coach will ask you questions, they also need to be able to provide some direction and guidance. The greater the reserve of knowledge and experience to pull from, the more beneficial it can be to you.

In addition, you need a business coach who has proven systems to help you reach your goals. There are multiple pieces to the online puzzle and I help clients with creating products/services, positioning themselves as an authority, attracting buying visitors, writing sales copy, creating email follow-up sequences, optimizing their campaigns, and putting systems in place to earn more while working less. This gives me a lot of freedom in the content I share since I can cover any of these subjects and link them directly to my various levels of coaching.

If I do a series of Youtube videos on copywriting, I can talk about systems like the Golden Glove and I can tell stories about the letters, videos, and webinars I've written and promoted over the years. I not only have experience in writing copy for my own business, but I've written copy for others and reviewed thousands of pieces of copy for clients over the past two decades. Then I can promote my Email Conversion Kit as an opt-in gift to get people to join my list. This free training series is giving them foundational information, demonstrating my authority, and guiding them toward working with me as a client long-term.

Let's say you're a real estate agent. Your goal is to attract more clients who list their homes with you. What do they need to understand to make a good decision? They likely want to know how to sell their home for top dollar in the quickest time possible. You could put together a special report on this subject. But you wouldn't want to just list 7 tips for getting maximum dollar. You also want to integrate your message and story into this. You've already written down your Hero's Journey that got you to where you are today. What is it that you do for your clients? What is your mission and how does it connect with selling your home for top dollar?

Perhaps you specialize in a specific neighborhood. You know everything about this neighborhood. You've sold 5 homes there in the past year. You send out mailing pieces to every home in the neighborhood. You run low budget Facebook ads in a 2 mile radius around the neighborhood (*so only people who live in that neighborhood or visit that neighborhood see your ads*). You'd want to bring up the importance of specialization in your report. That's what would make you stand out to your audience. No one else knows their neighborhood or sells more homes for higher value here than you do.

That's the key principle. When you're sharing content, it's not just about sharing content. It's about also positioning yourself as the best choice for your target buyer. What if you had to put together a report on how to choose a real estate agent? What would you include? Depending on what you bring to the table yourself, you might talk about experience, volume of homes sold, a step-by-step marketing system, help with finding financing, references, etc. You could provide a list of questions they should ask every real estate agent (and of course you'd be prepared to pass this test yourself with flying colors).

Free Previews For eCommerce Products

Let's hop in our trusty time travel device back to the door-to-door sales days. The 'friendly' neighborhood vacuum sales person shows up at your door. As surprising as it sounds, these still exist! Yes, with all the Internet tools available at our disposal, there are still people selling high priced vacuums door-to-door. Does the sales person just show you a picture of their vacuum and tell you how wonderful it is? Not a chance. No, if you allow them in, and that's a pretty big IF, they start cleaning your house. It would be a pretty good deal if you didn't have to listen to them while they were doing it.

They clean your carpets, your couch, and your bed. And if it will sit still, they'll even want to vacuum your cat. They're demonstrating the product in action. It's the only shot they have. When they're selling a vacuum for $3,000 and you could buy one down at Walmart for $200, they need every advantage possible. They tell you about the warranty. They tell you why it's better than anything else on the market. But the demonstration is center stage. They have to show you how it can pick up dirt your other vacuum misses.

Online you're not going to be invited into their house. You're not going to be able to vacuum their rugs, but you can show your vacuum in action on video. Show everything it can do. Demonstrate using another vacuum and then show how much more powerful yours is right after it. Pick up some of the most difficult dirt you can find. Imagine the worst situation you could possibly find and demonstrate how your product can win against that.

You may even be able to create viral sensation if you can come up with an interesting way of demonstrating your product benefits. For example, check out this website owned by Blendtec: **www.willitblend.com**. It became a viral sensation after they started showing how their blender can blend dozens of popular products including iPhones, skeletons, golf balls, baseballs, garden hoses, iPads, and more. They're demonstrating a competitive advantage of their product versus the competition. Instead of telling you what it can do, they show it in live action.

Of course you'd never need to blend any of these items, but this again goes back to the raspberry stain test. If their product can blend a golf ball, it can definitely blend any drinks or foods you throw at it. It goes beyond anything you'll ever need. This viral campaign not only increased sales of their blender, but it also became so popular that they started marketing "Will It Blend" themed merchandise.

If you're selling a product that doesn't have an impressive demonstration, you still may want to use video to show it in action. You could discuss the benefits behind a pair of shoes while showing them from every direction. And for a pair of hiking boots, you could also show them in action as you're hiking up to the top of the mountain. You could show your clothing on a model. You have a disadvantage online because you can't feel the material against your skin. But you can take advantage of video and demonstrate just how good the clothing looks.

The importance of video became obvious to me when I was looking for a German Shepherd breeder. Those who showed videos of their dogs and puppies had an immediate advantage. The majority of websites showed a few pictures of their dogs and puppies, but those who went the extra mile of showing the dog in action peaked my interest. They showed them at home, in training, and interacting with each other. These breeders were selling expensive puppies for $1,500 to $3,500 each, and the majority of them didn't even take the time to shoot videos of their dogs. In the land of the blind, the one-eyed man is king.

What if a video demonstration of your product won't show your product in its best light? This was a problem Joe Sugarman faced with his

BluBlocker sunglasses in the 1990's. The competitive advantage of his product was that it blocked out both UV rays and blue rays. By blocking blue rays, it made objects appear sharper and clearer. While people could see the difference between his sunglasses and the normal sunglasses when they put them on, this difference could not be demonstrated on video. And his primary sales method was through infomercials.

Instead of demonstrating the product itself in action, they focused on people's experiences. They let people try on the BluBlocker sunglasses in person and they recorded their reaction. You weren't seeing the demonstration yourself, but you were seeing social proof. This made the viewers even more curious about how the product worked. The product went on to sell millions of copies through infomercials based on these social proof demonstrations.

If you can't demonstrate your product in action, can you demonstrate social proof? For example, do you have clients who can talk about the amazing results they've received on video? Are there respected individuals in the market who could review your product in action? The best videos for car manufacturers often aren't the ones they produce themselves. They're the video reviews produced by car magazines and websites. An independent third party is giving their uncensored opinion about your product. You could contact the reviewer and ask for permission to feature their review on your site or send out an email to your list linking over to the review.

Free Previews For Information Products

Many of my clients sell information products like books, ebooks, video courses, home study kits, and membership sites. One of the big keys with a free preview when you're selling an information product is to introduce contrarian content. There are some 'internet experts' who will tell you to give your absolute best information away for free, but I disagree. If you give your best information away, why would someone want to buy from you?

One of the key selling triggers for information products is CURIOSITY. Don't underestimate the power of this. I've personally purchased high-end information products simply because of a few bullets in their sales copy that teased me with a few secrets I didn't know. If you give away your best information, and the viewers know this is your best information, you're giving up the curiosity factor...your strongest selling tool for information products.

Have you ever seen a movie trailer that included all the funny scenes in a comedy? You felt kind of ripped off at the theater, didn't you? Your clients will get the same feeling if you give everything away for free. Instead, you need to learn the art of the tease. Start off by giving away information that's contrarian to what everyone else is saying.

The most likely buyer of your product is NOT someone who is making their very first purchase. There may be a few readers of this book who have never purchased any other marketing book or course before, but the vast majority will have purchased multiple products before this one. And it's likely you've been disappointed in other products in the past. If all I did was present "More of the Same" to you, you never would have picked up this book...and you definitely wouldn't have made it this far into the book.

I had to present you with an idea that's different from what you commonly hear. Perhaps you picked up this book because you're frustrated with the over-aggressive sales techniques you've heard from others. Or you're tired of trying to promote your business online and not getting any results. Or perhaps you've even given away your best content, and you're not making any sales. You're looking for a different answer than you've heard in the common places.

That's the type of content you want to share for free. You want to share content that makes you stand out in the marketplace. You want people to look at it and say, *"Why hasn't anyone told me this before?"*

If you go through **www.mymarketingcoach.com,** my blog, you'll find I share a lot of inspiration. I also talk a lot about going against the grain. I was talking about paid traffic and Facebook ads long before Facebook started limiting our organic reach. I've talked numerous times about how important curiosity is when you're sharing content with your audience.

Your audience is looking for Infotainment. Information isn't good enough alone. Constipated content is boring. They want to be entertained. This means you want to have a little drama by sharing personal stories. You need to inspire them with your mission. Combine that entertainment and personal connection along with a little content that can help them benefit immediately.

One of the free preview strategies you can use is giving Step one away for free. There has been a very popular weight loss promotion online for years that is based on 5 'healthy' foods you shouldn't eat. The title of that content alone grabs your attention because you want to know what these foods are. It's contrarian since these are health foods you've been told to eat. But knowing what you shouldn't eat is only step one. That's useful but incomplete content. Now you need to know what you SHOULD eat! That's where their paid information product comes in.

A great free preview leaves a prospect curious and wanting more. And the only way they can scratch that itch is by purchasing your product. Some of the most successful information product websites are benefit and curiosity packed bullets. These are short one to two line teasers about what's included inside your product.

You can go even further with the free preview and SHOW them inside your site. This works especially well for membership sites. After you've put together your full membership site, record a screen video using either Camtasia Studio (for PC) and Screenflow (Mac). Invite them inside your membership site and video what is just behind the paywall. As soon as they become a member, they'll be able to access X, Y, and Z. This works best for large membership sites which have a lot of content, bonuses, or an active group inside the membership area.

Another strategy you can use is a free webinar. This is usually a 45 to 90 minute free training session. Don't make the same mistake with these that I did in the beginning. You don't want to teach your entire step-by-step system in a free webinar. If you do, there is nothing else for them to buy. Instead, think heavily about your Hero's Journey. Tell the story of where you started and where you are now. Look for 3 major tips you can give along the way. If you try to give too many tips, your audience will simply get lost. I've found that 3 major tips with an example for each is often the sweet spot for a webinar.

These 3 tips will be valuable content they can use immediately. At the same time, they're incomplete. Let's say I was teaching a free webinar on how to attract coaching clients. Perhaps I talk about how to find hungry buying audiences on Facebook. That's my first tip including a demonstration of how you find these audiences along with sharing some of my personal results running ads on Facebook. Perhaps I talk about how having a free discovery call application on the landing page. I show an example of what the website looks like. Finally, I talk about the steps to follow on the free call itself to demonstrate my value and persuade prospects into becoming paid clients. That's all great information.

What didn't I share? I didn't share the exact ads to use to generate the leads. Knowing how to target the right audiences is only part of the advertising method needed. Without knowing how to write the ads, you're not going to generate anywhere near the kind of results I personally generate. In my course I give you a template for the landing page and I share the exact script I use on the video to persuade people to fill out the application. I'll also share exactly what types of questions to use on the free discovery call. I'll talk about the journey you take a prospect on the call to demonstrate the value of your services and attract hungry buyers.

The webinar is useful but incomplete. This is vital with any type of information products. There is an overwhelming amount of information available on the web totally for free. If you're going to entice people to pay for yours, you're going to have to tease them while demonstrating enough value that shows how you're different from the competition.

Free Previews For Consultants and Coaches

A consultant or coach can apply similar techniques to the information publisher because you're attracting clients based on your expertise. Anything you do that demonstrates your expertise can be used to attract pre-qualified clients. When a client is attracted by your free preview content, gets on your list, reads your emails, and watches your videos, they're already pre-sold by the time they talk to you. They've been immersed in your systems already, which also makes them a much more compliant client. You don't have to 'convince' them to follow your systems. They wouldn't have hired you as their coach if they didn't already agree in what you teach!

If you follow the systems throughout this book, you can quickly flip the script. Instead of you hunting for clients, they'll be tracking you down. My own one-on-one coaching program is usually sold out. And since my clients often stay for years, I only let in new clients a couple of times per year at most. You can see the waiting list I have for clients here: **www.mymarketingcoach.com/one-on-one-coaching**

If you're just getting started though, the easy Free Preview method to use is the Free Discovery call. Set-up an application page on your website where people can apply for a free consultation with you. While you want to talk about the benefits you can deliver on this page, primarily you want to turn the 'selling' process around and have them sell you on why you should select them as a client. Here are a few of the questions I would ask when looking for clients who are interested in growing their Internet based businesses. You can modify these questions based on your market:

- Full Name
- Email Address
- Phone
- Mailing Address

- Website Address
- Currently Monthly Profit From Your Business (Multiple Choice of Income Ranges)
- Your Target Monthly Profit From This Business (Multiple Choice of Income Ranges)
- Please Be Honest. Why Do You Feel You Haven't Hit Your Target Monthly Profit Yet?
- Who is Your Ideal Customers and What Kind of Results Do They Receive From Your Offer?
- Which Goal Do You Most Want to Accomplish With My Help? (Multiple Choice: Generate More Traffic, Improve Conversions and Funnels, Reduce Costs, Improve Profit Per Customer, Work Less Hours)
- What Would Ideal Success of Working Together Mean to You?
- Why Would You Be the Perfect Candidate to Work With Me?
- Is There Anything Else I Should Consider When Looking At Your Application?

The majority of these questions are open ended except for the ones marked multiple choice above. Yes, I'm having them fill out a pretty extensive application as I want them to pre-qualify themselves. I'd also recommend using text similar to what I've used on the page:

> Below is an application where I ask you some basic questions about your business.
>
> I will personally review your application and decide if we might be the right fit for each other before we spend time on the phone.
>
> Please be as descriptive as possible as I have an overwhelming demand for my service...and am only choosing the clients who are ready to experience breakthroughs.
>
> If I decide we're not a good match, I'll let you know politely by email. If I decide you might be a good match, I'll contact you by email and we'll schedule a time to speak.
>
> No salesperson will call.

You and I will speak personally and we'll decide together if there are hidden opportunities for you to Earn More, Work Less, and Enjoy Life!

No pressure to join. And you'll walk away from the call with at least 2 to 3 new ideas to grow your business.

The goal of the application is to get them selling you on why you should take them as a client. To 'sell' them on filling out the application, I recommend using a short video where you describe what you can do for them as a client AND run as many testimonials as you have on the page. Written testimonials are great, but audio and video testimonials are even better. Let others demonstrate the results you've generated for them. Check **www.mymarketingcoach.com/one-on-one-coaching** out to see some of my testimonials and get an idea of the types of testimonials that grab the interest of clients.

You'd attract people to your application page through any of the content methods we're discussing throughout the book. This means you could be publishing videos on Youtube, writing blog posts, or running content rich ads on Facebook, Youtube, or any other advertising network.

You'll review each application that comes in. NOT everyone is worthy of you. If someone just zips through the questions without providing good answers, I'd respond back to them that you don't think you're a good fit for them right now. That's right. You're NOT going to say "Yes" to everyone. If someone doesn't take the time to fill out the application appropriately, then it's also likely they'll be a difficult client. Thank them for their application and their time, and quietly thank them for letting you know they're not a qualified client before you wasted any time on them!

When you approve an application, you'll schedule for their free call. When you get on the call together, start off by asking them questions about their current situation. You want to know why they came to you for help. Here's a basic script for starting the call, *"First I'm going to ask you a few questions to get really clear on where you want to go. Then, I'll let you know if I can help you. If I can't, that's OK too. You can ask me questions anytime during the call. Does that sound fair to you?"*

I'm going to suggest not having the entire call scripted. Don't be a 'telemarketer' desperate for a sale. You're a high-end consultant or coach. You're interviewing them to find out if they qualify to be a client you can actually help. You're not selling them on your service. They're selling you on choosing to work with them.

Don't assume their goals are the same as your own. That's a major mistake I made originally. Some of my clients wanted to get their business to seven figures as fast as possible while others wanted to create a lifestyle business where they were only working 3 days a week. One of the easiest questions to find out their goals is this, *"If we were having this conversation 12 months from today, what would have had to happen for you to be happy with the results?"*

Ask your question and shut up. Let them speak. Once they finish, ask them if there is anything else. If you're in business consulting or coaching, they're likely to bring up money. If they do, make sure they're specific about the amounts. No matter what you're discussing, be specific. Having general goals doesn't do anyone any good. Help them know exactly what they want.

Next ask them why this is important to them, *"What's important to you about that?"* You've got to find out their WHY. Success isn't easy. If you've been working with clients, you've probably seen that getting clients to implement is much tougher than getting them to pay you. Let's find out what motivates and keeps them moving forward.

Start asking them about their current obstacles. For me, this means I'd ask about how much their business earned last month, how much traffic they're generating, which products are selling, etc. You want to investigate where they're at right now so you can identify what's holding them back and the right course of action for them right now.

You'll be tempted to prescribe the solution for them right now, but I'm going to recommend you hold off on this. It's much more likely that they'll implement your advice if you come up with the solutions together. Basically, you want to use the Socratic method of teaching where you ask questions to brainstorm together on the solution. For example, I may ask...

- What if we tested some new headlines for the landing page?
- Is there anything else your customers likely want to buy?
- Where could we free up 2 hours of your day almost immediately?
- Have you tried Facebook advertising, and if so, how did it work?
- If we added an additional $10,000 offer, how would that influence your bottom line?

These are all prescriptions I could easily make based off of their goals and where their business is currently, but we want it to be done together. Next you'll prescribe the solution. You've investigated the problem, and you've brainstormed the solutions together. Now you'll put together a plan of action. After giving the outline for the plan of action, you can ask, *"If we did this, do you think we could hit your goal?"*

You want a YES answer here. If you don't get it, do a little more investigation and see if there is something else that needs to be added to the prescription. After you've helped them see the path, now you can ask if they would like your help with implementation. This is where your ongoing services come into play. You've given them an in-depth Free Preview of what you will accomplish together. You've got them thinking about the current challenges and where they could be in the next 12 months.

They could take the plan and implement it on their own. You gave them value without holding back for the time you were together. Obviously, there will be a lot of moving pieces in this plan, and they could use you beside them coaching them and providing support.

This is where you bring in your services and price. What will you do for them exactly? How does your program operate? And what are the costs involved? They've agreed with you on the plan. Now is the time to get them to agree on your services. Take their credit card immediately over the phone. Or have them pay you in your online system while you're still on the phone. If you have a contract to sign, you can email it over to them and go over it with them on the phone right now. You don't want to 'pressure' them in any way, but you do want to continue the momentum from the call. These are their goals and you can help them reach them.

At the same time, there will be potential clients which you don't want to work with. You'll uncover this throughout the call. They're combative. They don't have goals you can help them with. Be willing to get to the end of the call and tell them this isn't a situation you believe you can help them with right now. If you have a product or know another coach who may be a better fit for them, let them know this other solution. Thank them for their time. DON'T sign-up someone for your services if you have that uneasy feeling about them. I've made the mistake of getting the wrong client in my program before and it's not worth it.

The goal of this process is to sign-up clients who add energy to your life. The wrong client will drain you and potentially even sabotage your energy for working with other clients. Guard your practice and your life by choosing the right clients!

Free Previews For Service Providers

The process is almost exactly the same if you're a service provider. You can do the free discovery call, ask about goals, and review their current challenges. Let's say you have an Adwords advertising service. You'd follow the basic outline for the consultants and coaches, but you'd also want to access to their Adwords account. Preferably check out their account before the call so you have very specific advice you can give on the call.

Go through the goals questions. Find out what they've already tried. Look at their current results. And come up with a step-by-step plan together for them to reach their goals. After you've laid out the plan, get their approval that this can help them reach their goals. Then go into what you will implement for them and the costs involved.

No matter what type of service you're offering, you can follow a system like this. In some scenarios, such as a chiropractor, you will be giving them your 'report of findings' directly instead of asking for their feedback. You might ask them the problems and do x-rays to help identify the root cause. The key principle in this scenario is make sure they understand what they can expect from the full treatment plan and the importance of getting started now.

When you're first starting out, you would do these discovery calls and investigations for free. As your practice grows, you may want to switch over to a paid initial consultation. This will weed out the lookie-loos and you'll find a majority of those who come in for the initial call will convert into long term clients. The negative of course is that you'll generate less initial consultations. So you can use a paid consultation process as a way to turn down your flow of leads when there are too many leads coming through.

Yes, having too many leads is seriously a problem you too could soon be facing! That free initial consultation can be turned into a $25, $75, or $100 consultation. One of my clients charges $250 for the initial hour long consultation with him. You could even bump the price up and charge as much as $500 to $1,000 for the initial consultation. You are giving a ton of value in that first contact. You're giving them the step-by-step system to follow. Your help with implementation is just the next step in the process.

Let's say you choose $75 for your initial consultation and you're a Facebook advertising service. You would ask them questions about their Ideal Client and their product offers. If they're already running ads, you'd ask for access to their account and you'd review their current ads. You'd help them identify the exact audience they should target. And you'd come up with the initial advertising plan which includes the theme of the ads, image concepts, and what you'll test initially. You may even cover how you'll continue to optimize the account after they get started.

They could take this step-by-step process and run it on their own, or they could pay for your service and you'll handle it all for them. If they don't feel they got their money's worth from the consultation, tell them to let you know before the end of the call and you'll refund them the $75. If they want to follow the system on their own, you'll thank them for their time and let you go on their way (*hopefully the $75 eases some of the pain from not working with them*). If they decide to go forward with you (*and the majority should in a paid consultation*), you'll apply the $75 they already paid toward their first month's fees.

They win no matter what they choose. If they don't get advice that benefits them, they get a refund and owe nothing. If you give them a system they follow on their own, they got it at a discount price of only $75. If they decide to go forward, the consultation didn't cost them anything since it was applied directly to your fees.

On your side, the consultation eliminates the tire kickers and makes sure you only have serious prospects on the phone. It completely eliminates the feeling of being a salesperson since you're in the role of a paid consultant providing them the exact advice they need to succeed.

Again, I would only move to the paid consultation once you've tested the free process first. You want the additional volume a free consultation will generate in the very beginning. You're still taking the position of a consultant or coach who is helping them find the right path. Without the fee, the application becomes vital. You don't want to waste your time on the phone with everyone. Either they've filled out your application or they've paid you for the consultation. Make sure they've done something to qualify themselves before getting on the call.

Action Steps

- The key question to ask yourself is, *"How can I demonstrate results in advance?"*
- Stop thinking in terms of "Free Content." Think about giving a "Free Preview" instead similar to an ice cream shop giving a taste of what they sell.
- You could give your client a full step-by-step system of how to do something, and sell services, software, or products that make the process easier.
- Redefine the root problem. Everyone thinks the problem is X, but you know from experience the real problem is Y (which your product or service solves).
- Another method of delivering a Free Preview is to educate a prospect on how to make a good buying decision. What do they need to know to choose correctly (and it may not be choosing you)?
- Is there a way you can implement video to demonstrate your product in action or the end results of your offer?
- Forget "Information." Focus on Infotaintment: information that is useful, entertaining, and positions you as the authority.

How to Create An Attention Grabbing Lead Magnet

The money is in your list.

That's one of the most common cliché's in the online world, but it's still true. More accurately the money is in your relationship with a list. There are a LOT of platforms you can participate in online. Facebook is one of the most popular. You may use Twitter if you're targeting younger users or you're in a tech field. Linkedin is for B2B. Instagram and Pinterest are popular for photos. Youtube is king for video overall while live video is big on Facebook and Periscope.

I could continue this list almost indefinitely, and you could get lost in social media literally forever. The question is whether this is the highest and best use of your time as a business owner. While you will want to have a presence on a limited number of social media sites (Facebook and Youtube for example and Linkedin for B2B), never focus on them to the exclusion of your own list.

You are a GUEST on Facebook and any other social media site. They can decide they don't want you there any time they want. They can cancel your ad account, your Facebook page, and your profile at their whims. You have no recourse. It's in their terms of service you agree to. In fact, there have been several times Facebook has reduced the organic exposure of Facebook pages. If you're counting on Facebook to let you reach your audience, you're making a serious mistake that has already failed several times.

Instead, you need to focus on building your own list. Marketingsherpa did an online survey in 2015 that showed 72% of adults in the US preferred email as the contact method with companies they did business with. The next closest was postal mail at 48%. Only 11% preferred mobile apps and 7% online video. Combine this survey along with the reality of the online world where you don't own those Facebook Likes (*they belong to Facebook not you*), and email is the only obvious choice.

Every client I work with focuses on their email list. We want visitors to our sites to raise their hands and join our list. We want those we interact with on social media to visit our sites and join our lists. The majority of those feelers and content pieces we put out in the marketplace online are used to pull people back to our sites and onto our lists.

This is where your Lead Magnet comes in. Just telling someone to join your list and get your emails isn't very enticing. Seriously? Who goes online and says, *"Where can I go today to get signed up for more lists and get more email?"*

Absolutely no one says that. You're going to have to 'bribe' people to join your list. Their email address is valuable. You're have to give them something valuable in exchange for their email address and permission to follow-up with them.

Your Lead Magnet is the gift you give when someone subscribes to your list. It could be a free PDF report or white paper (*free report is often used when marketing to consumers while white paper is used when marketing to businesses*). For example, check out the free gift I offer at **www.mymarketingcoach.com**. It's my Free Email Conversion Kit. This is a report that covers how to multiply the profits you generate from email along with several Cheat Sheets and Templates that give you 64 story starter ideas, a 7 step system for putting together emails, and popular email subject line templates.

And a free PDF report is just one possibility. You could give away an audio interview with an expert. This is an easy method for someone who is just getting started online who doesn't have their own credibility. They interview someone who has already positioned themselves as an authority on the subject and they tap into their credibility.

You could give away a free video. This is a popular gift that many of my clients have used because video is such a great medium for making a connection with your viewer. Several clients give away a free video lesson when someone signs up for their list and they immediately link to one of their products or services directly under this free video.

You could give away a 5-day email training series where a new lesson is delivered each day by email. Or you could even send out an email that links over to a short video lesson for the day. A key element here is that the first day's lesson needs to be extremely strong to both get them to subscribe to your list for the instant gratification and to get them to pay attention to the rest of the free series.

You could even give the subscriber a coupon for 10% off or Free shipping on their first order. This works best in an ecommerce product type business. You're giving them a reason to immediately buy after joining your list.

Find the Hook For Your Lead Magnet

The first goal of your lead magnet is to hook a visitor's attention. The majority of my clients run their paid advertising directly to a page where a visitor joins their email list. It's the first transaction a visitor makes with them. Then we usually transition into going for an immediate sale. Getting people to join your email list is the first 'sale' you have to make.

What is ONE piece of information you could share in just 5 minutes that would truly knock someone's socks off? Five minutes here is just a suggestion. You want to share a concept that can be quickly explained when possible, but whether it takes 3 minutes or 60 minutes (*such as a webinar*), it's not the length that matters. What matters is providing a clear answer to a question a large portion of your buying audience is already asking.

The content needs to be contrarian. It can't be the 'common wisdom' they're hearing from everyone else. In fact, the content that works best often lays out why the common advice they've likely already been following hasn't worked for them. It teaches more in depth about the 'real root problem' that's holding them back.

In my '1 Weird Trick for Selling High Ticket Products and Services," the secret is selling a low cost paid consultation first. You deliver a ton of value on the consultation with the client. That's an easy first sale to make. You can offer a 100% refund guarantee to make it zero risk to the client. And the paid consultation pre-qualifies your leads giving you a much higher closing rate for your higher ticket offer. The actual giveaway is a 20 minute audio, but I can explain the basics of the strategy in just one paragraph.

Is there a case study you could share that would demonstrate how to solve their problem while also building your credibility? This could be a story about you or one of your clients. It illustrates the problem and shows at least one (*or more*) steps to take in solving the problem while providing a form of proof for the end results. A good case study covers the problem, promise, and proof all together. You or your client had a specific problem. You had a turning point and solved the problem by doing X, Y, and Z. Now you have experienced these results.

The more specific your case study, the better it fits for a lead magnet. You don't want your whole life history. Instead you just want to get into the specifics. For example, I could do a lead magnet about my $96,250 email (*now that I'm talking about this I can't believe I've never done this offer yet*). It would cover the set-up of why I was doing the email, how nervous I was doing it live, and the results. In addition I could show the exact email and explain why it worked so well....giving them a basic template to follow. It would be the perfect lead-in into my full email marketing course.

What template, cheat sheet, or tool could you provide that will save them time or money? In my example Lead Magnet at **www.mymarketingcoach.com**, I'm including several cheat sheets and templates. These are tools that help prospects get results faster.

One of my clients gave away the free video content piece on his landing page...and the lead magnet was a cheat sheet that went with the 20+ minute video. People didn't want to watch the whole video. They wanted the 1 page cheat sheet instead!

Cheat sheets and templates can be some of the most effective lead magnets. When you're selling an information product, people often buy them for the tools you include. They're overwhelmed with information already. It's the same way with your lead magnet. They'll subscribe to your list not for the information, but for the template, cheat sheet, or tool you provide them with.

You could provide them with a series of recipes (*like the recipe book mentioned previously*). It could be a list of the most effective conversation starters. Maybe it's a flow chart of how to set-up your first Facebook ad campaign. Or you give diagrams of 3 easy to learn self-defense techniques for women. Or it's a price guide of how much to charge for different types of copywriting. Or it's the 'magic words' to use when your wife asks you if these pants make her look fat (*this is a dangerous scenario indeed*).

The Forgotten Job of the Lead Magnet

Your lead magnet has to hook a prospect's attention and get them to subscribe. But that's only its first job. Its second job is just as important. It has to set-up the sale. It should naturally lead a prospect from where they are now to where your first product/service offer is the only obvious choice for solving what they perceive as their most desperate problem right now. It's a Free Preview for the first product or service you offer.

Forgetting this is the most common mistake with lead magnets. It's the same mistake I've personally made multiple times. Yes, you want to deliver value. Someone should feel you gave them something they didn't get anywhere else. At the same time, you want the information to be useful but incomplete. It's leading them toward your product or service.

Accomplishing this goal depends on what you're selling. If you're offering a done-for-you Adwords service, your first paid offer could be a $75 Adwords Optimization session. In that session you'll personally review their account, give them several tips they could use immediately to increase their profits, and offer your complete done-for-you service that's priced at 20% of ad spend (*minimum $500 per month*).

With this type of personal help and service, you could reveal a lot of information in your lead magnet. Obviously you can't provide a complete Adwords course...as that would be overwhelming for them and you. But if you had permission from a client, you could share a case study showing a 378% bump in ROI in just 3 months...focusing on 3 of the main improvements made to the account.

What if you're selling a course on losing weight with paleo? The product you sell will likely cover meal plans, exercise, eating out, etc. You don't want to 'give away' what you're selling in the freebie, but we still need a strong hook.

Maybe you focus a free lead magnet on the 5 health foods which are sabotaging your weight loss. Or perhaps you focus on the first week with a short guide on How to Lose 3 Pounds in 7 Days or Less. Or maybe you give away 10 of your favorite Paleo Recipes For Losing Weight. Or it could be a guide on the 7 superfoods that jumpstart your weight loss. Or it could share how Susan, your client, lost 30 pounds in the past 2 months along with a couple of her struggles and specific steps taken. Perhaps you put together a 'weight loss calculator' where they enter their current weight, height, and goals to see how much weight they could expect to lose over some time period.

When you're selling a service or software tool, you can 'give away' the farm. You can teach the inner workings of what you sell because people will still pay to have results quicker and easier.

When you're selling an information product, one of your core selling tools is curiosity. While you want to give useful but incomplete information, you don't want to completely let the cat out of the bag. There still has to be an element of drama and curiosity. While they may know the first step to success in your system, you need to keep some of your tricks hidden behind the curtain (*basically there needs to be a feeling that there is a lot more available which you haven't shared yet*).

When I review client's lead magnets, I'm always looking for the contrarian content elements. For example, let's take weight loss again (*it's a popular subject and I reviewed two different client projects in this market recently).* Pretty much every product is going to tell you to eliminate processed foods, exercise more, and drink more water. That's not going to stand out and position you as an authority.

You can get more specific with this information and teach people they can eat as much as they want of your healthy food list...while only exercising for twice a week at home for 20 minutes at a time. Now we're saying something that stands out a little. Or if you focus on how stress literally adds extra pounds to your body...and you can burn more calories automatically by reducing the stress...now we're being contrarian.

Your customers should be able to say, *"Why hasn't anyone ever told me this before?"* Or if you are talking about things they've heard, their response could be, *"Why hasn't anyone put together a system this simple and easy to follow?"* If all your free content does is repeat common wisdom, you've lost the chance for the sale. You're no different than anyone else.

At onlinetennisinstruction.com, they give a video tip on how to improve your serve after someone joins the list. They don't give you all the videos from their course or they'd overwhelm you with information and likely sabotage their own sale. Instead, they give you a useful and valuable tip specifically for your biggest problem. Then they sell their full collection of serve power tips. The tip they give you focuses on one of the most common problems their prospects have with their serve.

If you already have a lead magnet in place, how well is it delivering your core marketing message? If it's just there to generate new subscribers, it is only doing half its job. The second job is just as important...educate your new subscriber and lead them toward the sale. It's either repositioning the problem or sharing your unique promise with the goal of making you the obvious choice in the marketplace.

What Type of Lead Magnet Should You Create?

Think about your lead magnet in the overall flow of your business. What is the first product or service you're offering? How can you best educate and lead your customer toward this opportunity? Here are a few of the lead magnets you can create:

1. **Specific Promise**: Make a very specific promise: "How to Add 1,000 New Twitter Followers in 7 Days or Less," "Add an Inch of Muscle Mass To Your Arms in 8 Weeks," or "1 Weird Trick to Save 30% or More On Your Electric Bill Next Month."

2. **Case Study**: Share a case study: "How a Brand New Online Marketer Added 8,367 Subscribers to His List In Just 30 Days," "How this Work-At-Home Mother Earned an Extra $545 In just 3 Hours of Her Spare Time," "How this Desperate Nerd Found the Love of His Life in Just 56 Days"

3. **Cheat Sheets**: Show a short cheat sheet of 1 to 5 pages or less: "Quick Start Guide for Your First Facebook Ad Campaign," "15 Superfoods Guaranteed to Jumpstart Your Weight Loss," or "Twitter Essentials Cheat Sheet."

4. **Template**: Give them a template or tool: "Facebook Post Swipe File," "21 Proven Headline Templates," or "Product Launch Email Sequence."

5. **Coupon**: Give them 10% Off, $20 Off a $100+ purchase, Free shipping, or some other purchasing incentive. This is a great selection for ecommerce type businesses.

Which lead magnet is right for your business? It depends on your audience, what your competitors offer, and what you're selling. The goal is to bridge the gap from what your visitors currently think about the problem to them choosing your product or service. You also want to make sure you're not offering something that simply looks like a 'me-too' version of a competitor's offer. It has to have your own slant or angle to it.

If you have a strong case study that directly relates to your offer, this can often be the best solution. If you're dealing with an overwhelming subject (*what isn't overwhelming online today*), a cheat sheet can be a great tool to help your subscribers implement the first steps. A template is always popular…and can be a lead-in if you're providing training that also includes additional templates and tools. A specific promise is the default method in any market if none of the others jump out at you.

The 'size' of your gift also relates directly to the price point of your offer. If you're offering a $19.95 product, it doesn't make sense to put together a one hour webinar. Nor would you give away a 60 page ebook. That could be larger than the product you're selling! And it may be tough to persuade someone to your $2,000 offer with just one 5 minute content video. When you sell a high ticket product or service, that's when you put together full webinars or a series of 'pre-launch' style videos.

With those higher price points, you may put together a collection of the above. Your 1st video introduces your hook and covers the first step to fulfill on your specific promise. The 2nd video shares an in-depth case study with additional tips and value. In the 3rd video, you give them a template and share how to use that to get results. Throughout all 3 videos you're teasing them with the full solution to the problem which you will fully share on the 4th video. That's where you go into your full sales pitch.

You don't need to go into such an extensive sequence with a lower ticket item such as a product under $50. In fact, several clients have tested this over the past couple of years. We originally thought we could generate a higher number of sales by giving value over several days before making the pitch (*just like we do on high ticket items*). If there was anywhere this would be true, you would think it was Facebook. But in all of our tests across several different markets (*both B2B and B2C*), we LOST money whenever we waited to make the sale. It was much more profitable to go for the sale immediately.

You have to make an offer when your prospect is hungry. You grabbed their attention with your ad. They clicked through to your landing page. You have a short squeeze page that entices them to join your list. You send it to them by email. And then you tell them to wait till tomorrow for more? You just broke all the momentum you built up in the process. Now you have to grab their attention all over again tomorrow after they've been exposed to another thousand advertising messages!

Could you imagine any sales person getting your attention, answering your questions, making their offer, and then immediately saying they'll call you back in a few days to take your order. That's crazy! Of course you can say NO when they make their offer. And a large portion of your subscribers will do exactly that. When someone says "No," you'll follow-up on them again tomorrow. No sweat. But to stop your momentum right in the middle just because you don't want to be 'too salesy' is crazy.

Since we want to go for the sale immediately, that means you want your lead magnet to be something people can consume quickly. This could be a 5 minute video. It could be an 8 page report. Maybe it's a 20 minute audio podcast. Present your hook, give them the value, and share the next step they need to take (*the why of your offer*). Again, remember that if we're selling a high ticket product or service, it's likely the freebie will also be larger in size.

How to Create Your Lead Magnet FAST

If you you're going to be selling an information product, swipe content directly from it to create your lead magnet. You want your freebie to be based around the same basic hook as your product anyway. What's the most unique concept about your product? What is your strongest case study? If you already have cheat sheets in place, can you use one of these as the giveaway? What about using one of the already done templates?

The purpose of the freebie is to give value while teasing them with your full course anyway. Share something of value without giving the full payoff from your product (*make sure there is still some 'curiosity' hidden behind the curtain they pay to access*).

If you're creating new content from scratch, put together a very simple outline for it. Lead with the hook...

- What is wrong with the current approach everyone else recommends?
- What happened to help you discover a better way (*you stumbled on a solution, you had a mentor, you tested it yourself, you read it in a long lost book, etc.*)?
- How did your results change? Tell your story or the results someone else received.
- What are 1 to 3 tips you could share to help them immediately? The easier they can get a QUICK Win, the better.
- What is the next step? Or how will your paid product continue or improve on the results?

I'm always tempted to give away too much. Adding additional tips makes sense on a high ticket offer where you need to build up more credibility, but even there you're often better off sharing more case studies and results.

If you share too much information, you run into the danger of overwhelming your prospect. You want your advice to be quick to implement...not an encyclopedia of techniques. The only exception is when doing a cheat sheet you may give a list of techniques, but you don't go into the details of how each one operates.

If you're an affiliate promoting someone else's product or service, the best solution is creating a case study of your own results. How has the product or service helped you? What problem did you have? What specific results have you achieved? And what tips can you share along the way?

Or you could do a short audio interview with the product owner. If you've researched your audience, you should know some of the most common questions they have. Use those questions to put together an interview with the expert. Now you can focus your lead magnet on answering their biggest questions around X. Of course, talk about the paid offer at the end of the recording.

Action Steps

- A Lead Magnet is a gift you give people as an incentive to opt-in to your email list.
- Your Lead Magnet should be a Free Preview for the initial product or service you will offer in your email sequence.
- Any of the lessons we covered in the Free Preview chapter also apply to your Lead Magnet.
- Create your Lead Magnet quickly by using the 5 step simple outline given to you in this chapter.

How to Create Money-On-Demand With Email

Customers hate being sold, but they love to buy.

This is a major distinction that applies directly to your email list. The first few emails you send out to a subscriber shouldn't be a list of bullet benefits for your product or service. Could you imagine a clerk walking up to you in a store...and immediately spouting off all the benefits of their product in bullet form? You'd think they were crazy and you'd want to run for your life!

That's not what a good clerk does. Instead, they ask you what you're looking for today or how they can help you. They start with questions based on your desires. You don't feel pushed into the purchase. They answer any questions you may have. You, the customer, are in control of the buying decision. Buying something new should be a pleasurable experience.

It's hard to imitate that one-on-one conversation by email. Encourage your subscribers to respond to you by asking them what they want, but only a handful will reply directly. I'll show you how we solicit feedback and replies once we get into the emails in a few minutes. You can also send out 'smart emails' that segment people to different lists based on links they click. For example, my tennis client asks his subscribers which stroke they're most interested in (*forehand, backhand, etc.*). This email segments the audience onto different lists written to send them content and make an offer based on their choice.

You can also write emails that are a direct answer to questions your subscribers send in. Those are some of the easiest emails to write. Simply repeat the question they asked and answer the question. If they're asking the question, other subscribers on your list are thinking the same thing.

But since many customers won't reply, we're forced to write emails based off of what we know about our Ideal Client. What problems does your ideal buyer run into? What frustrates them? What pain points caused them to look for a solution to their problems? What caused them to search for and join your email list today? What is the 'desperate problem' that motivates them to action?

Write about those problems. Expose those problems. Write about the root cause of those problems. Demonstrate you have EMPATHY for what they're going through. You understand what they're going through, and you're here to help.

If you're standing there in front of a prospect, you can ask questions to reveal the pain points. We don't have that luxury with email communication except for those who reply to us. Yet, we want to expose all the potential problems and struggles our prospects may be going through.

I could say , *"You may be in debt and have creditors calling you all hours of the day and night...and you're looking for any solution out of this mess."* But that isn't going to resonate with my audience. Some of them probably aren't in debt. I don't know their situation. If I get it wrong, I've lost them because the message doesn't connect with their situation. Instead of trying to tell my prospects what they're going through, I tell my own personal story that will identify with a portion of them, *"I was in debt and had creditors calling me all hours of the day and night...and I was looking for any way out of that mess."*

Some subscribers will identify with that. Others won't. The majority will have went through some type of financial problem in the past so they can at least relate. I'm making a connection by telling about the problems I went through and how it felt to me. Even if my readers didn't go through that intense of a situation, they can still feel that bond through this story. We have shared experience.

What if I never personally experienced the problem in question? Then I could talk about a customer, client, or even someone else I know about, *"One of my clients recently told me about how he was in debt and had creditors calling him all hours of the day and night. He was looking for any way out of that mess...and that's when he joined my list."*

You're not selling the prospect on your benefits here. You're just telling your story or someone else's story. You're agitating the problem. One of the popular copywriting formulas is Problem, Agitate, Solve. You bring up the problem. You agitate the problem with all the repercussions it has on your life. Finally you solve the problem with your product or service.

Strong emails often focus on the first 2/3rds of that formula. You bring up the problem and you agitate the problem. You then drop a link over to your website for where they can find the solution to the problem. That's another key you'll see in the emails I'm about to share with you. I bring up the problems, especially if the root cause of the problem isn't what they think. That's illustrated by the phrase I regularly use, *"You don't have a traffic problem. You have a conversion problem."* If you can convert visitors and subscribers into buyers better than the competition, there are many sources of traffic available to you.

You're giving valuable content to your subscribers when you do this. Many internet marketers waste years looking for the holy grail of traffic when there are tons of traffic sources just staring them in the face. The problem is all of those traffic sources have a cost to them. Instead the correct approach is to better understand the audience along with their desperate problems, and connect those individuals to products and services that solve those problems.

We also position ourselves as a trusted authority by giving 'free samples' of our content. Sometimes I'll pull a short excerpt from my paid newsletter to send to my email subscribers. It gives them value and tips they can use immediately to grow their business, but it's not the full course meal. They're not getting everything they need to succeed on the free list. When you go to the ice cream shop, they give you a taste of the ice cream. They don't give you the full banana split. They want to give you just enough to leave you hungry for more.

Interest equals Benefit Plus Curiosity. In an information business you have to give free subscribers enough that they can gain benefits, but you have to leave them curious for what else you have hidden behind the curtain. Never forget the power of curiosity in selling.

If you're selling a physical product such as men's clothing, your free information may take a different direction. You can teach them exactly how to dress, what looks good on their body type, and how to make good choices. Essentially, you're giving them a 'Buyer's Guide' that's spread out over dozens or even hundreds of emails by integrating in your own stories, stories from other customers you've helped, and even business tips about confidence and dressing for success.

Instead of 'selling' your product or service, you simply drop links in as resources that can help them solve the problems and achieve the results you're sharing about. I only send out an email without a link a couple of times per year at most. The majority of links go directly to my products or affiliate products. Other times I'll link over to a free video, audio, or blog post that shares additional value and then links over to my products or services.

Email Broadcasts Vs Autoresponders

Your website doesn't have to be complicated. It could be as simple as a landing page where you offer a Lead Magnet. People join your list. They're sent out an immediate thank you email and given their free gift for joining. From here on out, you could simply send broadcasts that mix personality, content, and offers together. That's what I was doing when I first started online, and I've worked with several clients who started up a very successful business based on this simple foundation.

There are two types of emails you can send out: broadcasts and autoresponders. A broadcast is when you create an email and you either send it out immediately or schedule it to go out to your list (*or multiple lists*) at a specific date and time. An autoresponder is an email that is automatically sent out when a new subscriber reaches that time frame. They receive your first welcome email immediately. You may have your 2nd message programmed to go out 1 day later and then your 3rd message 2 days after that. Every new subscriber will receive those emails in the order you set them up.

The majority of my clients have a mixture of autoresponders and broadcasts. Several of my clients have autoresponder sequences that extend out for 3 to 5 YEARS. But they didn't get there overnight. Those emails were created as broadcasts over time, and they reinserted their successful broadcasts as autoresponders. You'll find many email services such as Aweber allow you to schedule autoresponders only to go out on specific days.

You'd want your welcome email to always go out immediately so you wouldn't schedule it for a specific day, but you could schedule any of your other autoresponders for specific days. For example, let's say you want to write new email broadcasts on Tuesdays and Thursdays. You could set-up all of your autoresponders to only go out on the other 5 days of the week.

None of your autoresponders would be sent out on Tuesdays or Thursdays except your initial welcome one. That would keep someone from getting two emails from you in one day (*getting two emails in one day isn't actually a problem if they're entertaining to the subscriber and they're looking forward to your emails*). In Aweber, this is called a "Send Window" and can be found under the "Settings" option on any follow-up message.

If you have a successful, entertaining broadcast email that gives value and sells your products and services, why would you want to waste it by only sending it once? You can easily plug it back into your autoresponder sequence so you can get maximum value out of it for years to come. There's a reason why I talk about working once and getting paid on it forever!

I'm subscribed to more than a dozen email lists of top marketers through my Gmail account. I have filters set that have all of these emails skip the inbox and are filed into a "Newsletters" folder. I'm not distracted as they come in and I can review them at my leisure.

I noticed a popular email marketer recently sent me a subject line that seemed familiar so I did a search of this folder for this exact subject line. He had sent the EXACT same message to the same email address 4 times in the past 2 years. So either he is rebroadcasting these messages or he has plugged that email into his follow-up system multiple times.

I wouldn't plug the same autoresponder in multiple times, but you could if it's a big winner. Why not take your 'best of the best' evergreen email broadcasts and plug them back in as autoresponders so everyone gets to experience them? One of my clients runs at least one limited time special offer for his various products each month.

He now has 12+ of these he's written over the past year, and he is broadcasting those specials out during the exact same time period this year. He has 5 emails in his Black Friday special sequence and he will send out those same emails on Black Friday this year just like he did last year. And he'll use the same sequence next year, assuming the special continues to work (*and there is no reason it wouldn't work in his evergreen market*).

Setting the Tone for New Subscribers

Don't try to create a long email sequence when you're just getting started. That's too difficult. You don't know your customers well enough yet to capture all their interests. Instead, just focus on the initial sequence of 3 to 7 emails. That's all we need to get started. In fact, you could get started with just one Welcome email and do everything else by broadcast. But I'm going to recommend doing the first few emails to help you set the tone for new subscribers on your list. The rest of your autoresponder emails can be inserted over time as you write more broadcasts and keep an eye on your stats (*open rates and clicks can be important, but the most important stat to watch is sales*).

Here's the basic outline I'm going to give you below:

- **Welcome Email**: You want to deliver your promised gift immediately. Then tease them with some of the benefits they can expect with upcoming emails. You may want to save writing these bullets until after you've written the next few emails. End with a link to an introductory offer for them to purchase or a higher end offer as an anchor to position you as premium service provider (*making your lower cost offers easier to sell*).
- **Feedback Question**: Repeat the promised gift to remind them of why you're emailing them. Now ask them what their biggest question or challenge is. The whole purpose here is to get to know them better so you can produce better content and potentially even personally offer them a product/service that fits their needs right now.
- **Challenge Common Wisdom**: In my example in this chapter I bring up the common advice of "Follow Your Passion" and talk about why it's wrong. I'm also bringing up the desperate problem. You could also take the route of ranting about a common lie/mistake in your industry.
- **Useful But Incomplete Tips**: Give your readers a few useful tips they could use immediately. In this email I start out with a strong hook/promise for the tips and then give the tips. I also note that I can't cover all these methods in an email. I'm just getting them started here.
- **Origin Story**: You want to get your origin story in quickly. In this sequence I share it over several emails and I'm only including the first one here. Your origin story reveals the desperate problem and the end solution while demonstrating what makes you different from others.

There's nothing magical about the order of these emails. You could send your origin story in the 2nd email and the feedback question in the 4th email. Or you could move the order around however it best fits the message you want to share. But I would try to get these core themes into the beginning of your email sequence: feedback, challenge common wisdom, useful but incomplete tips, and your origin story.

We're not directly promoting your products and services, but any or all of these messages can lead into a link to your offer. Instead of sending promotional emails right out of the gate, you're focusing on them and their interests. Don't just tell them you're different. Demonstrate it. We're including your Hero's Journey origin story so they can make a connection with you personally. You're illustrating the unique advantages you can offer through your story.

Your content doesn't have to be written either. We could shorten any or all of these emails down and simply link over to a video or audio on your website where you share your message. Perhaps you don't want to write your full origin story. Instead you get on camera and you tell it. Or if you're in an industry where demonstration is vital such as golf, showing them on video how to fix their golf swing would be much more effective than simply sharing a couple of tips in an email.

Post that video on your blog or website. Create a short email of just a few paragraphs that links to it. You could include a link under your video over to your offer. I have a couple of clients who follow that exact system right now. Each of their initial emails links over to a video content piece, and we have the link for their offer immediately under each video. Subscribers buy from all of these links.

Email #1 (Welcome & Teasers)

Here's the first email I've been using in one of my sequences for years now. I have made a few changes to it recently when I started testing a different lead magnet. All that changed were the first few lines where I tested the new gift. Here's the original email…

> Subject: 7 Email Stories to Double Profits – Info You Requested
>
> Thank you for requesting the "7 Email Stories to Double Your Profits Today" plus the bonus cheat sheets.
>
> There are also a few other naughty little surprises reserved for you… **www.mymarketingcoach.com/thank-you/**
>
> Download your complimentary PDF version of my $49.95/month hard copy newsletter along with all your other goodies.
>
> Print it out. Keep it as a reference.

They make creating emails much easier.

Over the next few weeks, I'll be sending you even more free tips and techniques to earn more, work less, and enjoy life...

Here's just a taste of what you will receive for free...

- Discover the #1 secret that launched me from pizza delivery driver into an Internet Lifestyle expert back in 1996.

- Why "passion" is a horrible way to choose a market and what virtually guarantees online profits instead.

- Why content isn't king...and how one little email earned $96,250 with only "OK" sales copy.

- 21 tips to sell more products today (a collection of quick income boosters).

- The devastating business mistake that almost made me quit the internet lifestyle for good.

- 5 Keys to Simple Internet Profits - how to eliminate overwhelm by focusing on what's really important.

- How to use both free and paid traffic to grow your business...and why you may be focused on the wrong one.

- If I had a gun to my head and I had to succeed in the next 30 days, what would I do?

Wait till you see the other gifts coming soon.

If at any time you don't feel I'm 100% over delivering and earning the trust you've shared with me, simply scroll to the bottom of any email and remove your name from my list.

Hopefully you'll never leave as I have so much to share with you about the Internet Lifestyle.

Your Marketing Coach,
Terry Dean
"The Internet Lifestyle Mentor"
Earn More. Work Less. Enjoy Life!

P.S. Subscribers are always asking how they can work with me personally...

There are two options for mentoring with me:

Option #1: One-On-One Mentoring

This is the crème-de-la-creme. You work directly with me and can ask any questions you need about developing your Internet lifestyle online: Traffic, Conversion, Product Creation, and More.

BUT I only take 20 clients at a time and you have to qualify. The rates are $500 to $1,000 per month for email and phone based mentoring:

www.MyMarketingCoach.com/one-on-one-coaching/

Option #2: Monthly Mentor Club

This is my group coaching program that anyone can afford. You get my BEST advice, group webinars, and a password protected group coaching board. Plus $853.80 in gifts just for giving it a try with a full money back guarantee.

www.MonthlyMentorClub.com

The subject line is the title of the free Lead Magnet they were promised on my landing page with "Info You Requested" added to the end of the subject line. Don't get cute here. Just tell them exactly what they signed up for so they can identify your email when it comes in. The first sentence thanks them for requesting the gift by name again. Then I give them the link to the download page for their gifts.

The next few paragraphs give a few details about the gift and a quick benefit statement, *"They make creating emails much easier."*

From here I go into teasing them about what I'll be sending in future emails. Some people subscribed just for the free gift, so I'm letting them know what kind of content they can expect in the future. I'm teasing them about what's coming in these bullet benefits.

After mentioning the upcoming emails, I let them know how they can unsubscribe at any time. If they want to leave my list, I'm OK with that. And I want them to know how to remove themselves instead of getting upset or hitting the SPAM button in their email provider. You could link over to one of your offers in the PS of the email. You don't want to be in their face about an offer in the first email or you can drive new subscribers away. But casually mentioning you have products or services for sale is good. Your subscribers already know you have something to sell, or you wouldn't have a business online.

If you have a low cost offer, you could run that here. Or you could link over to your book if you have one. Books are credibility builders. You're not just another person with an email list. You're also an author. In this situation I'm offering one-on-one-coaching which isn't even available at the time. Instead it has a waiting list you have to join. I'm putting it here as an 'anchor' since it costs more than the other products I'll make available in future emails. I've had clients who listed their high-end mastermind here or their $10,000 coaching day for the same reason. In addition, this builds credibility for me since my premium coaching is sold-out.

I link to this club as a secondary option for those who want group coaching instead of one-on-one and of course it's much lower cost than my private coaching. I normally wouldn't recommend making two offers in an email unless one of them costs significantly more than the other. In other words, the one-on-one coaching is for credibility and serves as an anchor to sell the group coaching.

Email #2 (Find Out Their Biggest Challenge)

I've played with this email in several different locations. You could use it several weeks into an email sequence after you've provided content and made a connection with your subscribers. You're asking for help here, and they may be more likely to help after you've provided value to them first. But this email is also my secret weapon for both generating new ideas and making sales to your subscribers. So now I'll often use it within the first few emails.

Email is a conversation…like pretty much every other marketing technique today (social media has changed marketing as we know it). You want to elicit a response out of your readers. Get them asking questions you can answer in future emails. Get them to reveal their pain points so you can better serve their needs. Respond to them individually and personally (or have someone on your team do it) to help them find the right products and services for them. Plus you get the additional side benefit that email services see people replying to your emails…which makes it more likely you'll get through their filters.

Subject: I need your help

Hopefully you had the chance to download "7 Email Stories to Double Your Profits Today" plus the bonus cheat sheets yesterday.

If not, here's that link again:
www.mymarketingcoach.com/thank-you/

I care about each and every one of my subscribers and I'd love to hear how I can best help you.

What is the biggest challenge you're facing online right now?

Just hit reply to this email and let me know.

I personally read every email sent to me.

It could take me several days to get back with you, because I receive a lot of emails daily.

Thank you,
Terry Dean
"The Internet Lifestyle Mentor"
Earn More. Work Less. Enjoy Life!

I start off mentioning the free gift they requested yesterday so they can remember who in the world I am. If you use a different style of email here, I'd still add that note about the free gift. Then I immediately ask them what their biggest challenge is. Notice that I'm not sending them over to a survey. That would be less personal and also generates a lower response. All they have to do is reply which also sets up the potential for the conversation to continue. You demonstrate empathy by actually replying to them and showing you care about their unique situation (*their challenge feels unique to them even if it's the most common problem in your market*).

You could also take the first two lines about the free gift they downloaded and move it to the PS instead. Then you'd start the email off with, *"I care about each and every one..."* If you already have a list, try an email like this as a broadcast to find out more about how you can help them. Have you run a survey or a question like this to your list within the past 6 months? You could word it like this when going out to your current list, *"I'm creating some cool new content for you right now. What is the biggest question you have about online marketing?"*

> **Advanced Tip**: This tip is for those who use an email service which provides "Smart Links" inside your emails such as Infusionsoft, Zaxaa, or Aweber combined with Aweber Pro Tools. You could use a short email like this as a way to segment your audience onto separate lists that are more relevant to their interests. Change the question to something like this, *"Which of these five statements best describes what you're struggling with the most right now?"*

You would then write 5 descriptive statements underneath the question. Each of these sentences would be a clickable smart link you can use to add the subscriber to a relevant list for their interest. The link itself could take them over to a survey form where they can give you more details about the issue and what it means to them personally. Or you could take them directly to content related to their issue.

Email #3 (Challenge Common Wisdom)

You need to demonstrate early on that you're not like others in your market. You can do this by asking them a question and actually replying to their email. You're a real person who cares about them instead of another faceless person hiding behind a website. Another way to demonstrate your difference is with your tone and message. What are the biggest myths, mistakes, or misconceptions in your market? What is a LIE that everyone seems to repeat? What is it about the industry that frustrates you and other customers…that NO ONE seems to be talking about?

There's a scene in the old movie "Network" where the news station is struggling and about to go off the air within a couple of weeks. The anchor Howard Beale goes on camera and rants about the state of society and gets his audience to yell out their window, *"I'm mad as Hell, and I'm not going to take it anymore!"* What in your market that gets you angry like this? What do you want to rant about? You can check out this scene on Youtube: **www.youtube.com/watch?v=ZwMVMbmQBug**

One of the struggles online marketers face is choosing their market. It frustrates me when I see people wasting months or even years trying to choose which market to go into. And one of the biggest lies in our industry is to *"Just follow your passion."* With advice like that, it's no wonder people get stuck trying to figure out what they want to do. Our interests often change as you get older.

I'm not passionate about the same subjects or hobbies that interested me 10 years ago. And just because you're passionate about something doesn't mean you have experience, credibility, or any kind of advantage in that market. That's why so many people start selling 'internet marketing products' even though they have little or no internet marketing experience. It's what they're passionate about today! That's why they're studying the subject. We end up with the blind leading the blind...and an industry that's full of half-truths and wild theories.

Instead of just going after what you're passionate about, think back to your personal experience and skillsets. Where can you share value with others? Combine value you can share with a buying audience that's easy to target. Add in a little bit of passion for the subject (*I definitely wouldn't recommend going into a market you hate*). And now you have the right kind of mix to be successful.

So one of the emails I've used for years is about this subject. The text of it is below...

Subject: Is a niche market worth your time?

Imagine your website is an oil well.

The analogy isn't too far off...if you set it up the way my clients do.

Do you drill your oil well because it "sounds" like a good idea at the time?

Do you dig your well because it "feels right?"

I hope not.

You dig your oil well where you discovered oil ...just waiting to be tapped into.

A lot of wet-behind-the-ear rookies tell you to "Follow your passion."

Sounds like a lazy platitude masquerading as wisdom.

What if your life depends on your decision?

What if there was a guy with a gun threatening to end your life if you didn't get results in the next 30 days?

You can bet your booty I'm not going to just follow my passion.

I'm NOT going to wing it and hope something works out.

I'm going to go where the money is.

That's how the situation felt when I first started online in 1996.

There wasn't any gunmen forcing me to get results, but there was a soul-draining pizza delivery job for Little Caesars paying me a lousy $8 an hour.

There were over $50,000 in debts...and a mailbox full of late credit card statements staring me in the face.

It felt like being thrown in the deep end.

Either this works...or I'm done.

There was no other option.

In that situation, you can't even think clearly about your passion.

All you know is you need to go where the money is...and fast.

Find a hungry crowd that's already buying. Their credit cards are out and money is flowing.

All you have to do is offer them a better, improved, or even just a new solution to their problems.

Quit looking for an empty market.

Competition is a GOOD THING. It means people are buying. I get nervous and run the other direction if there are ZERO competitors in a market.

Zero competition equals zero customers!

Love your competition. Join their lists. Read their websites.

They're leaving clues about how customers spend their hard-earned dollars.

Your competitors are successful because they're selling what your customers desperately want.

If you want to be passionate about something, become passionate about the CUSTOMER.

Fall in love with your customers.

Become intimately acquainted with their hurts, their pains, and their desires.

Tomorrow you'll discover 3 ways you can uncover your buyer's hidden motivations for free.

If only it was THIS easy when I started all those years ago…

But 99% of entrepreneurs never learn this secret.

See you tomorrow. Same time. Same channel.

Your Former Pizza Delivery Driver,

Terry Dean

Internet Lifestyle Mentor

Earn More. Work Less. Enjoy Life!

P.S. Yes, I do one-on-one coaching, but ONLY with 20 clients at a time.

This means it's an exclusive group with a waiting list that currently numbers in the hundreds. The rates start at a minimum of $500 to $1,000 a month…and many clients have been with me for 6 years or more.

Get on the list ASAP if you want any chance of working with me this year:

www.MyMarketingCoach.com/one-on-one-coaching/

"I STARTED WORKING WITH TERRY DEAN AS ONE OF HIS PRIVATE COACHING CLIENTS MAYBE 2 ½ YEARS AGO NOW. AT THAT TIME, MY BUSINESS WAS DOING ABOUT $7000 TO $10,000 PER MONTH. AND WITH TERRY'S ASSISTANCE, I ACTUALLY INCREASED MY BUSINESS FROM $7000 TO $10,000 PER MONTH TO $20,000 PER MONTH. THEN ACTUALLY FROM $20,000 PER MONTH TO $100,000 PER MONTH."

Lee McIntyre/GetMoreMomentum.com

This email starts off with the visual imagery of an oil well. Word pictures are a powerful way to get your message across. I transition into the myth everyone talks about, *"Follow your passion."* I then move into additional visual imagery of a gun being held to your head. I first heard Gary Halbert and John Carlton talk about 'gun to the head' copywriting where your copy absolutely has to produce for you. It applies in this situation to show the importance of making the right decision.

I drop a tidbit from my own story, *"That's how the situation felt when I first started online in 1996."* I don't go into my full origin story, but I identify with the pain here that's part of my origin story. I know how it feels to be thrown into the deep end (*notice that imagery again*). It's been mostly emotion up to this point, but the next part is the content where I talk about reviewing the competition and falling in love with your customer. It's a change of view from what you'd normally hear in the 'internet marketing' space. Finally I end with a teaser for the next email they'll receive. I also drop the same PS here about my one-on-one coaching.

Use this email as a model when you talk about a myth in your market. Provide contrarian content. As you do this, you have to capture the emotion and the pain. The biggest mistake I make, and you're likely to also make, is to provide reasonable and logical content. But humans are irrational. They don't make decisions just based on logic. We make decisions based on emotion and justify our decisions with logic. It's the heart strings that lead to action. That's why this email taps into emotion and imagery. Sending out content to your audience is good, but sales are generated by sending out content that's mixed with personality, emotion, and authority.

Email #4 (Useful But Incomplete Tips)

"Useful but incomplete" means your content is useful. Subscribers gain value and can get results from following it. But it doesn't feel complete. You gave them a thousand-foot overview of the whole process, but you didn't get into the little nitty-gritty details. Or you gave them the first step to take. They do it and get results, but now they need to move into step two. You help them solve their first problem, and now they need to solve the next one…

> Subject: 3 Ways to Uncover Your Buyers Secret Language
>
> What if your best customers offered to write your websites and your emails for you…for free?
>
> They write the EXACT words to say to lead them into a buying decision.
>
> No more stressing out over a blank page.

You just use your customer's own words...freely given to you.

Because let's face it.

Sometimes writing sucks.

Hemingway said, "*There is nothing to writing. All you do is sit down at a typewriter and bleed.*"

Maybe that's what you've been taught...bleed all over the page.

But there's a much easier way where you use your customer's own words to persuade them.

It's impossible to share the complete step-by-step technique in an email, but I can get you started on the right path.

Buyer's Secret Language #1: Amazon

What sets Amazon apart from Google, Bing, Facebook, and other top sites?

Only BUYERS visit Amazon.

BINGO.

There are rumors Amazon has over 200,000,000 credit cards on file.

That's like heaven to a smart marketer.

Here are just a couple of techniques you can use today on Amazon.

Visit any category in Amazon and find the top selling products. What titles pull the most interest?

Click on those top sellers. Read the customer reviews.

What do customers say positively or negatively about this product?

It gets even more exciting. Each review actually lets other customers VOTE on whether a review was helpful.

That's right. Other customers are voting on whether the language in that review helped them make a BUYING decision.

I have to stop here or we could be here all day with everything you can do with this information.

Two more quickies...and then I have to run until tomorrow.

Buyer's Secret Language #2: Forums

Dig into the popular forums in your niche.

Most of them allow you to sort all the threads by popularity. The threads with the highest readership and replies hit a nerve in the market.

People CLICKED on those subject lines.

I hope you just grabbed a major hint for your emails in that last sentence...

Buyer's Secret Language #3: Search.Twitter.com

Twitter is basically a social media site where your future customers go around shouting out everything on their minds all day long.

Try typing in phrases that match up with what you do, what you sell, or even competitor's names.

Ignore the marketers and look for what customers are saying about the subject.

They'll give you clues here about exactly what you need to say on your website and in your emails.

Can you tell this topic gets me excited?

I'm always looking for shortcuts that actually work.

You can create winning websites and emails using OTHER people's language.

In fact, this is the EASY way. Quit struggling and often getting it wrong on your own.

If only this had been available to me when I was starting out...my success would have been even FASTER!

I ran through these 3 techniques at lightning speed in this email.

If you'd like to hit the ground running and discover how to immediately tap into ALL of your customer's buying language, check this out…

www.AutoresponderAlchemy.com

And that's just one of the advanced modules.

Watch the very first video in the course. Create your first email using one of my proven templates. If you don't agree this is the quickest and easiest way to multiply your income online, just return it for a full refund. No questions asked.

This Stuff Is Out of This World,

Terry Dean
Internet Lifestyle Mentor
Earn More. Work Less. Enjoy Life!

I open up the email with a strong promise about customers telling you what to say for free. Then I drop into the problem of stressing over a blank page. I hope this sentence jumped out at you from this email, *"It's impossible to share the complete step-by-step technique in an email, but I can get you started on the right path."* I'm telling them this is useful but incomplete before sharing the actual tips. Then I do 3 quick tips, before going into a 'soft' pitch for my product here.

This is content email you can easily model and use over-and-over again…

1.   Give a promise for the email in the first sentence.

2.   Talk about the problem this promise solves.

3.   Let them know this isn't the complete system.

4.   Give them 1 to 5 rapid fire tips they could use.

5.   Tell them how to get the complete system.

Email #5 (Origin Story #1)

You need to tell your subscribers what makes you different from the competition. But just coming out and saying you're better because of X, Y, and Z feels too salesy. Sure, there's a time for that, but an even better way to get your message across in the beginning is through your origin story.

There's a reason why you started this business, got into consulting, or created the product you sell. What's the story behind it? I'm in this business because I was looking for any way out of the financial mess I was in at the time. When I came online, it was email that set me free. But it wasn't just about building a list and spamming them. It was about sending emails full of hidden persuasion techniques.

My clients also work their origin stories into their emails and their copy. For example, Florian Meier at **www.onlinetennisinstruction.com** discovered a very unique method of coaching tennis players to improve their technical game. He shares this method throughout all of his online courses, a monthly continuity program, and live clinics. Marcus Santamaria at **www.SynergySpanish.com** discovered his unique Spanish speaking methods while teaching English in Mexico. He has a complete origin story of how he struggled with languages until he discovered these unique tricks for English speakers to learn Spanish at any age.

Paul Wright at **www.healthbusinessprofits.com** has used this statement dozens of times, *"For more than 20 years he owned multiple successful health clinics in Australia, whilst still spending more time at home than his wife preferred, never missed a school concert or sports carnival, and visited his clinics for only a few hours each week – at one stage he didn't even live in the same city as five of his clinics."*

It's part of his origin story and I'm sure he gets tired of telling it times just like I get tired of telling mine. We continue to use them because these true stories give the WHY behind your mission, add credibility to your message, and demonstrate what makes you different from the competition.

Subject: #1 Secret to Internet Income

I stumbled upon the #1 secret to Internet income in my first month online.

www.AutoresponderAlchemy.com

But it wasn't till six months later that I realized just how powerful this secret is.

I agonized over what to do each day when I got home from my soul crushing $8 an hour job delivering pizzas for Little Caesars in 1996.

We had a pile of debts...many from previous failed businesses like direct mail, door-to-door sales, and network marketing.

What else could I do to get out of that nightmare?

Truly, was there any hope left for me?

That's when it happened. There were rumors of people using the Internet to make a living.

I said to myself, "*I can do this. I know I can.*"

I used my last remaining credit card to buy my first PC from Best Buy.

Took it home and trained myself to use this computer-thingy. It wasn't easy!

My very first offers were tiny little self-help reports and videos which I licensed from others.

Surprise, surprise.

A tiny little stream of income started coming in. First it was a few bucks here and there, but it quickly grew to an avalanche.

And it was all because I had two flashes of brilliance that first week online.

Secret #1 is....wait for it...

Build a targeted email list.

Hopefully you've heard that before. It's foundational.

But are you doing it CORRECTLY?

Here is my second secret...and this is what makes the list work.

LOVE your customers.

On a recent interview I was asked to define love.

The best way to describe it is this.

Love is a commitment to ADD to everyone's life that comes in contact with you...whether they buy from you or not.

Give them value. Improve their life. Never subtract from them...and never tear them down.

It could be a simple daily email tip.

It may even be something as small as giving a word of encouragement to those around you.

Let that be a guiding light in everything you do.

When offering products, it could mean letting customers know who they're for…and who they're not for. Your products aren't for everyone.

Who is the RIGHT customer that gets the best results from what you offer?

For example, "Autoresponder Alchemy" isn't for everyone.

It's designed for those who want an EASIER way to create million dollar email systems.

www.AutoresponderAlchemy.com

You get my proven templates along with my simple email creation system…even if you're not a writer.

If you're looking for a sit back and do NOTHING system, this isn't it.

Once you have the system in place, it works for you like clockwork.

But you are required to at least watch the first video, model the template, and push the "send" button.

Do nothing. Get nothing. That's the bottom line.

Your Plug-And-Play Email Coach,
Terry Dean
Internet Lifestyle Mentor
Earn More. Work Less. Enjoy Life!

The link for the course is in the very beginning of this email. You'll get more clickthroughs with a link up top than near the bottom, but that doesn't necessarily mean you'll get more sales. I'm including it here because I already mentioned this course in previous emails. I then go into the pain point (*Desperate Problem*) of my origin story. My mini-story here transitions into a very simple secret of building an email list. That tip isn't enough on its own because EVERYONE in my market has heard that before. It was too predictable. That's why the email continues into the second secret of loving your customers and it talks about the definition of love in this situation.

This is not just about giving information. I'm also creating a 'qualifier' for who should buy my product and who shouldn't. I'm calling out to those who actually care about their customers and want to add value. It's not about doing hard sales pitches or pressuring people into the purchase. Yes, I use techniques that motivate the right people to take action, purchase, and use the course. But I also want to repel those who reject that message...and are just after a quick buck.

As I analyzed this email, I spotted a mistake I never noticed here before. It's this line, "*It's designed for those who want an EASIER way to create million dollar emails systems.*" While that would be a good line to use in another scenario, it feels like a disconnect here. I was talking about loving your customer and choosing 'million dollar email systems' is the wrong transition. It would be better to write about selling without being salesy or making sales while providing value and content.

Watch out for the tone in your email. Read all your emails out loud and try to feel the emotion being carried at each point. It's easy to drop out of the flow, even when you've written thousands of emails before. I've coached many clients over the phone where I'll read something, and my first response is that something just feels off about the email. Sometimes you can't quite put your finger on it. We'll try rewording several ways until we find something that connects with the message that's being shared. We even pull up a list of synonyms online for a few of the words to see if we can find a better match.

I don't do this for every email. Money is attracted to speed. You might write many of your broadcasts quickly. Read them out loud. Make a few edits. Load it into your email system and hit send. But if you're going to be using an email as one of your first few follow-up messages that will be seen by tens of thousands of leads, you owe it to yourself to go through it for the right words and emotions.

Money-On-Demand Emails

The next email in my sequence continues with my origin story along with some of the mistakes I've made along the way. Sharing your mistakes is a great way to connect with your readers. You don't have to project an image of perfection. They know you're not perfect anyway. They're likely making some of the same mistakes you did. After this I share a case study about how one of my clients used scheduled email broadcasts to live the Internet Lifestyle while traveling the world for 6 months. This illustrates the dream many subscribers have and again connects back to my email course.

You can continue on with the themes I showed you in these initial emails. Keep the content 'alive' by connecting it to your own experiences and stories. You're not going to attract buyers if all you do is send out dry content. They need to feel like they know you. I was shocked when I attended my first internet marketing conference. People came up to me and repeated some of the stories I told in my emails. They wanted to know more. Even though I had never heard from them individually, these subscribers felt like we were friends since they had read so many emails from me.

One man told me about how he printed out each of my emails and took them with him over to the park where he ate lunch every day. This is someone who listened to me, purchased from me, and felt like he personally knew me because we spent so much time together. And the whole relationship was simply through the emails I broadcast out to my list. That's the power of email.

These day-to-day emails are the first piece in the puzzle. You're also going to run special offers with deadlines. I always launch my products at a special discount price for just 5 to 7 days. But any occasion can become a good time for a special. Retailers are experts at this. Every holiday equals a new sale: Easter, Mother's Day, Memorial Day, Father's Day, 4th of July, and on through the year. Get to Thanksgiving and Christmas and those sales become major events with Doorbusters and limited stock.

Although we don't like to admit it, we're motivated by deadlines. There have been many times where I've received an email about a special offer, checked the deadline for it and put it off to the side for later review. Then I forgot about it. I expect you've done the same. Here's a basic outline for a 5 day special offer you could broadcast out to your list...

Day 1: Big Discount with REASON WHY you're making this offer (*why is this such a good deal now*).

Day 2: Focus on an additional benefit (*talk about the unique promise and secondary benefit*).

Day 3: Case Study or Testimonials related to offer (*the middle day is a good place for a story*).

Day 4: Time is Running out (*repeat core benefits and remind them of the upcoming deadline*).

162

Day 5: Last Chance (*this is a short email giving them one last chance to order*).

Many of my clients run multiple emails on this final day. One runs in the morning, another in the early afternoon and a final one when there are only about 6 hours left. I've had many specials where over half the orders came in on the final day...a large percentage of those coming in the last 6 hours. If you teased people in advance about the upcoming special, you'll see orders coming in immediately on the first email. The sales will decline as you get into day 3 in the middle of the special and then the orders pick back up as you get close to the deadline.

These types of offers are easiest to run as broadcasts since they're based off of limited time availability. But you can also run evergreen specials in your autoresponder sequence by plugging in one of the countdown timer scripts such as:

- **www.scarcitysamurai.com**
- **imwenterprises.net/start-everywhere,**
- **scarcitybuilder.com**

Any of these scripts can be used to be a timer that's set to expire at a specific date and time if you're running a special for the next few days by broadcast. You can also also set-up evergreen timers and specials that are coded to when a visitor first visits the page or joins your list (*Scarcity Samurai can be triggered when someone joins your list in a few email providers while the other two trigger only when someone first visits the page*).

You could run a series of emails like the first five I showed you in this chapter, and then plug-in an evergreen special for the next five days to promote one of your products with a special offer. The "Reason Why" behind this offer is that it's a special for new subscribers. Obviously you can't connect it to any holiday or big event. New subscribers could be joining your list at any time. But this is an introductory offer for new subscribers to get a fast start in your subject. If they don't purchase by the deadline, they miss out on the special offer. Getting an evergreen special in your sequence early is a great way to help you pay for the expenses of generating the list!

Action Steps

- The easiest emails to write are simply answering questions sent in by subscribers.
- Share your story and agitate the desperate problem your subscribers are already feeling.
- Every email should have a call-to-action. The majority of these will be an opportunity to purchase a product or service.
- Create an initial set of emails for all new subscribers. These emails share your core message, introduce your story, and demonstrate a Free Preview for your initial product or service.
- At least one of your initial emails should ask your subscribers to respond back to you with a question or challenge they're facing. Sending a personal reply to these emails can set-up additional sales.

Why EVERYONE Should Have a Blog

Everyone should have a blog. Not everyone needs a Facebook page, Twitter account, or a Youtube account, but everyone should have a blog. You may have a great looking website that has been designed for your business or you could just have a simple landing page where people can join your email list. Either way, you should still have a blog, even if you never call it by that name.

A blog by this definition is simply a section of your site where you can easily add new content. You don't need to know HTML. You don't have to use any fancy design tools. You can just post new content and updates yourself in just a few minutes...anytime you want. The tool I recommend for this is Wordpress which is completely free.

Your blog is your home base. Social media is exciting. You can attract visitors over to your site from participating on Facebook, Twitter, Linkedin, Instagram, and other social media avenues. The problem with social media is you don't own your profile. You pretty much sign over those rights when you create your account. If Facebook decides they don't like your business for whatever reason, they have every right to cancel your account. Those 'Likes' on your page, they're not yours. They belong to Facebook.

Facebook has proven this to us multiple times the past few years. They keep reducing the organic reach of business pages. That means all those Likes you've worked hard to build up on your Facebook page, you're not reaching them...unless you choose to advertise. A social marketing firm, Locowise, did a research study in 2015 to determine the average Facebook post reach. It was a pitiful 2.6%. The more Facebook likes your page has, the smaller percentage you reach of your audience. A Facebook page with less than 1,000 Likes reached 22.8% of their audience while pages with over 1,000,000 likes only reached 2.27% of their audience. Those with 50,000 to 100,000 likes reach 9.62%. Those with 500,000 to 999,999 reached 7.74%.

Those numbers are pretty low, and Facebook has further reduced organic reach since that time. Larger, more effective brands are essentially punished for their success. You work your butt off to build your audience on Facebook, and you don't even get to reach them. You might even be spending money on Facebook ads to build that audience. If you want your post to reach this audience you've earned, you'll have to hand over even more money for Facebook ads.

That's why you can visit social media, but don't live there. Build up your followers, but concentrate instead on attracting visitors to your site and getting them to sign up for your list. Post content to your Wordpress blog. Share it on your Facebook and other social media sites. Your website is your home base for everything you do online. It's what you own. Your email list is your online audience. This is where the money is. Everything you do in social media is designed to get more people over to your site, onto your list, and buying your products or services. It's NOT just to build a large fan base.

How to Install Wordpress

If you're not technically inclined, you may want to ask your webmaster to install it for you. It's a pretty easy install and shouldn't cost much for the install itself. There are a lot of both free and paid 'themes' you can use along with it to get the kind of design you want. If you want to match the design up with the rest of your site, then you may need to pay your designer to create a custom theme. A simple free design may cost you under $100 installed. A premium theme could cost another $100 or so if you wanted a little fancier design with more features. If you need a custom theme designed or you need to match the theme to the rest of the site, you can expect it to cost $1,000 or more.

If you want to do-it-yourself, a basic install is pretty easy. Many web hosts have Wordpress built right into their system and you can install it through their control panel. You just fill in a few details and it is installed for you. If your web host doesn't have this, then you can install it through FTP with software tool such as Filezilla. You can download the Wordpress software itself from **www.wordpress.org** and then grab Filezilla software from **filezilla-project.org**.

Once you have Wordpress installed, it comes with a few basic themes (*the design of the site*). You can view and download thousands of free themes from **wordpress.org/themes**. Or you could install a premium theme which includes even more features. Vendors can be found all over the Internet. My favorites are **www.studiopress.com** and **www.ithemes.com**.

One of the beautiful things about Wordpress is that you can change from one theme to another without that many hassles. All the content you have on your site will immediately appear inside the new theme. The only things you will lose are any of the customizations you've made to the theme. This makes it easy to get started with a basic free or premium theme. Then you can have someone design a custom theme for your brand at any time in the future. It doesn't matter whether you have 3 posts on your site or 3,000. Your content moves to the new theme with you.

If you're having a website built for you now or you're going to have one designed in the near future, ask your designer if it would make sense to build the entire site in Wordpress. There is no reason why simple websites like a local business owner, consultant, or author would use shouldn't be designed entirely in Wordpress.

Wordpress allows you to use both 'Pages' and 'Posts.' Pages are intended for static content. Your home page, About Us, and Contact Us could all be built as Pages. Navigation can include or exclude any specific page that's created on the site. The benefit to you of having your entire site designed in Wordpress is the ease of editing. Once your site is up and running, it would be easy for you to go in and make small edits to your content. If your hours change, you wouldn't have to hire a designer at premium prices to fix this. You or anyone on your team who has the username and password for the site can go in and make this edit in just a few minutes. Wordpress makes it easy to keep your site up-to-date.

If you need more advanced features for your site such as a large ecommerce website with thousands of products, you'll likely find other solutions can be a better choice. But that's only a small portion of website owners. For the rest of us, you never have to be held hostage by a website designer again. Have someone get your site up and looking good. Then ask them to show you how to make minor edits to it yourself.

Wordpress pages are for static content. You can also create Wordpress posts. These are likely what you're expecting when you hear blog. These are automatically organized for you in chronological order (most recent posts first) in whatever categories you choose. They're designed for updated content. Think of this as the 'News' portion of your site. Each time you add a new post, it will show at the top of the list. For example, an accountant would want to post about recent tax changes. Those posts would be shown at the top of the 'blog' section of the site. Each time you add a new post, it goes to the top of the list so visitors see it first in this section.

What should you post to your site? This matters what other type of content you're producing (and we'll get into that later). For example, whenever you post a Youtube video, I'd recommend grabbing the embed code from your video and creating a post on your blog that allows visitors to play the Youtube video without leaving your site. If you publish a podcast, create a copy of it as a blog post. Write a few short bullet benefits about it and give them the link to play it or download it.

The majority of my clients and I post copies of the email broadcasts we send as Wordpress posts. When I write a personal story and connect it to my offer, it gets sent by email and posted to my blog. When I send out a content piece about how you can generate more visitors to your site using Youtube, that gets posted to the site also. About the only emails that don't also get published on the blog are limited time specials. You should be sending out regular and consistent emails. If you published just one email a week and posted that to your website, that's 52 posts over the year. What if you published daily emails? That's 365 new posts a year on your site.

We're not going to dig into everything about search engine optimization here. That's too big of a topic and it changes over time. Each of these posts is giving you additional search engine fuel to attract visitors to your site. The majority of visitors you get from the search engines won't be from a few big terms. Instead it comes from long-tail phrases that could be three, four, five words or more in the search query.

Whenever I look at Google Analytics, I'm always surprised at how many visitors came to my site from a unique search term. That means there was only one search that landed on my site from that exact phrase in the past month. There are often thousands of these types of long-tail search results in your Analytics reports. And that comes from having a volume of posts of your website.

The Amazing Power of Plug-Ins

We've only tapped the surface of a Wordpress blog so far. In addition to the ability to create posts and pages, there are literally thousands of plug-ins (*many of them free*) you can use to add additional capabilities to your website. For example, you can install social sharing buttons on your website using a free plugin. These plug-ins can create those little Facebook, Twitter, Google+, and other social sharing buttons at the top or bottom of each of your posts. These make it easy for your visitors to share your content with their friends. Instead of recommending a specific plug-in here, I'll give you the link to where you can search the Wordpress database itself for plug-ins: **wordpress.org/plugins/**

Do a search for "Social Sharing Buttons." A large list of social sharing plug-ins will come up that have been rated by other Wordpress members. I'd recommend only considering plug-ins with hundreds of reviews and an average rating of 4 or 5. This is a popular subject, so all the top plug-ins will have a lot of reviews for them. If you're looking for a plug-in that's a little less common, you might not have that volume of reviews. Personally I wouldn't want to be the first person to test out a new plug-in, so I'd still zero in on those with more reviews in the 4 to 5 level.

You can add plug-ins to your site that make it easy to install Google Analytics on your pages, publish your own podcast, use pop-ups to ask visitors for their email address, protect your site from hackers, create a message board, and more. There are so many options here that it can blow your mind. Many of these plug-ins are completely free, but there are even paid plug-ins you might use to expand the capabilities of your website.

For example, here are a few of the premium Wordpress plug-ins I've personally purchased:

- **Wishlist Member**: This plug-in allows you to turn a Wordpress site into a paid membership site, protect any or all of your pages and posts, and manage your members from inside Wordpress itself.
  www.mymarketingcoach.com/wishlist
- **Survey Funnel**: You can create a survey on your website that asks a series of preset questions you select, and then segment your audience to different pages of your site and onto different email lists based off their answers.
  www.mymarketingcoach.com/surveys
- **Icegram**: This plug-in creates pop-ups, headers, footers, and even allows you to install opt-in box right inside your posts themselves. This is a great way to generate more subscribers from the visitors to your Wordpress website.
  www.mymarketingcoach.com/icegram
- **WARNING**: It's easy to go overboard with plug-ins once you see all the options available. Each one can add additional

capabilities to your site, but they can also slow down the loading of your web pages. The one weakness of Wordpress is that it's database driven and can be a little slower loading than other types of websites. Adding dozens of plug-ins can make this even worse.

A second negative of having too many plug-ins active on your site is they can have conflicts with each other. You'll install a new plug-in (*or your webmaster installs it for you*) and it won't run. Or you'll see some other error on the site. Many times this is a conflict between plug-ins and the way to fix it is to turn off all the plug-ins and see if that fixes the problem. If it works without plug-ins, slowly turn on the plug-ins one-by-one until you find the one causing the error.

Instead of adding everything you want to your site, think about what you actually need. Use a minimal amount of plug-ins that add benefits you want. None of my websites have more than a dozen active Wordpress plug-ins on them at a time. Of course this isn't a limit set in stone. It's just a principle. Only install and activate plug-ins that add a capability that helps you attract more visitors, get more people on your list, or sell more of your products and services.

Turn Visitors Into Subscribers and Buyers

Visitors to your website are good, but subscribers are even better. Buyers are the next step up. And we could talk about the hyper-responsive buyers who purchase everything you publish. Our goal is make the ascension through these levels as convenient as possible for our audience. The first step for most visitors is to raise their hand, request your free Lead Magnet, and get added to your email list. This means our priority in the design and use of your website is to get people on your list.

Take a look at **www.MyMarketingCoach.com**, my main website. I offer my Lead Magnet above the fold. While there is navigation at the top of the page, the opt-in offer is pretty much all your see before you scroll down the page. You don't see my product offers until you start scrolling. This could be the only time a visitor comes to my site. I may only get one shot. And making a sale to a cold prospect is a tough game on their first visit. If they join my email list though, I'll get another opportunity tomorrow, the next day, and the day after.

Now visit **www.mymarketingcoach.com/blog/,** my blog page, where all the new posts go (*these are mostly copies of my email broadcasts*). You'll see the Lead Magnet opt-in offer on the top right of the page. Click on any of the articles on the main blog page and you'll again see the opt-in offer to the top right of the page. And another opt-in offer at the bottom of the content. It should be pretty obvious what I want you to do at this point.

You could even add a popover that asks for a visitor's email address (*you may or may not see one on my website based on what I'm testing at the time*). If you use one, set a delay on it for 15 seconds or more so that a visitor can get attached to the content first. If you pop it up in the face when they immediately land on the page, it can be a good reason to hit the 'Back' button and go somewhere else.

Concentrate on your list. I can't say that enough. That's why you're publishing content on your website. Attract visitors and get them on your list. Your calls-to-action for your list should be the most obvious thing on the page.

Some of the content you post on social media should bring visitors back to your website. We'll get into more detail about how to use social media correctly in a later chapter, but a portion of your posts will bring visitors back to your content pages. Once they're here, one of your goals is to get them on your list.

Basic Search Engine Optimization For Your Website

Google is king when it comes to search, and they're looking for 'authority' websites. There are multiple signals Google is looking for when indexing your site. These include the age of your website, whether other high quality websites link to you, and your overall brand (*do people search for your brand name for example when looking for keywords in your topic*). It's not very fair for those starting out, but the more popular you are, the more likely Google will send even more traffic your way.

They're looking at not just the number of other sites linking to you, but the overall theme of those websites and the words they use when they link to you. If we jumped in our trusty time machine and went a decade back in time, Google's algorithms weren't that great about sifting and sorting sites. The website with the highest volume of incoming links using their keyword often ended up the winner and ranked on top.

That's NOT the way it works today. Google found people were gaming the system and putting up hundreds of sites just for the purpose of linking back to their own sites. Today a few good links from high quality authority sites on your topic are worth considerably more than thousands of low quality sites. Getting a few mentions and links from high traffic blogs in your category could be enough to catapult you to the top of the rankings for less competitive terms. And if every site links to you using the same keyword phrase in the link itself, that can actually be a negative. You're much better off with a 'natural' link profile of people linking to you over time using multiple keywords and phrases.

That's one of the reasons why we'll talk about making connections with influencers in a later chapter. Getting on top of Google isn't about tricking the search engines. It's about getting connected with others online. Some will tell you search engines are all about great content, but that's not really true. Getting ranked is about popular content which is linked by other authority websites and shared on social media. Google takes into account whether visitors to your site are sharing your content with others. They judge that if you have a lot of shares, then you're likely producing stuff others want to read. That's why you want to add the social share buttons to your website so it's easy to share your stuff.

Authority sites are often deep sites with a large number of pages on the topic. That's another reason why you want to post the majority of your emails as posts on your blog also. As you build up a network of hundreds or thousands of posts on your site, you're not only giving Google more ammo to work with in terms of long-tail search terms, but you're also building a deeper and more informative website overall.

Google wants visitors to have a good user experience when they come to your website. How fast do your web pages load? People are impatient today. If your site takes too long to load, they'll simply hit the back button and visit another website in the search results. Do visitors stay on your website when they visit or do they immediately hit the back button? That's a huge black mark against your website if visitors click back to Google as soon as they land on your pages. Either your website isn't really relevant to the terms they have you listed for, or visitors weren't comfortable on your pages. Either way, your website isn't the authority they're looking for on this topic.

Is your website mobile responsive? Mobile is becoming more important all the time. If your website isn't built to display properly on all devices, you're throwing away a large portion of your marketing! Google will 'punish' your site when people are searching on mobile if your site doesn't display properly for their devices. You can check if any of your individual web pages or posts are mobile responsive here: **www.google.com/webmasters/tools/mobile-friendly/**

Make sure whichever theme you pick for your Wordpress website is mobile responsive. The majority are today, but you can still find a few hold-outs which won't pass this test. Look for the term "Mobile Responsive" when selecting the theme.

What Can You Do On Your Website Itself to Increase Your SEO?

Write about the topic you want to rank for. I know that sounds obvious, but it is the first step. Including the keyword phrases you want to target in the title of your post is important. If you want to rank for "lose weight with paleo," include those words in your title. Also include the phrase several times throughout the body of the post.

Don't use that exact same phrase a bunch of times in the post,because Google has advanced ways to spot those tricks. Instead write for the visitors. Google is watching those people who click back from your article, and they're also looking at the overall clickthrough rate to your article. If the title of your post is so persuasive that it attracts more clicks than the other results in the search engine, that's another little boost for your ranking. Remember the tip from the email marketing chapter in regards to subject lines. Attract people by sharing a Benefit plus Curiosity. Get them curious enough that they have to click to find out more.

You can also influence your search engine results with both internal and external links. External links means linking out to other authority websites. Don't go overboard with a bunch of links to your site which send your visitors away. Good external links are simply links that refer to another resource on the topic, especially when it's an influencer you're trying to connect with. In other words, share the love with them first by linking to them. You link to XYZ's in-depth research study on the current trends on real estate prices from your real estate website. This is useful content your visitors will appreciate that's relevant to the topic and published by another authority website. Google looks at your overall 'neighborhood.' Do high quality websites link to you and do you link out to other high quality sites?

Internal links are links to other pages and posts on the same website. For example, you create a post on your website that mentions real estate values in your city. You link it over to the in-depth post you already have about how real estate values in your city have changed in the past year. You're adding even more weight to that older real estate values page. You're letting Google know it's important information on your website. Not all of your pages are going to rank equally in the results. Link over to the ones you most want to rank. And you can also share some of that 'search engine juice' with other pages on your site by linking back to another relevant post from the high ranking one.

Links inside your site should be natural just like external links. You're linking when it makes sense for visitors to want to know more about the topic. You can also think a little about SEO when creating categories on your site. With our real estate blog, we might have categories about selling your home, buying a new home, first time home buyers, moving to your city, etc. As you add new posts to your blog, you can add those posts to the appropriate categories. This will help visitors find what they're looking for, and this internal link structure can also provide you with a small additional benefit on the search engines since Wordpress naturally creates pages for each of your categories.

What I've shared above is simply an introduction to search engine optimization. It's not a big part of my own personal strategy, but it can generate some extra visitors, leads, and sales using the exact same content you're already creating. When you get an influencer to share your website on social media or link to it from their own website, you'll pick up visitors through their direct links. At the same time, you're building your overall authority with Google and other search sites for additional free traffic and leads. That's the same reason I'm posting the majority of my emails to the website. It's leveraging the content you're already creating for additional exposure and reach.

10 Content Templates For More Content In Less Time

You may be asking what you could write emails about or what you could write posts about? How can you come up with interesting content for your site? That's a common question. The good news is that this is pretty simple. Here are 10 basic ideas you can tap into no matter what market you're in and who your audience is…

- **Personal Story**: Tell a story from your personal life that illustrates something you want to share. For example, I've often talked about my dogs in my own emails. They're a part of my family and they do little humorous things that can turn into good stories. I've even written a post called, "Marketing Lessons From My Dogs."

- **Case Study**: Share the results one of your clients received. These are some of the most successful content pieces you can write. Not only do you share content, but you add credibility for your message at the same time. Share the problem they originally experienced, a couple of steps involved in solving the problem, and how it feels for them to have solved the problem today.

- **How-To**: It's easy to break up a how-to post into 3 to 7 steps. What is the problem you want to solve? What are each of the steps in solving that problem? Write out the steps involved first, and then come back and write a paragraph or two about each one. Super-simple to put together.

- **Create a List**: That's what I'm doing right here. I'm giving you a list of 10 content template ideas. I simply looked back at the types of posts my clients and I have written, and made a list of them. Then I wrote one paragraph about each.

- **Book/Product/Video Review**: Review someone else's product. Is there a good book you've read on the topic? This allows you to share advice from another topic while building up your own credibility on the subject. If they have an affiliate program (*or the book is available in Amazon*), you could also link to them as an affiliate for a commission.

- **Rant**: These are some of my favorite emails and posts to write. What lies are robbing people in your audience from success? What mistakes, myths, and misconceptions keep them from experiencing everything available to them? I've often ranted about the 'business opportunity' shysters online when they promise success with no work. They keep people from success, and others see their pitches and shy away from anything involving online marketing.

- **Feedback**: Your subscribers and customers will send you questions about your emails, posts, and products. Simply start your email or post by repeating their question and the rest of your content is your answer to the question. Write the answer just as if you were talking to them individually. Feedback is awesome because it helps you create new content!

- **Pop Culture**: Use a movie, song, or the current news as a launching point into your content. Marketing is all about connecting with the conversation already going in the head of your reader. What can you use to illustrate your point from a subject that your subscribers are already thinking about?
- **Multimedia**: Create a video and embed it on your blog. Then link to it in a short email. If you were interviewed on a podcast, share that on your blog. Hire someone on Fiverr to create a infographic with a list you created. Share something in a different format from your common style.
- **Resource Links**: Link to resources from others. What are the 5 best blog posts you read this week about your subject? Write a quick paragraph about each and link to them. You're sharing good content with your readers and you're doing something good for other influencers.

These are just 10 ways you can create content for your audience. Inside my Email Conversion Kit, I share an in-depth mindmap including dozens of types of emails you can create no matter what market you're in. In addition, I share template subject lines, introductory sentences you can use to get started fast, and 64 story starters so you're never lacking an idea for your content. You can grab your free copy over at: **www.MyMarketingCoach.com**.

What If You're NOT a Writer

At this point you may be thinking, *"But what if you're not a writer?"*

No problem. First of all, if you can talk, you can write. Good writing online is not like writing in college or for a professional publication. There are no real rules to online writing other than making yourself understood by your target audience. Throw out your $20 words and focus on writing like you speak in your day-to-day life. It doesn't matter how intelligent or well educated your audience is, they're distracted online. They may have several browser windows open at once. They may be visiting your website on a tiny little mobile screen. Or they might be quickly scanning an email you sent them while sitting at a traffic light. Use short words and short sentences. Use everyday language. Make it a fast moving thrill ride. Drop in little tidbits about your day-to-day life to demonstrate you're a real person.

Whatever you do, don't fall into your 'writer voice.' Just talk to your reader like a normal person. If you struggle with typing, there are several very good voice recognition programs out there. I use a PC and Dragon Naturally Speaking works well. Personally, I feel more comfortable with typing so I don't use it often, but some of my clients swear by it. I shared it with a friend who was struggling to write a book. After practicing with it, he produced a 300+ page book in the next 30 days. It just poured out of him the moment he could speak instead of having to sit down and write.

There's nothing that says the content you produce needs to be written at all. The Internet is quickly moving toward video. Cisco has estimated that Wifi and mobile devices will account for 66% of all Internet traffic by 2020. Video is expected to be 82% of global traffic by 2020. If you don't feel comfortable writing, you can produce videos instead.

Video doesn't have to be a fancy production where you hire a studio and professional videographers, especially not for day-to-day content. Start small. It's likely that your cell phone has a good enough video camera on it to get started. Or you could simply use a webcam attached to your computer. Write down a few notes about a subject to talk about and sit down in front of your webcam to shoot a short video. It's easy to put content together today. You can even record directly to Youtube. And Youtube allows you to edit the video online.

If you want to edit your video in more depth, there are easy-to-use tools like iMovie available on the Mac or iPads. On PC, Sony Vegas Movie Studio is one of the best options although it is not nearly as easy to use as iMovie.

The easiest way to improve the quality of your online videos is through a separate microphone. Most camcorders and mobile devices shoot good quality video, but they have poor audio. Buy a separate lapel mic you can attach to your recording device. If you're using a webcam, you could buy a USB microphone such as the Blue Yeti series of desk microphones. I have one and it produces excellent sound for video or audio recordings.

If you're going to record video regularly (*such as creating one short video each week*), look into buying several lights also. You can purchase three box lights or other soft type lights that give you good lighting without glare of shadows for less than $200. Do a quick search on Youtube for "low cost video lighting" and you'll find multiple options including how to set the lights up in small spaces.

What if you don't feel you have the face for video? Then audio it is. Podcasts can be an excellent way to share content with your audience. Several of my friends and clients produce their own podcasts and share the majority of their content to their email lists in audio format. There are free podcast plug-ins you can use on your Wordpress site to make publishing audio content easy. Instead of writing a long email, send out a short email teaser that links over to your audio post.

Audio is easier than video to produce, and you can also invite guests on your 'show.' You can bring in guests for video also, especially through online tools like Google Hangouts, but you'll find it a little more difficult. Recording audio interviews can be as simple as calling someone over Skype and using a free audio recorder such as mp3Skyperecorder at: **voipcallrecording.com/MP3_Skype_Recorder**

Audio interviews are one of the methods we'll talk about as we start reaching out to influencers online. Instead of asking them to promote your website or link to you, you tell them how you've already linked to them or you invite them for an interview. You'll share their message with your audience. This has the additional benefit of giving you additional credibility since your name is seen alongside other experts in your industry. You must be an authority if you hang out with other authorities.

All of the content methods I've mentioned throughout this chapter apply to both video and audio also. You can use whatever methods is most comfortable for you. The key is sharing Infotainment with your audience. You want to share entertaining content that promotes your products and services. Whether it's in written, audio, or video format isn't what's most important. Getting it done and sharing your unique voice is what will separate you from the competition.

Action Steps

- A blog is your home base online. Everyone needs a blog, but you don't need a profile on every social media site.
- Having a free or premium off-the-shelf Wordpress theme shouldn't cost that much money. Expenses increase dramatically if you have a theme custom designed for your site. Make sure it is mobile responsive and you're able to do basic editing.
- Wordpress plug-ins can add a lot of useful additional functionality to your site, but they can cause conflict and slow down your website speed.
- Don't get carried away with search engine optimization. Write about popular topics, but focus first on your audience. Write for real readers, not for search engines. Create a useful and easy to navigate website full of information your audience is looking for.
- Video or audio can be even more engaging than written content such as blog posts. Go where your audience is and produce the kind of content they're looking for.

How to Create One Year Of Content In 30 Days or Less

Creating content doesn't have to be a long, time consuming process. If your goal is perfection, then yes, you're going to waste a lot of time here. If you listen to some of the blogging gurus who tell you every post has to include 4 hours of research before spending 4 hours writing your masterpiece, you're not going to get very much done.

You might produce a few posts like that, posts that become pillar content designed specifically for others to link to them. But you don't need to create those starting out. In fact, trying to find your 'voice' in your very first few posts is tough. Instead I recommend a READY – FIRE – AIM approach where you get started producing content and find your voice along the way.

Creating great content that attracts a hungry audience is not just about regurgitating a bunch of facts. It also needs to be mixed with your personality. It's NOT your goal to become an unbiased news source. That's just an illusion perpetrated by the media. No one is unbiased. Every single source of news you receive daily is biased by the writer's opinion. If it was produced by humans, it is biased. It's especially easy to manipulate surveys and even scientific studies are influenced by the end results desired by whoever is funding them.

This is an important principle because so many people try to remove their emotions from the content they produce. And you want to do the exact opposite to attract your audience. Share your opinions. One of my proven subject line templates is *"My Uncensored Opinion About X"* where X is the subject you're covering. For example, *"My Uncensored Opinion About Facebook Ads"* is a subject line I've used with great success before.

You've went back through the reason you're in this business and discovered your Hero's Journey. That's the story you have to tell. That's what your audience wants to hear. They don't just want to be overwhelmed with more facts and figures. There is already more content online than we know what to do with. It has to have that human-interest story.

We live in a world today that is infatuated with celebrity. They read about where their favorite celebrities vacation, what they eat, and even who they endorse for political office. When you look at it from a logical perspective, none of that should matter at all. Just because someone is an actor, singer, or athlete doesn't mean they know a thing about finances, politics, or anything else that affects your daily life. Yet people care. That's the power of celebrity.

You can position yourself as a celebrity no one outside your market has ever heard of. You get the benefits in front of a buying audience without being hassled by the paparazzi. Think about the tabloids and how they follow celebrities around. There's an ongoing narrative about the popular celebrities as they give you a peek inside their lives.

That's NOT what you're doing. You're giving content and value. People come to you because they're interested in discovering more about the subject. They stay with you because they connect with you. They identify with what you share. You drop little tidbits of your story throughout your emails, blog posts, or videos. Your focus is on your message, but you are a part of that message. Nobody cares how much you know until they know how much you care. A little authenticity and even a little vulnerability can go a long way to establishing a relationship with your audience.

It's about more than just information. It's infotainment. Give value to your audience, but mix that message with entertainment and personality. Be yourself. One of the biggest mistakes I see online is when someone takes on their 'formal' writing voice. They talk to you one-on-one like you're a normal person, but the moment they start writing they put on professional airs. One of the greatest compliments people have given me is they can hear me personally speaking when they read something I've written. My writing voice is the same voice you'll hear when speaking to me in person.

We covered your Authority Architecture in a previous chapter. You'll integrate in elements from this throughout your content. You might have an email that highlights a mistake you've made in the past. Another one might be you ranting about a villain in your industry (*remember this doesn't have to be a person – it can often be a lie or something else that's holding your clients back from their desires*). You'll tell a story from your personal life that illustrates a lesson you want to share. You might tell about a mentor who has influenced your life.

The point here is to deliver engaging, entertaining content with a slice of your own personality. Be yourself. Get real with your audience. And get passionate about your topic. If you can do that, you're already most of the way there.

Where to Start With Content When You KNOW Your Message

One of the biggest challenges in getting started with "content marketing" is coming up with ideas about what to create! Where should you start? What should you talk about? Are you even qualified to talk about this topic?

The best-case scenario is where you already know what makes you different from the competition. Maybe you've invented a new method that no one else is using. Of course you talk about this in your content. For example, one of my clients teaches his clients how to speak Spanish faster by focusing first on words that are easy for an English speaker to use and remember along with words that tie sentences together. With a very small vocabulary, you can create tens of thousands of common phrases. His method is totally different than the textbooks which gives him a reason to constantly talk about this, give examples, and tie the theme directly to his products.

If everyone in the market is trying to solve the wrong root problem, then you could talk about this instead. I put out a training course a few years back with Dr. Glenn Livingston called the Total Conversion Code. When I published content about this product, I continually talked about how traffic is NOT your problem.

Everyone thinks their problem is that they're not generating enough traffic. If only they could get more traffic to their site, all their problems would be solved. The truth is that if you have a large enough potential audience and you know how to turn visitors into subscribers and buyers, there are dozens of great sources of traffic. You can buy traffic from Google, Youtube, Facebook, Twitter, and literally hundreds of other places. There is no lack of traffic IF you can earn more per visitor than it costs to get those visitors to your website.

There was a weakness in this message though. It only attracted a small portion of the market. Smart marketers realized the importance of conversion and they were drawn to the message, but the majority continued with their dreams of more free traffic.

This type of message is even more effective if it lines up with what customers are ALREADY thinking about their subject. For example, there are a lot of dog trainers who teach how to train your dog using methods such as choke chains, prong collars, or even shock collars (*of course they rarely call them shock collars anymore*). If you teach only positive training methods, you could make that the theme of much of your initial content along with showing those training techniques. This is a message that would immediately appeal to a portion of the audience who only wanted to use positive methods with their best friend.

If you know your message and how you want customers to perceive you, you can start here with your content. It's going to allow you to build your 'public persona' faster because people will see what sets you apart in your first few content pieces. You'll be attracting the right audience out of the gate. But you might not be sure about your message yet. What can you do in this scenario?

How to Quickly Come Up With Your First 100 Pieces of Content

Let's say you're just getting started with content, but you're not 100% positive on your message or how you want people to perceive you yet. Where should you start with your content? This is an easy method that I first heard from Travis Cody who talks about this in his book, **"When a Book is a Goldmine."** He uses this method specifically to write a book, but you can use a very similar system for coming up with any type of content.

Set a timer for 10 to 15 minutes. Write down every question your audience is asking about the subject. Don't stop to judge any of the questions. Just keep writing questions they're asking about the topic. This exercise is easier if you've been interacting directly with the audience by answering questions from clients, chatting at conferences, or even lurking on Facebook groups and in forums. What questions are people asking? Write every question you can come up with.

Get up and take a quick break. When you come back, set your timer for another 10 to 15 minutes. Now you're going to write the questions your audience SHOULD be asking. This is based off your knowledge of the topic itself. Your audience often doesn't even know the right questions to ask. What are the most important elements to know about your subject? You're the expert, so you can GIVE them the questions to ask.

You should have dozens of questions written now from these two short writing sessions. All of these questions simply came from what you already knew during those two sessions. Now you can expand out from here and do a little research. Visit a few of those Facebook groups or discussion boards. What questions do you see people asking? Write those down. Open up your email. Do you have any emails from clients? If so, scan through some of those previous emails for questions clients have asked you directly. While you're at it, you could even look at email newsletters you may subscribe to. What subjects are they writing about?

You can use the Amazon trick here also. Look up a few of the bestselling books in your category. First click on the "Search Inside" feature by clicking on the image of the book near the top left. Scan through the table of contents. Write out a few quick questions based on the chapter titles. Scroll down and look through the reviews. What questions are being asked in the reviews or in comments on the reviews? What do people say is important to them?

Follow these same steps for another book about your topic. You can continue with this theme by looking for popular content about your subject. Do a search about your subject on Youtube. Use Buzzsumo.com to search for your keyword and see which posts are the most popular. Of course you could even simply do a Google search to see what comes up on top also.

Invest around 30 minutes on the two short writing exercises. Invest no more than around 90 minutes total in doing additional research. In just 2 hours, you can come up with 100 or more questions that your audience wants to know about your topic. If you were to write 2 pieces of content per week, that's almost a few years' worth of content all in one sitting.

You're including the questions your audience are asking, so you know this is what they're interested in. There is another advantage to the Question and Answer method. One of the biggest mistakes people make when writing their content is to take on an overly professional tone of voice. If you sound like a boring professor, you're going to lose your audience's attention. Instead you want to share a voice that is more personal. It sounds like you're speaking in person with your audience.

Imagine one of your audience members asking the question and then you answer it. You may or may not include the questions itself in your content. There are times where I'll start an email, blog post, or video by saying, "*Here is a question that a subscriber recently sent to me.*" Then I repeat the question and answer it. But you could also simply allow the question to be asked off-screen. Someone asks the question and you go right into your answer in your content.

I'll repeat the question IF it was an actual question a subscriber or client recently sent me. I'll just go into my answer when it's a question I wrote down using this method. Having every piece of content start with a question sent to you by a subscriber can get boring. It's just too predictable.

How to Sell Without Selling

It could work on a Youtube video channel, but I'd mix it up in email or on blog posts. Start with a question at times. Use a story intro. Create a list of tips or steps.

Remember good content is not just about content. It's about Infotainment. You have to keep your audience interested in what you're sharing. They need to connect with you as a person. You're providing value, but at the same time you're entertaining them. They see something in your personality or lifestyle that they can admire. It could be your courage of standing up to the establishment. It could be your authenticity and willingness to share the mistakes you've made. It may be the challenges you've personally overcome.

How to Sprinkle In Personal Stories For Connection & Illustration

Your audience may forget the 5 points you share in an article, but they'll remember forever some of the stories you tell. This is something I discovered by experimentation over the years, especially with email. Personally, I'd rather just rattle off a bunch of facts. Here's how this works. This is step one. This is step two. And so on down through the list. I wish that was the type of content that worked best for attracting a hungry tribe of buyers, but it's not.

Your prospect is already overwhelmed by content online. Over one hour of video is uploaded to Youtube EVERY second. That's 86,400 hours of NEW video per day. This is across all subjects and markets, but there is no way anyone has time to watch all the new videos about their topic. And that's just video. What about when we add in Facebook posts, Twitter updates, Instagram photos, blog posts, and more. There is FLOOD of new content online daily.

Why should someone not only be attracted to what you create, but be hooked by it? They can't get enough. They read all your emails, buy your products, attend your events, and pay for your services. They join your monthly membership site and stay in it for years. Yes, giving value is important. If you truly give people stuff they can use, then you're ahead of the game. But it's still not enough on its own. The next secret is to sprinkle in stories and an ongoing narrative with you as the star.

Think about an ongoing series of novels, a long-running TV series, or a movie franchises. We go to the movies to watch an entertaining story that connects with our emotions. It doesn't matter whether it's a drama, thriller, horror, or a comedy. It was created to tell a story and affect your emotions. Have you ever paid attention to how a good movie toys with your emotions, especially in its use of background music to set the scene?

A long running movie franchise has to do even more than tell a story. You have to connect with the character. James Bond has been played by 12 actors in over two dozen movies. While each actor brings their own take to the role, they keep many of his traits the same. He has to be confident, intelligent, charismatic, well dressed, and dangerous. He's a man to be admired. He's going to end up in situations where it appears like there is no way out, but he finds the solution using both brains and brawn. And he has his little idiosyncrasies which are carried throughout his continued appearance.

In an age where you're surrounded by competition and overwhelming content, one of the ways you separate yourself is by becoming that confident character. What does your audience admire about you? What have they come to expect from you? What if there was a James Bond movie made where he didn't conquer? It would be a surprise ending, but it wouldn't be the surprise his audience is hoping for. It would likely be a flop because it went against everyone's expectations for the character.

But how do we know what to expect from James Bond? We've seen his stories through movies and books. We were never told what to expect. Instead, it has been demonstrated to us through stories. You can't tell people to *"Trust me."* You can't just say, *"I'm reliable."* And you can't say you're a genius and expect your audience to just believe you.

You have to demonstrate it through the stories you tell. A marketing consultant who wants their audience to see their genius would tell stories about the breakthroughs they've engineered. They'd share detailed case studies from their clients about the 'miracles' they've performed. They will tell you about the challenges they've faced and how they overcame them time and time again. They're not telling you about their genius. Instead, they're demonstrating it in story form.

Some of the most powerful stories you can tell are case studies. These can include both your own case studies and results you've generated for your clients. In a case study story, you set the stage by talking about the Desperate Problem first. You tell about other ways that you or the client tried to solve the problem and how those didn't work. Then the breakthrough moment occurred. The solution was realized. Perhaps there were a few other challenges along the way. And finally you hit the end results, the unique promise of the story.

Case studies are awesome because they contain the 3 P's of the Golden Glove (*Problem, Promise, and Proof*) along with a mix of content *(the solution you talk about)* all in a memorable story form. This is one of the most powerful forms of storytelling. You're giving value while demonstrating your expertise and persuading your audience.

I've helped clients who primarily monetized their website through affiliate promotions. They didn't have any products or services of their own. Instead they promoted other people's products for a share of the profits. Sharing a case study about the product you're promoting will set you apart from all the other affiliates who are likely just using the company's provided promotional materials. You actually used the product and generated results from it. It's not just an ad. It's a content rich endorsement.

6 Additional Types of Stories You Can Tell

Case studies are just one of my favorite types of stories. There are six more story formats my clients and I commonly use in our emails, blog posts, videos, and social media. How can you use each of these to communicate your message with your audience?

#1 - Who Am I:

This story brings in something from your background to illustrate why you've become the person you are today. Maybe it's something your grandad told you before he died. Or it's a lesson you learned as a child. Perhaps it's a story about going to college, meeting your spouse, or seeing your child for the first time. These are emotional events that leave a life-long impression on who you are.

It could be about mistakes you have made to get where you are today. A lot of the lessons I've learned about online business were birthed out of my own mistakes. For example, I spent 6 months of my time to develop a business growth course for small business owners. When it came time to launch, there was very little interest. Yes, I sold a few copies. It was profitable, but it wasn't worth anywhere near the time I invested in the course.

I was coaching a dental consultant at the time, and that gave me an idea. I took the course, only made slight changes in it to change it from focusing on all small business owners to speaking directly to dentists. This meant a change in title, adding in specific phrases referring to dentists and patients, and modifying a few of the examples to the dental market. I bought the InternetForDentists.com domain and rolled out the offer with a couple of JV contacts I had in the market.

The course started selling. My ad copy had very few changes other than focusing on dentists instead of all small business owners. I no longer offer this specific course, but the principle has stayed with me until now. People are looking for a specific solution to their unique problems. Most entrepreneurs don't consider themselves 'small business owners.' They're dentists, chiropractors, accountants, etc. This lesson has also enabled to help many of my B2B clients target a specific industry in their marketing.

And this lesson can also be applied to any type of marketing. An accountant for example may serve any business client, but they could create a campaign specifically targeting chiropractors. They send out a direct mail package to local chiropractors that talks about how they've helped other chiropractors, includes testimonials from chiropractors, and possibly even includes a special offer designed specifically for chiropractors. A member of one of my coaching groups owns an IT firm and wrote a book specifically for those in health type practices. While he can serve any type of business, he specializes in health practices. You can use niche targeting to generate higher conversion rates in most marketing campaigns.

#2 - Reason Why:

This type of story can be used to explain why you're making such an incredible offer. Are you making an offer that seems a little too good to be true? By explaining how and why you can make an offer like this, you build credibility and believability. Perhaps your prices are lower than all your competitors because your overhead is so much lower. You can tell your customers why you have lower overhead and what influenced you to run your business this way.

One of the big email promotions I often talk about is when I generated $96,250 in sales in one weekend in front of a live audience. If you were to go back and analyze that promotion, the email itself only briefly mentioned the offer. The majority of the offer was explained after you clicked through the email to the website. Around 2/3rds of the email was WHY I was making such an incredible offer that was only good from Friday till Sunday.

I gave my readers two reasons why I was making this offer. The first reason was because I was standing in front of a room full of over 130 entrepreneurs and I had promised to show them how much money my email promotion could earn that weekend. That was obviously true as all of my subscribers would have seen my previous emails promoting the conference I was speaking in front of. And they would have seen my promises about the email demonstration they would see at the conference. No one wants to look stupid in front of an audience, so it's very believable that I'd want to offer a great deal to get people to respond to my offer that weekend.

The second reason I was making such an incredible offer was because my wife and I were looking at new homes in Arizona. We were tired of the cold weather and the snow in Indiana and we wanted to move to somewhere we'd never see snow again. The profits from the promotion would become the down payment we would use on our new home. My wife had just came back from looking at homes in Arizona, but we ended up not moving out west. Instead we moved to Florida a couple of years later, but we were looking for homes in Arizona at the time and we intended to use the additional profits to help pay for the new house.

You might think that nobody would care why you're making an incredible offer. They just want the great deal, right? But they do care. You have an ongoing narrative about who you and your business are. And telling people why you're making an offer like this builds your credibility. You're not just another salesperson who marks down their prices at random. There is a specific reason you do what you do.

Over the years I've used many Reasons Why for my promotions. These include popular holidays such as Black Friday, Christmas, Valentine's Day, and the 4th of July. But they've also included events such as my business' anniversary, my birthday, my wife's birthday, and our anniversary. You could even connect to strange holidays such as 'Talk Like a Pirate Day' if it makes sense with your offer and your audience.

#3 - Rapport Building:

A rapport building story is about sharing a common bond. You could tell a story about your parents, spouse, or children. It could be about a vacation you enjoyed. It could be about sitting out on a boat. If you're cautious about it, you could even bring up religion or politics (*be careful here*).

Since I don't have children and don't really like to travel, I've often tapped into my love for dogs. I'll share lessons I've learned from my dogs or emotional moments I've experienced with my dogs. They've brought so much love, joy, and heartache at times into my life.

My blog post which received the most comments and my Facebook post which had the most comments were both about times where my dogs had died. I simply shared what had happened from my heart. I didn't make an offer either time. I didn't try to sell. And I honestly was upset and in tears when I wrote both of those, but my dogs are a part of who I am. To not mention or include them into my business wouldn't make sense.

One of the comments I remember most was a woman who said she was going to pay even more attention to my emails and products because she could see how much I loved my dogs. That built a connection and a rapport with her. Those messages were not about business or profits. They were simply a part of who I am which I was sharing with my audience.

Share your love, your joy, and your excitement with your audience. Share your heartache at times too. Be a real person they can relate to.

#4 - Counter Objections:

What are the most common reasons people don't buy your products or services? They might not see how your product is any better than the competition. Or they simply don't believe you. Case studies help with the believability factor. Improving your offer and giving them a reason why you're making this offer can demonstrate why your product is better.

What other objections do they have? Maybe they're worried about the price. You could tell a story about another customer who was worried about the price and what happened when they made a decision to go forward anyway. Or you could talk about a time where you were worried about the price of something (this can be totally unrelated), and how you made the right decision of moving forward anyway. Tell them the fear and emotions you felt, and then how it felt once you said YES anyway along with the end results of the decision (*it worked out great, right*).

Perhaps they're afraid of how much time it will take. Share a story about how little time it took another customer. Or share your own story overcoming this fear in another situation. They could be concerned about how many other products they've tried without results. Tell about the customer who tried everything or tell about your own experience where you tried everything only to find the solution at the end.

Survey your audience. Find out what objections they have and what challenges they're facing. If you have the opportunity to speak to clients in person or over the phone, use those opportunities to find out what objections they have to your products and services. Tap into stories where other clients have had similar objections or when you've faced a similar challenge in making a decision for something else.

#5 - Vision:

What is your vision for the future? You're on a mission. How will you transform the world for good and what will that look like? For example, the Make-A-Wish Foundation has a vision of fulfilling a wish for every child that's suffering with a life-threatening illness. One of the most famous and inspiring vision stories came from Martin Luther King Jr. as he gave his "I have a dream" speech.

Maybe your vision is to help 1,000,000 students find the right colleges for them. Or you want to help train 100,000 dogs through your courses and your licensed dog training team. Maybe you're a chiropractor who wants to share the message of health with 10,000 people in your local area. Or you could even combine a vision story with a "Who I Am" story by talking about why your mission is to stamp out diabetes since both your parents died of it.

Here's a secret to a vision story. It needs to be bigger than you. It has to stop you in your tracks and make you say, *"How in the world will I do that?"* You need a team to accomplish it. More than that, you need your clients to come alongside you to help you accomplish the mission. Don't tell a story about a vision you can accomplish on your own. Vision stories need to be too big for you to be effective!

#6 – Entertainment:

You can tell a story simply for its entertainment value. Anything funny happen this week? What did your child say? What did the waiter say? Could you make fun of some silly mistake you made? Self-deprecating humor is great at humanizing you as long as you don't overdo it to where you lose your authority. Even experts make mistakes and you're definitely not an expert at everything (don't get me started on my home improvement stories).

I've often talked about when I first asked my wife out. When I was going to college, I worked up the courage and asked her if she would go out with me Friday night. She ignored the question and changed the subject!

After she went on and on about something that wasn't nearly as important at the time, I asked her again if she would like to go out with me Friday night. Her response was, *"Sure, I'm not afraid to go out with you."*

What a resounding vote of confidence...at least I didn't have that serial killer kind of look to me. The moral of the story is the importance of both boldness and persistence. It's a funny story that also illustrates a point. If you're going to be an entrepreneur, you're going to experience some rejection. How will you handle it? If something like this would cause you to go hide, then you may simply not be cut out to succeed in today's Internet world.

How to Schedule Your Writing

You know what you're going to create content about and you also know how to insert personal stories to create that human connection with your audience. Next you have to schedule when you'll create the content. This depends on what you're going to create. I'm a writer. That's my preferred content method. I create emails and blog posts. In addition, I do a decent number of videos.

When I create videos, I almost always write them out first. If it's a promotional video, I write out a full word-for-word script which I read from a teleprompter. For a content video, I usually don't have a full script, but I do have a very extensive outline. In many cases, I'll actually write an article about the topic right before I produce a video. That way I'll reuse much of the written content in the video itself.

Writing is my method. You might prefer audio content such as podcasts. And you could even produce audios first and have them transcribed to turn them into written content also. Voice recognition software such as Dragon Naturally Speaking does a pretty good job of turning audio content into written content, although you're definitely going to have to go back in and edit it, especially adding punctuation. Or you could hire a transcriber from Upwork.com to create a higher quality written publication of your work. If you love the interaction of having someone else on the audios with you, then you could focus on interviewing experts or even partnering with another entrepreneur to run your own ongoing 'show.'

When you're doing audio, your recording times will be scheduled with your partner or your interviewee. But what about writing? How do you schedule that into your day and your week. People are always asking me about my personal schedule, so I'll mention my method first and then I'll share the other common writing method you'll hear from many prolific authors.

My writing preference is blocking off long writing periods. For example, I might schedule Monday, Thursday, and Friday afternoon as writing periods from 12 PM to 4 PM. In one day's time block, I might knock out 4 to 6 emails for the next week or two. Or over several days I'll write my monthly print newsletter. Or I'll try to finish at least half a chapter of a book like this.

The 'time block' method requires you to have good control over your time. If you're going to have employees, children, or your spouse bugging you during these periods, you won't get nearly as much accomplished. You'll get pulled out of the flow. Several studies have shown you lose 15 minutes of focus from even a short interruption. If you're constantly getting interrupted, this method simply won't work.

Focus on your writing for 25 to 30 minutes at a time. Then take a short break of 5 to 10 minutes. Get up and walk around. Do some pushups or some chin-ups. Being stuck at a desk is NOT good for your health. I'll also get up and play with my dog which he definitely appreciates. There are times where he lays there watching me, and jumps to his feet whenever he sees me move my chair away from my desk. He's anxiously, but quietly, waiting for the next play time.

The legendary copywriter Eugene Swartz used time blocks like this to create 9 books, hundreds of successful ads, and who knows how many articles. And he did it all working just 3 hours a day, 5 days a week. That's a pretty nice part-time schedule!

He always worked from the same desk. When he sat down, he set and egg timer for 33 minutes and 33 seconds. During this time, he was allowed to drink coffee, write whatever he was working on, or stare out the window. He was not allowed to get up and he was not allowed to do anything else. And he did this at a time where he wasn't faced with the constant distraction of the Internet.

Today you'd want to add the additional rule that you need to turn off all your digital devices, close all your browsers, and turn off any instant notifications. All you have is Word or another word processing program open in front of you. Write or don't write. Don't do anything else.

Even if you felt like you had 'writer's block' you'd eventually get bored of sitting there and you'd start writing something. That's all you're allowed to do during this period. Don't open Facebook, and you might not get any writing done today! You just wasted all that 'money making' time for something of much lesser importance.

When the timer went off, he'd get up and do something else for 10 to 15 minutes. After taking his break, he sit back down and start the timer again. The same rules apply. If you can string together 4 to 6 writing periods like this, you will get a LOT of writing done.

Of course your attention span could be longer or shorter than Eugene Schwartz. While I'm much happier to live in the time period we have today, with ability to have pretty much worldwide knowledge at our fingertips, it's also easy to see just how hard it is to focus today. There are so many buzzing devices surrounding us. Social media is calling to you about that exciting new thing you just don't want to miss. Microsoft recently did a study where they found the average attention span has dropped to just 8 seconds today. It's hard to focus!

You may find you have to start with a shorter writing period such as 15 minutes. As you practice, you can increase the time, matching Eugene Schwartz's time of 33 minutes and 33 seconds or adding more time such as 45 minutes on each work period. You can improve your ability to focus through practice!

Plan your writing periods based on your schedule. Eugene was consistently writing 5 days a week. Personally I have a couple of days per week where I block off 3 to 4 hours for writing. Other days I may be more focused on working with clients or presenting on a webinar.

Many writers like having a specific time each day where they sit down and know it is time to write. One popular method is the 'pay yourself' first method where you schedule the first hour of the day to write. You don't check email or your phone. That's being reactive. You're basing your actions off of other people's demands of your time. Instead, that first hour or each day is carved out for writing.

This method has several advantages. First of all, it puts you in a consistent routine. You owe yourself that hour each day for writing. If you get up an hour before everyone else, it's also quiet time. No one is calling and no one is expecting you to email them back yet. Your family isn't up and bugging you yet. You don't have to get the kids ready for school until writing time is over.

This means you're moving your business forward every single day. By just scheduling one hour per day 5 days a week, you'll have written for 5 hours by the end of the week. BY the end of the year, you'll have written for 260 hours. Think about all the content you could have finished and out in the marketplace building your authority and attracting new clients if you dedicated 260 hours this year to this plan. What if you had invested 260 hours for each of the 3 previous years? What would be the effect on your business? You'd likely be further ahead of where you are right now.

This doesn't mean you're ONLY limited to just this one hour each day. It's simply investing the first hour in yourself. You could schedule additional time blocks if you want and you're able. You might dedicate the whole weekend for several weeks in a row to finish off a book. Or you might block out a couple of additional afternoons to finish a new online training course. But that single hour invested daily can produce huge dividends in your business.

Create a Content Calendar

Don't waste time trying to figure out what to create each time you sit down at your desk. Over the years, I've probably spent more time figuring out what to write than actually writing. And you don't make money from 'getting ready to create content.'

The secret here is creating a content calendar you can follow. This means you know the moment you sit down what you'll be writing about today. In fact, you can glance at your calendar in the last few minutes of the day before, and your subconscious can go to work for you while you're enjoying free time with your family.

Here's the first method that several clients have found effective, especially for frequent email content. I mentioned in a previous chapter that your list will accept more emails from you than you expect, as long as they're entertaining. They'll reject one boring email a week, but hang on every word of entertaining emails sent every day. Hyper-responsive buyers in a market are interested in the topic, and they want to hear from you more often.

You may send one email a week, two, three, four, or even five emails a week. You might send emails every single day or even a couple of emails a day. Your first response may be that your audience doesn't want to hear from you that often. But the reality is that they want to hear from you IF you're sending out emails they want to read. The limit isn't based as much as on the subscriber as it is on you, the publisher. How often can you send entertaining, contrarian content that holds their attention and interest?

Here's the email method one of my clients follows. He sends 5 to 6 emails a week. He sends out video content on Monday. He shoots videos for the next month all at one time, during one of his time blocks. On Tuesday, he sends out a special discount for one of his products and services. Wednesday is an in-depth content piece. Thursday is a story or case study related to the product offer (this means entertaining content that provides credibility and proof for the offer). Friday is a scarcity closing today special for the offer. He may add in an additional scarcity email on Friday if the offer is a top performer.

That's a pretty simple routine he follows week-after-week. You can modify it to fit your own email schedule. Maybe you offer a podcast instead of a video. And you are so busy handling all your current clients that you only want to send two emails a week. You publish an email linking over to your podcast and another email that includes your content/case study for the week. Or maybe you don't do your schedule like this at all.

The other way to produce a publishing calendar is to plan out your themes over the next few months. What products and services will you be offering? Yes, we think about the calls-to-action first. The primary reason you're sending out content is to sell more of your products and services. Running a business is not a charity endeavor. Yes, people will get value out of what you send, but you have to keep your eyes on the prize. You want to sell without selling. And a consistent publishing schedule is how you do this.

Let's say you're a dental consultant and you'll soon be coming out with an online course that teaches dentists how to train their front desk team to retain clients, get them coming in more often, and generate more referrals. You know you'll be launching this course on January 30th. I would start talking about these subjects at least two weeks (if not longer) before the launch of the course. You might run a survey about the challenges dentists are running into in this area about a month before the launch.

You start producing content on this subject. Maybe your first piece of content is about the 3 phrases front desk staff can use to generate more referrals. The next week you do an interview with another dentist who has thoroughly trained their team to be more effective. You continue with this theme by sending out personal stories about when your front desk staff cost you patients and money.

As we get closer to launch (2 weeks out), you publish a step-by-step video of a technique the front desk staff can use to start seeing almost immediate results. You want your subscribers to implement this so they can see some results before you launch your course if possible. You also start teasing about the course you have coming out soon and how it relates to this technique.

Next you do an interview with one of your clients who has implemented this system already in their practice. They share their 'before' and 'after' story. You publish another video that relates your before and after story. You integrate in your Hero's Journey story here. You're prepping them for what's coming up soon.

You start getting a little feedback from the first tip you shared and you share some of those in your next email out to the list. Your final email before the launch is letting them know when this new product will be available and also includes another case study from a different client.

You've already 'sold' many of the people on your list before you've even launched the product. Your two best days of the product launch will be the first day and then final deadline right before the product is either sold out or the price is increased. Those who purchase on the first day were ready to buy before you ever started selling it. You sold them without selling. Those who buy on the final day are simply acting on human nature and getting in before the deadline.

I don't know about you, but I was one of the students who liked to cram on the final day before the test. Customers are like this too. They don't want to miss out on your special discount, additional bonuses, or the offer itself. Many of them take action right before the deadline.

Several of my clients create a full calendar for the year in advance. They know they will be releasing new products or services each quarter. Those 'launches' are written down in their calendar first. The content for at least two weeks leading up the launch will be about the subject along with all the emails during the week of the launch. NEVER change the subject in the middle of a special. Anytime you're offering any kind of special to your list, all of your emails need to be related to that offer. It doesn't mean you need to send hardcore pitches for the offer. It simply means any content, stories, or case studies you share during the special will be related to the special.

After they've filled in the launches, they write down what other specials they will run in-between these launches. You might decide to run a special for 7 days once a month. You'll plan out the content for those seven days and perhaps the week before also to be related to that subject.

After you've planned out your specials, you can then fill in the gaps with other pieces of content and stories you want to share. If you publish a print newsletter or a membership site, you might publish content related to your topic this month for the week leading up to when the content is released out to members. This is a great way to tease subscribers with why they need to become a member this month!

Here's one final tip on scheduling and creating your content. Continually write down ideas when they come to you. You could go old school like I do and write your ideas in a journal or you could record a quick audio note or reminder in your phone. You're out at a restaurant and the waitress says something funny that you know would connect well to your message. Write it down. You'll forget if you leave it for later. You watch a movie or read a book, and you want to share something from there with your audience. Put it in your notes immediately. Over time, you'll have a journal full of story starters and content ideas you can share about.

The last thing you want to do is sit down to write content without a clear goal and direction in mind. You can look to your schedule to see what you need to write about or look in your journal to pull out a story to share. If you review your calendar or your journal at the end of the day, you can let these ideas percolate in the back of your mind. When you come in to the office, they're ready to pour out of you!

Action Steps

- Become a celebrity no one outside your market has ever heard of. Provide Infotainment which is content mixed with entertainment and personality.
- Write down every question your audience is asking about your subject for 15 minutes. Then take a break.
- Write down every question your audience should be asking about your subject for 15 minutes.
- Research additional questions your audience may be asking in forums, groups, and on Amazon.
- Sprinkle your content with case studies and other stories that connect with your readers instead of just giving them 'facts' they quickly forget.
- Block out time to write or create content. Find what fits your schedule and your energy levels. My preference is large blocks of time such as 4 hours at once, and then divide them up into 25 minute focused sessions.
- Write down ideas whenever they come to you. It's tough to work with a blank page. Know where you're going to start before you sit down.

How to Reach Millions of Potential Clients By Tapping Into Other Peoples' Audiences, Connections, and Influence

Social media has changed the world as we know it. This applies double to the marketing space.

An example of this can be seen in Facebook advertising. Running a 'good ad' just isn't good enough anymore. Facebook uses a metric called 'Relevance Score' to help them judge the quality of your advertising. When viewers like, share, post comments, and click your ad, this adds to its Relevance Score. If viewers hide your ad, call it spam, or simply ignore it, these responses hurt your Relevance Score. An ad with a Relevance Score of 9 or 10 means it is well received by your viewers while an ad with a Relevance Score of 1, 2, or 3 is receiving a lot of negative feedback.

You will see your cost of reaching your targeted users on Facebook decrease if you have a higher Relevance Score. If you have a low Relevance Score, you're going to pay more to reach those same users. Facebook uses your Relevance Score as one way to automatically judge whether users are interested in your ad or not.

We've also found that Facebook can be picky about any 'strong' promises of benefits you make in your Facebook ads. You will want to review both your ads and any direct landing pages that visitors are taken to from your ads for the promises you're making. You may want to tone down any strong promises. Instead you'll often see better results in Facebook advertising by focusing on 'feel good' stories about results you or your customers have personally achieved. Instead of making promises of what someone else can receive from your products and services, simply tell them the kind of results others have already received. A case study can often be one of the most powerful forms of promotion.

There is another strategy we've found even more effective for our Facebook ads to cold users (*a cold user is someone who hasn't heard of you or your company before*). Instead of running an ad that sells a product or service, or even invites them to opt-in for a free gift, we often run ads that include content inside of the ad itself. For example, we might run a 2 to 3 minute video tip on how to fix your slice when targeting a golfing audience. At least 80% of the video is designed to actually give them valuable content they can use immediately to improve their game. Then we'll run a call-to-action to click to our website and register for more free video tips like this.

In other words, this is 'How to Sell Without Selling' in action. A couple of years ago we would have simply run an offer asking you to visit our website and sign-up for your free golf tips. After someone joined our list, we would have sent those free tips and included offers for our product or service. Since Facebook wants you to run ads that people share, we're moving the free content BEFORE someone opts-in to our list. There is free content in the video ad itself. Or we run a Facebook ad that takes them over to a blog post on our site that includes free content. Then we insert multiple opportunities to opt-in to our list throughout the blog post for even more free content on the same subject.

It's multiple step process. Someone doesn't know us. Running an ad in their Facebook newsfeed is an interruption in their daily process. They think, "*How rude! This jerk just came into my house where I'm socializing with my friends to sell me something!*"

You get better results by flipping the script. Instead of selling them something or even asking them for a small transaction of giving you their email address, you give them value right up front. My clients with large and profitable Facebook advertising campaigns are constantly getting their ads and their videos shared with others. The type of ads that work best are posts that viewers want to share with their friends. You're giving them a great golf tip, a delicious recipe, or sharing an entertaining video. This is the kind of stuff they're already sharing with others.

A business consultant could take visitors over to a blog post on their site where they show a 5 to 30 minute step-by-step video on how to attract more highly qualified clients to your practice. And they could publish a button right under the video where you can opt-in to their list to get a free Cheat Sheet that outlines the system in detail (*you'll find many people would rather opt-in to the list for a free Cheat Sheet they can scan through quickly rather than watch the long video*).

The key here is to think about what your audience would want to SHARE with others. A real estate agent could either link over to one of their listings in the area or show a video tour of a home for sale. This is the kind of thing that viewers would share with friends they know are looking for a new home. A restaurant could post a video showing some of their delicious meals along with a coupon for a discount entrée or a free desert.

A client of mine who owns a fine dining restaurant sees people sharing his ad with their friends all the time, asking them if they want to meet for lunch at his restaurant. An auto dealer could run a video review of one of their new vehicles or post about a recall notice on one of their vehicles. One of my clients did this and saw hundreds of shares as viewers told their friends who owned that vehicle about the recall.

In today's online environment, your best performing ads will be the ones that are useful and/or entertaining enough that people share them with their friends.

Understanding the True Power of Social Media

Social media allows you to get your message in front of millions of people who may never have heard of you before. It has decentralized the media. Instead of relying on just a few large, broad channels that control information, there are now millions of little channels all over the Internet. This means marketing has become more focused and audiences more specialized than ever before. If you want to reach females over 40 who are interested in paleo diet plans, you can reach that audience. There are blogs and Facebook pages they visit, podcasts they listen to, Youtube channels they watch, and Instagram accounts where they share photos.

Convince&Convert published a study that customers who follow a brand on social media are 53% more loyal to that brand. In addition, social media has 100% higher lead-to-close ratio than outbound marketing (*State of Inbound Marketing, 2012*). And social media allows you to contact your audience more often using more modalities (*video, audio, images, and text*).

But if you're like most business owners, you probably haven't been getting a whole lot out of social media. The common methods you'll hear from most social media experts are totally wrong, and essentially just a waste of time and money. You may have already experienced this. I've talked to business owners who have been on social media sites such as Facebook for years. They've paid social media gurus to post content daily to their pages. While they have some likes and shares, they're not depositing much, if any, money in the bank from all their efforts.

I frankly don't care how many followers you have or the number of views, likes, and shares you generate from each post. What I care about are the number of new buyers you've attracted through social media and the number of current buyers you've upgraded to additional purchases through your accounts.

Most business owners are simply broadcasting their message into an empty wasteland. From 2012 to 2014, organic reach on Facebook dropped from 16% to 6.5%. And it has continued to decline. Pages with more than 1,000,000 likes have an organic reach as low as 2.27%. Even if you're able to attract an audience on Facebook, your organic posts are only reaching a very small portion of them. And most business owners don't have that many likes to start!

The true power of social media, at least in the beginning, isn't in reaching the end consumer. It's in making connections with other influencers. If you've ever studied real estate investing, then you've likely heard of using other people's money to buy houses. Real estate can be a great way to build wealth because of the leverage available to you.

Social media operates off the same principle. Building your own audience from scratch is SLOW, takes too much effort, and is too expensive. The best way to profit from social media quickly is by tapping into other people's audiences. It doesn't matter whether we're talking about Facebook, Youtube, Pinterest, Twitter, or any other social media site. There are influencers out there who already have your Ideal Clients' attention. They might have invested thousands of hours and years of their time to create those audiences. And they have also tapped into other people's lists to grow their following. It makes ZERO sense to try to build your own audience from scratch when you can tap into audiences which have already been pre-built for you.

Yes, you want to grab the attention of your target audience, but it's even more important to make connections with these influencers, especially in the beginning. Without these connections, you're shouting your message in an empty desert. One share by an influencer can attract many visitors (*and qualified leads*) into your business than all your posts up till now.

Here are the big secrets of social medial. Connect with influencers. Be generous. Profit. Be generous both to your audience and to the influencers in your market. One of the most common social media models is called 411. This means you share 4 posts from other people (*usually influencers but could be anyone who posts good content*), 1 of your own content, and 1 promotion. So you're posting 5 content pieces for every promotional piece. And 4 of those content pieces are from others.

Maybe you're worried that sharing all this content from others will make you lose your audience? That is possible. If you're sharing content from someone who is directly competitive with your products and services, then yes, you could potentially lose out on business. But in most cases, you're not going to be sharing content from your direct competitors. Instead you'll be sharing content from people in other specialties...or people who serve your audience in a different way.

Let's say you run an Adwords management service. You may share content related to Adwords from popular bloggers and internet marketing consultants. Perhaps they offer products and consulting services, but these aren't directly competitive with your management service. Content about conversion and email marketing would also fit your audience and theme, but the influencers in those fields aren't likely to be running an Adwords service. All of these content creators could already have your Ideal Client inside their audience profile, but they're not selling a directly competitive service.

Let's change direction and say you're a local realtor. Your own content would be about the local market, finding your dream home, and how to sell your home for maximum dollar in minimum time. But you could share good content from numerous other sources such as financial planners, CPAs, interior designers, contractors, builders, etc. All of these subjects are related to what you do but are non-competitive with your services.

You're accomplishing two goals by sharing content from others. First of all, you're demonstrating to your audience that you're a source of good material. By following you, they get access to great advice related to their interests. You don't just share any old content. You only share content you know will be valuable to your audience. But the second goal is almost as important. You're tapping into reciprocity. By sharing other people's content first, you're opening the doors for them to share your content. You're a giver. You comment on their content. You share it. As we move a little deeper, you'll also be connecting with them by email. Over time, a portion of them will take notice and promote you in turn.

Create Your Home Base

Your Wordpress blog is your home base for social media. While Facebook allows you to set-up a page on their site, you don't truly own that page. Facebook could cancel and/or ban you for any reason. They probably never will, but why put yourself at their mercy. Over time they've reduced the organic reach of Facebook posts multiple times...making it harder and harder to reach your audience for free. Even though business owners worked their butt off to build up successful pages, Facebook has reduced their reach to those audience members whenever they wanted.

Never build your business to rely 100% on someone else's platform. This is true in both advertising and social media. I've seen entrepreneurs who built their entire business model on Google Adwords traffic. They didn't have any other sources of advertising, and they didn't concentrate on turning those Adwords visitors into email subscribers. Their entire business was based on Adwords. One day an Adwords reviewer took issue with something they didn't like on the website, and the entire business came crashing down. Google can turn off your traffic in an instant if they don't feel you're providing a good user experience. Facebook can and has done the same.

I've now been full-time online for over 21 years, and the secret to surviving that long is building your own platform. Your number one platform should be your email list. You should also have your own Wordpress blog. Go back to the previous chapter on "Why Everyone Should Have a Blog" for more on this subject. Your blog becomes your home base for your social media content.

If you're writing content, you're publishing the majority of it on your blog first. You might decide that you want to focus more on video instead (*this would be an excellent decision as the Internet is moving more and more toward video every day*). You set-up your Youtube channel and upload all your content there. At the same time, you should be embedding each video from Youtube on your blog also. If you promote this content on other social media sites, send them to your blog where you control the environment around your video. Instead of being distracted by a dozen other videos like they would on your Youtube page, visitors simply see the ads you've placed and your offer to opt-in to your list.

The same rule applies if you're publishing your own podcast. You'll publish your podcast over in iTunes, but you'll want to publish a copy of the content on your own blog also. This can be done with a free audio plug-in such as Powerpress at **wordpress.org/plugins/powerpress/**. Some people will want to subscribe to your podcast in iTunes, but others will want to listen right on your blog. Create a blog post for each podcast episode that includes the playable audio, a few bullet benefits about the episode, and a link to subscribe to your podcast in iTunes. And of course you'll provide a way for visitors to opt-in to your list on every page of your blog.

When following the 411 model, 4 of your posts are sharing other people's content. One of your posts will be sharing content from your blog (written, video, or audio). And one of your posts will link over to an offer you have available.

Make a List of 100 Top Influencers in Your Market

If you're going to connect with influencers, first you're going to have to find them! I'm going to focus this section specifically on those who want to write, but the same rules will apply for video creation and appearing on podcasts. Since we're focusing on writing, we're going to be looking for popular blogs in our market, especially those that accept 'guest posts'. A guest post is when you write epic content for someone else's blog simply because they'll share your byline and a link to your site. This can create a huge surge of traffic to your site immediately and it can also help you rank higher on the search engines as high quality websites link over to you.

If we were focusing on podcasting as our primary content method, we'd give a preference to influencers who had their own popular podcasts. Most podcasts accept guests, and you can drive a lot of traffic (and buyers) to your website by being a featured guest on podcast shows in your market.

Your goal is to find 20 or more high traffic blogs in your market (*or closely related to your market*). In 'deep' markets such as internet marketing or social media, you might be able to find 100 or more influencers, but that just isn't possible in most markets. That's why I'm giving you a goal of at least 20 high traffic blogs run by influencers you can connect with over time. This is a minimum. You can connect with more and likely will over time, but get started with at least 20.

As already noted above, they don't have to cover the same subject you will primarily focus on, but they should attract a similar buying audience. An Adwords management service is going to write all about Adwords, choosing keywords, writing ads, producing landing pages, little tricks inside Adwords, tracking your advertising, and even expanding out into long-term conversion of Adwords visitors into sales. They could find their Ideal Clients reading blogs about Adwords, conversion, copywriting, online media, ecommerce, email marketing, Facebook advertising, etc. They could potentially even connect with a CPA who runs a blog for entrepreneurs. The Adwords service is looking for entrepreneurs who already have a website and have the budget to attract more high quality leads to their website.

You might already know a few blogs that fit what you're looking for. They're the ones you're already reading about your subject. Go to their sites and search through their posts. Do a search of their blog using the term "guest post" to see if they have featured any guest posts on their site. If they don't have a search feature built into their blog, you can use Google for this also. Just use a search string like this, "Site:mymarketingcoach.com guest post". You can put any web domain where I have mymarketingcoach.com. You're asking Google just to search that specific site for the phrase "guest post."

What if you find a high traffic blog that never publishes guest posts? That's OK. Usually they'll have social media accounts also that you can click over to from their blog. Do they ever share other people's content on their social media sites? If they do, you're good to go. There are a lot of ways to partner with other influencers. Guest posting is just one of the possible methods. If you don't see guest posts and don't see them sharing anything from others, feel free to follow them...but it may not be worth your time to share their content or try to make a connection with them. There's nothing in it for you!

As you visit the blogs you already know about, look for links to other popular blogs in your market. Sometimes they'll have a 'blogroll' in the sidebar or they'll have a 'link post' where they're linking over to other people's content. By following their links, you can often find other influencers to add to your list. It's amazing how deep the rabbit hole can go. As you visit these other blogs, you can follow the same system and look for guest posts or see if they're linking out to other blogs.

Let's say you come to a dead-end and we need to do a search for more blogs. Go to Google and do a search for "keyword guest post." So if you're in golf, you would look for a "golf guest post." You're looking for high traffic blogs which feature guest posts. A few other searches you could look for include "keyword write for us" or "keyword contributing writer."

Another strategy is to let someone else do all the hard work for you. Once you've found a couple of blogs which accept guest posts, look at the names of the guest post writers. Search Google for their name like this: "Terry Dean marketing." Of course you're going to see their own blog, websites, and social media accounts. But you're also going to see websites which are featuring them in some way. Maybe they wrote a guest post, were interviewed on a podcast, or were part of an affiliate promotion.

How do you know a blog is high traffic enough that you'd want to write for them or spend time sharing their content? First look at the average number of comments across their posts, especially the ones by guest authors. If you see 30 or more comments on each post, then you're on a pretty high traffic blog. But 5 to 10 comments on each post could also point to a high traffic blog for your niche. It all depends on the market you're in and how active the participants are in that market.

You can also look at the number of social shares on each post. If one website averages 100+ social shares on each of their posts and another gets only 2 or 3, you know the first website likely has a much larger audience behind it. And of course you can also visit their social media pages to see what kind of follower counts display for them there.

Make a quick spreadsheet of the high traffic blogs, the name of the publisher, their social media accounts, and if they have any rules for submitting guest posts to their blog. You can also subscribe to the content they're publishing through an RSS reader such as **www.feedly.com**. An RSS reader makes it easy to manage content from dozens of blogs in one easy to use app. At the same time, follow and like these influencers on the social media sites you're participating in.

How to Attract Thousands of Hungry Buyers From Other People's Blogs

One guest post on a popular blog can generate thousands of visitors and hundreds of new leads for your email list. And that's just the immediate results, not even counting the increased search engine rankings you may experience and connections you can make with other influencers down the road.

Search each of the websites in your spreadsheet and see if they give any guidelines for submitting a guest post. Again you're going to use their site in a Google search phrase like this, "site:mymarketingcoach.com guest post guidelines." If they've published guidelines for submitting guest posts, then by all means FOLLOW those rules. If they tell you exactly how to submit to them and you do your own thing, your emails are probably going to end up in the trash.

Remember, you need the high traffic blog more than they need you. The majority of the blogs on your list are not going to have guidelines listed, and in these cases you're better off making some other form of contact first. Comment on their blog. Share some of their content through social media (*making sure to tag them in your post*). Send them an email where you thank them for a content piece they wrote that has influenced you.

An awesome way to make an initial connection with an influencer is through 'praise.' Tell them how much one of their articles influenced you or even send them an honest testimonial for one of their products and services. One of my friends has actually made some of his biggest joint venture deals with consultants he has previously hired to coach him on some of his projects. He teamed up with someone who influenced him in his life and business first!

Don't ask for anything in this first contact. And don't send a request for help immediately after either. Wait a week or two as you want to disconnect your first contact with your 2nd message. All you want is to create that initial connection where they'll open up your email when you contact them in the future. Opening up your emails is a pleasurable experience.

Another trick for getting their attention on first contact is to subscribe to their email list, and reply to their email broadcast. Most publishers have replies to their email list come to them personally and they're expecting feedback from their subscribers. Replying to their newsletter (*and keeping their subject line in place*) is a great way to grab their attention.

After you've made first contact (*and potentially 2nd and 3rd contact as you share their content on social media*), it's time to ask them about guest posting. Remember, if they publish guidelines on guest posting, follow those rules instead of what I'm outlining here. Always do what they find most convenient.

Keep this message short and simple:

Hi Sam,

I've been reading your blog for the past few months and I'm getting a lot out of it. Your posts on X and Y were especially helpful to me.

I know it's tough to produce epic content like you do consistently, and I was wondering if you might like a little help with it.

I've already thought about a couple of ideas that might fit your readers:

Idea #1

Idea #2

These are topics I've written a lot about, although they are coming from a different angle which should grab attention and benefit your audience. To see the quality of the content I produce, you can check out a few of the posts on my blog:

Great Content Piece Link #1

Great Content Piece Link #2

Great Content Piece Link #3

I'd be honored if you'd allow me to contribute to your site.

If not, no problem. I understand. Feel free to call on me anytime.

Thank you,
Terry Dean

You'll see a couple of important elements in this email example *(feel free to create your own)*. I mentioned at least a couple of potential ideas for hot topics. You could expand out to 3 or 4 potential ideas. Make sure these are attention grabbing titles that would grab their reader's attention. Some of my favorite would include *"How to..."* posts, case studies where you achieved a specific end result *"Case Study: How I Lost 33 Pounds in 60 Days With the Paleo Meal Plan"*, or list posts with *"35 Unique Methods to Attract Hungry Buying Visitors to Your Website."*

You'd come up with these ideas by looking through their blog content and finding some of their most popular posts. What subjects are their audience already interested in that you can write competently about? Again you're looking for a large number of comments or shares on these posts. Some sites will even have their most popular content listed over in their sidebar to make this super-easy. Make sure whatever titles you suggest are something you can deliver awesome content about.

Guest posts should be some of the best content you produce. You should really feel like you're giving away the farm on someone else's site. That's how you get published, and get others saying "Yes" when you ask to guest post on their site. In other words, bring your A+ game to any guest posts.

The 2nd element you'll notice in my email example is I link to other content you've already created. If you're showing content on your own blog, they should be some of your pillar posts, the kinds of posts that your audience has shared with others. Those are your try-outs for getting guest posts on other sites. If the content you link to doesn't impress the blog publisher, you're not getting your content published on their site. If you've already written some epic guest posts on other people's blogs, you could link to those guest posts instead.

Once they agree to your guest post, it's time to bunker down and produce the content. Invest the time to do it right. Give them a step-by-step system. Give away some of your best value. Make your guest posts home runs for their blog publisher. This could be your only chance to shine in front of their hungry audience.

At the end of your post, offer them a 'content upgrade' at your website. Link back to your blog, but don't just link to the home page. Instead link over to an opt-in landing page where you give away another piece of content that expands on what you just wrote about. If your guest post was about your amazing weight loss, then your free gift could be a PDF where you share a cheat sheet that included your shopping list and your step-by-step exercise plan to go along with the diet information you shared in your original post. If you shared 35 ways to attract hungry visitors, maybe your free opt-in gift could be a deep-dive on your favorite one of these techniques, showing step-by-step how you used it to drive an additional 100,000 visitors to your website.

In other words, give them a reason to come to your website and subscribe that connects directly with the content you produced for the guest post. The best case scenario is you produce a free gift that can be combined with multiple guest posts you write for different blogs. You can see that we're putting a lot of effort into each guest post. That's why it's so important that you go after high traffic blogs in your market. Putting in all this time for a low traffic site just isn't worth it!

How to Persuade Strangers To Promote You

If you send out emails asking popular bloggers to link to your stuff, you're not going to get a whole lot of takers. Most likely you'll simply hear the sound of crickets. No response whatsoever. Persuading influencers to promote you is similar to persuading strangers to do anything else. These influencers are tuned into WIIFM just like your customers and clients. They're asking, "What's in it for me?"

That's why you want to come to them from a direction that benefits them. For example, another strategy that could get your guest post published in a popular high traffic blog is writing a case study for something they teach. Have you been following them for a while? Have they published any posts, articles, or even products that you've put into practice in your own life? If you've followed one of their systems and achieved results from it, that creates the perfect opportunity to get published with them.

Contact them and thank them for the post, product, etc. Write a quick testimonial of your results. Offer to create a full 'case study' about how you followed their system in detail and the end results you achieved from it. This type of post is going to be really tough for them to resist, even if they don't normally publish guest posts. You're building their credibility in front of their audience. Giving you a little link in exchange for that credibility boost is an easy decision.

This applies to anything else you're doing. I've seen new online entrepreneurs create a product and immediately start contacting influencers to promote their product for them. There is absolutely ZERO motivation for a high traffic website to promote you starting out. You don't have a track record of proven sales. Sure, maybe you're offering them a percentage of the sales, but so is everyone else who has a product. And many of those competitors asking the influencer to promote have already built up a relationship with them first.

That's why you can get started by promoting others on social media first. Become an affiliate with the influencer and promote their product to your list. Send them a testimonial about how their products or services have benefited you. Do something for them first to put yourself on the map.

Let's say you're publishing a podcast or even videos on Youtube. How can you get an influencer to mention your podcast to their audience? Obviously going to them and asking them to promote your podcast directly just isn't going to work. There is no incentive in it for them. But what if you did a short interview featuring their work on your podcast? You're going to promote them with absolutely no strings attached. And this gives you the benefit of spending 20 to 30 minutes on the phone talking with them about their favorite subjects...themselves and the work they're doing right now.

The easiest way to become interesting to another person is to ask that person questions about themselves. Focus all your attention on them during the interview and ask them about what projects they're currently working on or have coming up. You have to put 'your projects' on the backburner initially to make the connections you need for long-term success online. As Zig Ziglar often said, *"You will get all you want in life, if you help enough other people get what they want."*

Here's a sample email you could model or use for contacting people for interviews. The best way to send this message is as a reply to their newsletter (you joined their email list – didn't you).

> Subject: May I interview you about ____ NAME?
> Subject: NAME!
> Subject: RE: All My cheat sheets in one place
>
> Dear (Expert First Name),
>
> I was recently impressed by your post about X (STATE SPECIFIC POST/PRODUCT TITLE AND WHY IT IMPRESSED YOU).
>
> I was wondering if you'd be up for doing a quick 20 to 30 minute interview where we talk about Y (THEIR EXPERTISE OR MESSAGE). I've recently done interviews with A and B who you may already know and they were very popular with my audience.
>
> You will receive a list of specific questions beforehand, and you can select the ones you feel most confident to answer, and/or revise and modify with questions you felt better suited to address.
>
> You don't need to reveal any "trade secrets," but if you could provide some advice to others about pitfalls, steps to take that will help them succeed, and any ways they can avoid mistakes you perhaps made… well, that would be wonderful.
>
> AND… of course you'll get to promote YOUR any website or product you choose. Right now I have X readers and I think they'd love what you have to share.
>
> In addition, I will provide you with a copy of your recorded interview which you may use any in way you desire. And I promise to make you look GREAT!
>
> Just hit reply to this email and let me know if you're up for the interview and we'll schedule a time that works best for you.
>
> SIGNATURE WITH FULL CONTACT INFO + WEBSITE!

This message is intended to be casual about the subject. You're starting off by complimenting them and pinpointing a subject they're an expert on. That's what you enter in the X above. You'll mention the subject of the interview in Y and it should be relate back to X. Enter names of other experts you've interviewed in A and B. The more well-known they are, the better. Or people who are somehow connected with the expert you're connecting with are also good. Make sure to give your website address (*where they could access other interviews*) along with all your contact info at the end of the email.

Will everyone respond to this email? Of course not, but you'll get a much higher number responding to an email like this where you're talking about them and their interests than you will for one where you're asking them to promote you. Build the relationship first. Help others get what they want. Then you'll get what you want.

This is Only the Beginning

I can't go into all the details and all the possibilities available in one short chapter of this book. My goal was simply to share the right mindset with you for contacting and getting influencers to promote you. In addition, I gave you a couple of template emails you can use to 'sell' people on promoting you. Persuasion is involved in EVERYTHING you do both on and off the Internet. And it always comes back to what motivates the person you're connecting with.

If you're trying to get people to do what you want, that's manipulation. Persuasion is finding out what people want, and helping them get it. Do that, and you'll create both a meaningful life but also a very successful business.

I also couldn't go into all the possibilities available with social media here because they change so fast. As I'm writing this, Facebook is still king. But there are quite a few up-and-coming challengers. Who will be on top one year, two years, or even five years from now? I have no idea. But the mindset and strategies I shared here will still be working for you decades into the future.

That's one of the reasons I've been so successful online for over 21 years now. In the very beginning, I focused on how to sell. Search engines have come and gone, but human nature and persuasion have stayed the same. We're using a lot more video in our marketing today, but the words we use on our videos aren't all that different than the plain text I used on my websites 21 years ago.

As new social media sites come into existence, your success won't be determined by understanding every technical detail of each new site. Instead it will be about understanding human psychology, connecting with influencers, and getting them to share what you have with their audiences. Instead of you spending all your time learning the inner nuances of each site, tap into other people's knowledge and influence.

That direction will leave you with a whole lot more time to grow your business...and enjoy your life!

Action Steps

- Give value upfront in your advertising instead of invading someone's living room and trying to sell them immediately.
- Here's the real secret to social media. Connect with influencers. Be generous. Profit.
- Create a list of 100 social media influencers your audience listens to who you would like to connect with.
- One of the best ways to connect with an influencer on your first contact is by authentically praising them for something that has helped you.
- Contact bloggers who feature guest posts and use the template email included to suggest several ideas for 'epic' content you could create for their blog.

30 Minute Content Marketing Blueprint

I've covered a lot of material in the last few chapters, and by now you may be feeling a little overwhelmed. That's OK. It's normal. Marketing online is a little like learning a whole new language. Even some of the words may be foreign to you. But you can do this. I've worked with clients as young as 13 and as old as 82 (*and there may have been older ones also who just didn't let me in on their secret*). One of the keys to success online is NOT trying to do everything at once.

If you try to participate in every traffic source, join every social media site, and try to put all the conversion techniques I share in place all at once, you'll go crazy. You'll be overwhelmed and nothing will get accomplished. It's not how much you know that's important. It's how much you implement.

Especially after the previous chapter, you may be asking yourself, *"How am I going to get all this done?"* If that's what you're thinking, this chapter is for you. I'm going to share with you a little 30 minute content trick several clients have used to maximize the value of every minute they invest in their business.

In the last chapter, I told you to focus your content on what you do best. If you're a writer, write. If you like to talk, do audio recordings. If you like getting on camera, shoot videos. All of these methods work, and each one can be used to attract a hungry buying audience.

But let's say you don't have much time to invest. You'd prefer to hand the entire process over to someone else and just wash your hands of it completely. Yes, you can hire ghostwriters who will write content and put your name on it. Some of my clients have used this method previously, but I've never been happy with it. It can work, but it's limited in results. And I'm going to recommend a different approach here in a minute.

What's wrong with hiring ghostwriters? If you hire high-end ghostwriters, such as those who cost $20,000 to $40,000 to produce a book for you, you can often get top of the line writing skills. They'll look at other things you've written. They'll listen to your recordings. They'll speak to you in-person until they understand your tone of voice. And they'll share that in their writing. People may never know you even used a ghostwriter if you use a great writer.

But rarely do most people hire those ghostwriters to produce content for their blogs or other online media. Instead, they're hiring much lower cost writers where they're paying $10 to $50 for a post depending on the experience of the writer and just how specialized your subject is. You're going to pay quite a bit more for someone to write about chiropractic than an article about the new Dodge Ram.

The big issue with ghostwriting isn't just the skill level. Often good ghostwriters are technically proficient. The content they create is good, possibly well researched, and is accurate. But the content lacks personality. It could have been written by a machine. You'll find any great writer has their little idiosyncrasies. They have common phrases they continually use. They have figures of speech that belong to them.

One of the best ways to explain this is when I was first studying copywriting intensively, I soon started recognizing sales copy which was written by Gary Halbert. I could even identify letters he wrote for his clients even when I didn't have any other clues the letters came from him. It didn't matter whose name was on the letter, I knew it was Gary by his writing style.

I've had close friends read something I've written and tell me they can hear me speaking to them. My writing is how I talk. You have a voice. And your audience begins to recognize that voice. A portion of your audience becomes hooked by that voice. When someone else writes in your name, they feel a disconnect. They may not be able to put their finger on it, but they can feel it.

In addition, most ghostwriting will miss out on your stories. People may forget your 5 major points and even your core lesson, but they remember the stories you tell. Professional speakers know just how vital their personal stories are. The audience will even come up to a speaker and ask them if they're going to tell the story about X. Even though they've heard that same story half a dozen times, they want to hear it again. It's the stories that set the message apart from cold, dry content which I refer to as constipated content. Constipated content doesn't sell. Your audience connects with your stories. They identify with your personality. And they keep listening to you because they like you as a person.

A really good writer can imitate your voice. They can tell your stories if they have access to them. Only those who pay extremely close attention may even notice the difference. But most entrepreneurs don't hire ghostwriters of this caliber to produce their online content. And there is an easier way.

How to Create All Your Content With Easy 30 Minute Interviews

This is a secret several of my clients have used to create done-for-you content creation packages in their markets. It goes a step beyond hiring ghostwriters, and it can often be put into action much faster than doing a load of research for the market. Let's say you had hired one of these clients to produce all the monthly online content for your business. They wouldn't immediately start researching the topic. They wouldn't read books about it. They wouldn't study other people's blog posts. You're the expert. It would be a waste of their time to try to be an expert on the topic when you already have all the knowledge that needs to be shared with your audience inside your head.

They prepare a list of questions based off the questions commonly being asked on forums. They add additional questions they have about your topic. Then they interview you over the phone or over Skype for around 30 minutes. They ask you to share some examples. They pull a couple of stories out of you. They lean on your knowledge of the topic.

They translate this interview into all the content you need for the month. If they wanted to produce twice as much content, they'd do a second interview with you on a slightly different topic. The interviews themselves can be edited and offered as a podcast. They can break up the interview into multiple subjects and turn them into blog posts and emails. They share your stories. Everything they write comes directly from your interview. It's your voice translated into written emails and blog posts.

The audio can also be cut up into separate topics and Powerpoint added to it to create videos for Youtube. Short 'sound bites' in the article can be pulled out and scheduled as Facebook posts and tweets. One 30 minute interview can easily become a podcast, 3 to 5 blog posts and emails, 3 to 5 videos, and 10 to 20 social media updates.

My clients have only offered these types of services in specific niched business-to-business markets. So I've just handed a new business idea to some of the readers of this book. You could put together a service like this where you interview the business owner, have your team members edit the content and turn it into articles, and post social media updates for your clients. You could easily charge $300 to $600 a month or even more for this type of service depending on the market you're in *(in some markets this could be a $1,000 to $2,000 a month service if you do several interviews for even more content)*. And of course you could add on a set-up fee of $1,000 to $3,000 to help them get their Wordpress blog up, social media accounts in place, podcast published, and more.

This type of service is perfect for busy professionals who want hands free content creation and production. And the beauty of the system is the content you'll provide will be so much better than they could get from anywhere else. It will have personality, include their stories, and appeal to a buying audience.

You might be the busy professional yourself. In that case, you could have someone interview you to create your basic content. Hire writers to translate your audio into several additional content pieces you can use. There is no reason you have to slave away behind a computer if you hate writing. Speak out your content and let other people do the heavy lifting. Upwork.com is a great place to find people who can do the writing for you based off of your content! You're going to hire them to create articles based off your audio instead of researching and ghostwriting from scratch.

How to Create Powerful, Inspirational Interviews

You're going to come into an interview with a list of question in most situations. For example, if you want to become a regular guest on podcasts or radio interviews, you're expected to have what's called a One Sheet. This one page document will include your quick bio for reading on the air, a few of the topics you cover, and a list of questions for the interviewer to ask you. The reason most experts seem like they have it all together and they answer the questions posed to them with ease is because they wrote the questions themselves! They know exactly what the questions will be and in which order. It's all scripted upfront.

You can create a list of questions like this by researching your market and finding out exactly what questions they're asking. In addition, you can use template questions like I'm going to give you in the next section to help round out your list of questions. There is no reason to be nervous going into an interview because you can have everything planned in advance to make you look good.

When designing your questions, remember you want to share stories and examples. Good questions help bring out these stories. For example, one of the template questions I'm going to give you is, "*How did you get started in X?*" That's a softball pitch for you to share your origin story. Another template question is, "*What has been most difficult for you personally in X?*" That's designed to help you tap into a personal story about the subject. Information is not enough. Interviews, just like any other form of content, should be infotainment.

You can get started with template questions, but they can only take you so far. The best interviews go a little deeper. They get to the heart of the matter. I recommend having a list of questions when you go into an interview, but be willing to go off the schedule. The interview can be edited. So if you get too far off track, you can simply delete that section. There's safety in knowing nothing you say has to go live. Some of my best audios have been when I've been willing to really dig into an answer of WHY something works the way it does. One question leads to the next and you end up sharing something of value you've never talked about before.

Two of the most important traits of a good interviewer are curiosity and empathy (*those are great traits for everyone in general also*). You're curious about the subject. You're interviewing an expert to help get your questions answered. You're listening intently to what they're saying. You're not just waiting for your next chance to speak. And you're not sitting there with your next question loaded up. Instead, you're listening with interest and willing to probe a little deeper to fulfill on that curiosity you personally feel.

Empathy means seeing the situation from their point of view. You're listening with both your heart and your mind. What are they really saying? You might ask them a question to help clarify such as, "*So what you're saying is X?*" You repeat back what you heard in a slightly different way to dig a little deeper. Or ask them, "*How did you feel when X happened?*" X would refer to a situation they just shared. You have to be present in the interview to spot opportunities like this.

When interviewing someone, I like to think of myself as an advocate for my listeners. What would they ask if they were here with the expert right now? Remember, if you're doing the interview, you are not the expert right now. Let them be the expert. You're just a curious student asking questions for the listeners. All in all, a good interviewer is a great listener. You can start with a list of questions, but be willing to flow with the conversation and pull gold out of them that they might not have even known was there!

Template Questions For Interviews

In just a moment, I'll give you a list of "template" questions for your swipe file of ideas to create your questions. These are your starting point, but you cannot rely on just the questions you've prepared.

REMEMBER that an interview is primarily a listening process. You ask a question. They respond. You LISTEN to them honestly asking follow-up questions on what they're talking about. In other words, we're not leading them. We're simply digging into their knowledge to find out more.

Example question:

What's the difference between a good _____ and a great _____?

What's the difference between a good interviewer and a great interviewer?

You could use this as a template in many cases. Let's say we were interviewing someone on model airplanes. The question would then be, "What's the difference between a good model airplane builder and a great model airplane builder?" It gets them to thinking about what separates the good from the great in their field...and often reveals some excellent information. All the questions below can be used in the same way. Let's go with another example. Let's say you want to make sure to clarify or make sure you understand something they said.

So what you're saying is _____ (repeat back to them what they said in another way to see if you understand it).

They may reply that you didn't quite get it and explain what they said in another way. If so, that's great news. They just shared the message in another way. Or they might agree with you that you're correct. This is great news because you just explained the message in another way. Either way, your audience gets a different perspective on the topic.

- How did you get started in _____?
- Why is _____ important to you?
- What excites you the most about _____?
- In your experience, what's the best way to _____?
- What do you do better than anyone else in your opinion?
- What do you wish you knew about _____ when you first started out?
- What has been most difficult for you personally in _____?

- Do you have any examples you can share about _____?
- Why is _____ so important?
- How do you know that? (*make sure this is not a confrontational question – it's a digging question*)
- If people could take away 3 lessons from today, what would they be?
- What's the biggest mistake you made in _____?
- When you said _____, what exactly did you mean?
- How would you explain that to someone who doesn't understand _____? (*for example if someone uses a very technical answer – always be on the lookout for the expert to say things that some of the audience may not understand*)
- How can our listeners get started in _____ this week?
- What tools do you feel are essential for _____?
- For someone listening, what is the very first step to take?
- Why do you feel this way about _____?
- If you only had 30 days to _____, how would you do it?
- In your experience, why is that?
- What are some good short-term and long-term goals for a beginner?
- What do you see as a coming trend in _____?
- What are some major pitfalls to watch out for when doing _____?
- Can you possibly offer our listeners a special offer?
- Is there anything else you'd like to add?
- Can you think of anything else?

Easy Methods to Multiply Your Content Reach

The easiest method of most people is to record an audio interview and use that as the basis for all your other content. It's easy to come up with the content as you can start out by answering the common questions in your market. Tell your personal story of how you got started in this market and some of the case studies you've personally seen. A good interviewer will allow the conversation to naturally evolve as they put themselves in the role of an advocate for the listener. They're curious about the subject and asking some of the same questions others will be asking.

From here, you can expand the content. You could hire a transcriptionist to turn it into written material. On Fiverr.com or Upwork.com, you can often get 'decent' quality transcriptions for as little as $10 to $30 for a 30 minute audio with 2 speakers. The work will require proofreading! Often I've done the proofreading myself so I can fix difficult to spell names and make sure the content is accurate. Or you could expect to pay another $10 to $30 for proofreading of the material.

You're going to be pretty surprised the first time you read through one of your transcripts. Spoken language is quite a bit different than writing. From here, you need to hire a writer to rewrite the material into several interesting articles. It's not as easy as just breaking up the transcript. In most cases it's going to need to be rewritten to publish it as a blog post. The price for a quality writer is going to vary by subject, but since you've already produced all the content, the prices could be as low as $10 up to around $50 each. Compare that to paying for a quality article to be researched and written and you'd be paying close to 10 times as much. And it wouldn't include your own personal stories. It would miss out on your personality!

Look through the content for several short 'sound bytes.' These are short memorable quotes. They're perfect for tweets or sharing on Facebook. You could add the quote to an image background (*beautiful scenery like mountains or the ocean are often chosen*) to create memes on Facebook or Instagram. This is again perfect for Fiverr. Do a search for "memes" and you'll find people who are willing to do 2 to 10 photo based memes based off your quotes for just $5! Images get a lot more shares than just written content on Facebook.

If you share content that could be easily turned into an infographic, you can also hire this out on Fiverr for $5 each. An infographic is an image that communicates quite a bit of content in image form. Instead of someone having to read an entire article, they can scan the image and get a basic understanding of the message. This is something I would never personally create for myself as I'm graphically challenged, but it's cheap to hire it out. Collect the information and tell them exactly what to include and what to communicate. And let a graphic designer do the rest. With Fiverr, it won't even cost that much.

With the above system, you're only needed for the original interview. Everything else in the process could be handled by others. Transcripts are produced and edited. Blog posts are written. Social media sound bytes are pulled out. Images are created. There's no reason why ANYONE couldn't become a content producer with these methods...even if you're not a writer.

This system can be personalized for you. For example, I enjoy writing. I create a quick outline of what I want to share. I'll write the initial content. When I want to produce a video, I'll create it immediately after writing it. If it's just a content piece I'll post to Youtube, embed on my blog, and email to my list, I'll sometimes record it free flow after writing it out. I don't follow an exact script which can make it a little more personal. If I'm going to use the video in my paid traffic funnels, then I use the article as a written script which I read from a teleprompter. This guarantees I keep my message on target for the audience I'm advertising to.

I can expand out on the content by doing an audio about the subject or recruiting an entrepreneurial friend to chat with me about it. We'll use the written content as an outline and starting point for our discussion but we'll often dig deeper into it on the recording.

I approach the system from a different order because I enjoy writing. Make this system work for you. Flow in what you do best. Outsource the rest.

Blogging to Your First Book

I'm sitting here writing the majority of this book, but several chapters and sections throughout the book have been pulled from my paid newsletters or other courses. Again, I'm a writer. It's what I do. But the majority of my clients who have published books did very little of the writing themselves...at least when it came time to put together the book.

First of all, why would you want to have a book? It's the ultimate form of content marketing. You're the expert because you wrote a book on the topic. Anyone could tweet about it or shoot a short video. Anyone could write a few blog posts, but it takes dedication and hopefully expertise to write a book. Try telling someone you're a writer sometime. They won't even give you a second glance. Even more entertaining will be if you tell them you're a blogger. So what?

Now tell them you've an author. You'll be given a little more respect. A lot of people claim to be a writer. In many cases, that just means you're a hobbyist or perhaps you're just unemployed. A lot of people think they have a book inside them, but that's exactly where it stays. An author is someone who actually finished their book. They've 'fulfilled' the dream.

Most entrepreneurs exchange business cards, but what if you instead hand people a copy of your book? If all other things were equal, would you choose the real estate agent who hands you his card or the agent who hands you a copy of her book about *"How to Sell Your Home for Top Dollar in 90 Days or Less?"* Of course there are other factors such as your relationship with this person, how you met them, and whether you click with their personality, but there is no denying the immediate advantage being a published author has.

Plus, it's much easier to get free publicity both on and off the Internet with a book. Interviewers want to feature authors (*again it's that aura of expertise given by the book*). That book can be your doorway to radio and podcast interviews. It can attract new subscribers and customers to you. And it can also be a pathway to higher consulting and coaching fees in your business. You're unique because you're the expert on this specific topic.

Writing a book is hard work! There is no denying that. Unless you enjoy the writing process, there has to be an easier way. And there is. I remember mentioning to one of my clients that he could produce a book. He agreed it was a good idea, but I could hear the hesitation on his side of the conversation. He just didn't have the time, and I knew this when I made the book suggestion. But he already had all the content he needed for a book. It was already written. He just needed to organize it in the correct order and hire an editor to make sure it flowed well.

All he had to do was compile the blog posts and articles he had already written. The amount of content available was more than he needed for one book. He could have put together several books. He didn't need to spend the next 3 to 6 months writing new content for a book. He had spent the past couple of years producing content that was perfect for a book. He just needed to go through it and choose which posts to feature in the book. If necessary, he could update a few of them to better fit the theme.

I've had clients who wrote their book this way. They started a blog with the intention of turning it into a book when it was finished. They did their research to better understand the market and the questions their future customers were already asking online. Then they put together an outline for their 'book.' But instead of writing the book in secret, they published each chapter of the book to their blog as it was finished.

This method accomplished several things at once. They were motivated to create the content because they looked at each chapter as its own individual goal. Once they finished the chapter, they could publish it as a blog post. This meant getting content out on the web, providing value for their audience, and attracting new leads to their business.

They also received feedback while they wrote the book. They weren't writing in a vacuum. Their subscribers and visitors posted comments. They asked questions. They gave additional suggestions. This gave them the opportunity to improve the content before the final published version.

In addition, this meant each chapter had to be customer focused. They were not only writing for the book, but they were also writing for the web with the goal of attracting searchers and readers. If a chapter didn't work, they could change the title. They could modify the content. They knew whether they were hitting the bullseye on the market or not.

When it came time to publish the book, the rough draft was already finished and already on the web. All they had to do was put it together and do their editing. Hand it off for review by someone else and have a cover designed for it. This is one of the easiest and most effective models of book creation for those who enjoy the writing process.

How to Create a Book WITHOUT Writing

The blogging model is great for writers, but you can also create a book without doing any writing. I've already given you the secret. Do your initial research just like the writer does. Create a list of questions your target market is already asking or should be asking. Put those questions in a logical order. Brainstorm out stories and case studies you have to share and where they fit inside those topics.

Instead of writing the book, you're going to have it interviewed out of you. Sit down with an interviewer for 4 to 6 hours and have them go through all the questions. The better the interviewer is, the easier this process will be. They shouldn't just read off your list of questions waiting for your response. They need to listen intently to your answers. They need to be curious about the subject themselves. This way they can ask natural follow-up questions as you share your message.

They should pull the 'gold' out of you during the interview. They need to encourage you to share your stories and your message in action. How would your audience apply this to their unique situation? If you don't have someone to do this interview, you could again turn to Upwork.com for a skilled interviewer. You want someone with experience such as a background in radio or even podcasting. There are also services you can search for online who will interview you with the goal of creating a book.

Once you've done the interview, have it transcribed. Pay for it to be proofread. Go through it yourself. And hire a professional editor. You want to go through it personally to make sure the message is on target, but you also need the editor to spot everything you're going to miss. Getting the book done right is too important to cut it 'too cheap.'

Instead of slaving away for months writing your manuscript, you can have the rough draft transcript done in an afternoon. From here on out, it becomes the editing process. The 6+ months that most writers take to create their book could be transformed into 30 days or less total once you include everyone else's contribution.

And in the end, you'll have a book that not only shares your message, but it comes with your stories and your personality. It's you in book form...ready to attract new high quality clients.

Action Steps

- The easiest way to create content without writing is with interviews. Create a 30 minute interview, turn it into a podcast, have it transcribed, and break in into posts and videos.
- The secret to powerful, inspirational interviews is CURIOSITY. You can come into the interview with a list of questions, but a good interviewer is actively listening and digging for the gold.
- Start outsourcing today by hiring someone from Fiverr.com or Upwork.com to transcribe your audio, produce a video, or design an infographic for you.
- You can use content from your blog to create a book. Instead of taking on a big 'book project' at once, you can produce content one bite at a time through your blog. Get feedback from your readers as you go.

How to Sell Without Selling With Paid Advertising

If a potential buyer has already done their research about product options available and knows exactly what they're looking for, you can lead them directly to a sale in your advertising. For example, if a customer knows they want to buy a Canon EOS 5D DSLR camera and that's what they're searching for online, you can take them directly to that product in your online catalog. Since they know what they want to buy, their choice to purchase from you or not will come down to the price, shipping options, and any value you add to the sale.

Taking them anywhere else, such as to a page that lists all your available cameras or asks them for their email address would be throwing distractions in the way. When a client knows what they want to buy, sell it to them. But the majority of visitors aren't at this point yet. They haven't made up their minds about what they want. Instead, they're just reviewing possible options.

This is especially true for many of the clients I work with. An ecommerce store that sells name brand physical products can take advantage of the advertising the manufacturers are doing for their brands, but many of my clients sell information products. No one gets up in the morning and says, "*I need to spend $100 on a course today to help me play better golf.*"

Consultants and coaches face the same challenge. Their clients don't get up and think about how they could invest $25,000 on an expert to help them with their online marketing. Instead, they want to achieve an end result. The client wants more visitors at their website. They need to convert those visitors into buyers. And they want to double their sales from $250,000 to $500,000 this year. They want the end goal, but they're not sure how to achieve it.

Local business owners I've worked with often face the same problems. Clients may search for a CPA when it's time to do their taxes, but the most successful CPAs are more than a numbers cruncher who helps clients with taxes. They offer bookkeeping services, Quickbooks set-up services, tax advice, and even financial strategy sessions. A potential client might not even know financial strategy sessions are available, not to mention what they could do for their bottom-line.

A chiropractor doesn't just help with back pain. They're also effective for migraines, shoulder problems, knee problems, and so much more. If someone is online searching for migraines, their first thought is probably a drug to take the pain away. Chiropractic treatment can go to the root of the problem and bring relief without the side effects of drugs. But they have to tell their story. They need to provide more than just a paid consultation offer. They need to share content that demonstrates the value of chiropractic and why it's a safe, effective solution for the desperate problem.

Since a potential client isn't specifically looking for the information product, the consultant, or the chiropractor, they're not likely to be ready to purchase immediately. Just putting up a 'sales page' that tells them about your offer isn't likely to have many takers with 'cold' advertising. They simply don't know you and they aren't ready to make a buying decision yet. There is no reason for them to trust that you can do what you say you can do.

If you go right for the jugular with strong sales copy intended to get them to order immediately, a portion of them will buy. You might get 1% or 2% of them to purchase with a sales website such as mine at **www.MonthlyMentorClub.com**. That means you're losing 98% to 99% of your visitors, likely never to be seen again. That's not an efficient use of paid traffic. The numbers just don't work in most markets. That's why we originally came up with a 2-step email opt-in model.

"Old Fashioned" Squeeze Page Funnels

Instead of going for the purchase immediately, we offered free information in exchange for an email address. Just give me your email address and I'll send you this valuable free report, audio, or video about the topic you're interested in. Visit **www.mymarketingcoach.com/free** and you can see an example in action. You'll get access to a free report on the "7 Unique Ways to Create Profitable Emails even if You're Not a Writer." All you have to do is enter your email address.

We call this a squeeze page because you either enter your email address or you leave. There are no other options and no distractions. It's a Yes or No decision. One of the biggest mistakes people make with their websites is offering too many options. Someone isn't sure what path to take, so they surf around a little before disappearing forever into the Internet universe.

Obviously I'll deliver on my promise by sending you the free report. In addition, you'll be added to my email list and you'll start receiving regular emails from me (*3 to 7 emails per week*). These emails are based on the system I revealed in an earlier chapter about Infotainment. They include entertaining information, personal stories, and links to my offers. This consistent follow-up allows me to build a relationship with my reader and break down the walls of resistance.

Some subscribers purchase immediately from the very first message. Others purchase in the first week. The majority purchase within the first 30 to 60 days. While still others lurk on the list, reading messages for months or even years before buying.

Depending on traffic source, we can get anywhere from 10% to 80%+ of visitors to join the list. Advertising such as Google Display ads are often on the lower side closer to 10%. Advertising like Facebook is usually in the 20% to 40% range. Youtube ads are 30% to 50%. And anything above 50% is usually because they met me in-person at a seminar or another influencer endorsed me to their list. Yes, the quality of the traffic is the most important variable for both opt-in conversion and sales!

This is the method that I've used for the majority of my marketing for well over a decade. You can see it in use on the above page. My clients and I also focus on going after the opt-in on our home pages such as you would see at **www.MyMarketingCoach.com**. You're able to click over to my offers for my Club or my coaching from this page, but I'm asking for your email address above the fold (*in the first screen of information before you scroll*). I also focus on the email address as the core call-to-action on my blog in the top right, and many times even have a popover in place to ask for the email.

These pages are not squeeze pages as there are other options available, but they're focused primarily on getting the email address. When advertising on Google, I've been forced to use soft squeeze pages that have links to other sections of the site: **theterrydean.com/free-gifts/**. This was a requirement by Google during one of their reviews of the site.

Get the email. Follow-up. Make the sale. If there was just one lesson you took from this entire book, that would be what I'd want you to walk away with. Once you have a subscriber on your email list, you can consistently follow-up with useful, entertaining content designed to sell without selling. That email list can turn suspects into prospects and prospects into clients.

No matter where I was advertising, I used a squeeze page or a soft-squeeze up until 2015. And I still use them in most of my marketing, but there have been some additional trends over the past few years which have reduced its effectiveness.

Opt-in rates from squeeze type pages have declined. People aren't as likely to give their email address to someone they don't know. It's become a more valuable commodity to them. In addition, some sources of advertising have made it much more difficult to advertise with a squeeze style page. Facebook specifically is the ad source which forced me to start testing other methods.

On Facebook, they have a metric called "*Relevance Score.*" They compare the positive and negative interactions to your ad and give you a score. Is your ad getting clicked, liked, and shared? Those are positive actions. Are people hiding or listing your ad as spam? Those are negative. A great performing ad that is well liked by your target audience may get an 8, 9, or 10 Relevance Score. An ad that is getting more negative feedback than positive may only get a 1, 2, or 3. Scores of 4 to 7 are middle of the road, and of course the higher you get the better.

Facebook's algorithm will expose your ad to more viewers at a lower cost if you have a high Relevance Score. If you have a low Relevance Score, your audience will be limited and you'll pay more to reach them. In addition, I'd avoid having an account that's full of low relevance ads as that can't look good for your entire account if you get pulled up for a review.

It's tough to generate a high Relevance Score when running an ad that takes visitors to a squeeze page. The only clients who have been able to do this consistently are in passionate markets such as raw vegans, scrapbooking, and muscle building. Honestly, those audiences are a little crazy! We've struggled with Relevance Scores especially in any type of B2B market.

In addition, we've often found ourselves receiving a large number of negative comments on ads that send a visitor directly to a squeeze page. You can hide these comments, but good comments are essentially an endorsement for your ad. And our best performing ads are also the ones that create a lot of social proof in the comments as people recommend the post to others.

To get a high Facebook Relevance Score, you not only need an ad that gets people to click and respond, but you also need for them to like and share. On cold Facebook ads, we've had better results in most markets by giving content upfront and then asking for the email address. For example, we'll give away a free video right on our landing page. Then we'll offer a free Cheat Sheet about the content in the video for those who opt-in to our list. Here's an example of this in action:

www.mymarketingcoach.com/authority-architecture-free-video/

The majority of people from Facebook don't want to watch a 30+ minute video right now, so the Cheat Sheet becomes a very enticing option. We've also done this with long, content rich blog posts sprinkled with several opportunities to opt-in to an email list throughout. Basically you're moving content BEFORE the opt-in to build more credibility. And you're giving people a reason to SHARE your ad. Even your advertising is useful to your viewers!

Another great way to do this is to use a short content rich video as your Facebook ad. That way you're giving contrarian content (*mixed with a story if you've been paying attention*) in the ad. It's even more likely to get likes and shares because the ad itself is useful.

How to Make Your Advertising Valuable

Gary Bencivenga, one of the world's greatest copywriters, has said the secret to advertising is, "*Make your advertising itself look, feel, and actually be valuable to your target audience.*" One of his winning controls for a health promotion mailed over 100 million pieces. It wasn't just a 'sales letter.' Instead, it was in paperback book form. Yes, they actually mailed out a book as promotion. That kind of destroys the theory some people have that buyers won't read long copy. People won't read long, BORING copy, but they'll read every word if it is all about them and their interests.

Putting the sales copy into book form made it look and feel valuable. In addition, he loaded the book with great nutritional tips along with his persuasive 'pitch.' So the promotion itself not only looked valuable, it also was valuable to the target audience.

Many of the most successful promotions of all time have included valuable content throughout. Here's a magazine display ad written by David Ogilvy:

www.mymarketingcoach.com/ogilvy

The headline is *"How to create advertising that sells."* It includes a byline of *"By David Ogilvy."* It reads like a magazine article and could easily be mistaken for an article in the publication. The very first paragraph is proof and credibility, *"Ogilvy & Mather has created over $1,480,000,000 worth of advertising, and spent $4,900,000 tracking the results. Here, with all the dogmatism of brevity, are 38 of the things we have learned."*

This ad was published in 1972. That one billion would equal well over 8 billion in today's money. What else do they need to say to demonstrate their overwhelming expertise in advertising?

From here, the ad lists the 38 advertising tips with a paragraph or two about each. At least 80%+ of the ad space is real, valuable content you could use. If you were in advertising, you'd want to pull this page out of the magazine and stick it to your wall. They are guidelines and rules you'd want to remember. So you're going to have to SAVE their ad to refer back to it. It was probably better information about advertising than all of the other articles in the magazine put together.

The final subhead in the ad says, *"Is this all we know?"* The final paragraphs read...

> *These findings apply to most categories of products. But not to all.*
>
> *Ogilvy & Mather has developed a separate and specialized body of knowledge on what makes for success in advertising food products, tourist destinations, proprietary medicines, children's products – and other classifications.*
>
> *But this special information is revealed only to clients of Ogilvy & Mather.*

Then the ad ends with their logo. There is NO call-to-action whatsoever. And you're not even given contact information other than their physical address. You're going to have to work to contact them by either mailing a letter or looking up their phone information another way. No enticement of a free consultation or anything else to get you to respond. They call-out some of the industries they work in, but they don't ask you to contact them. In fact, their ending makes it seem exclusive. The specialized information, that goes beyond the 38 tips you just received, is only for their clients. You're left wanting to know how you can become a client.

When someone does the work to hunt them down, Ogilvy & Mather aren't going to have to sell the clients on their services. They've turned the tables. They're the ones being pursued. You'll have to qualify to be one of their clients. Maybe they'll even make you sell them on why they should accept you as a client.

What if you put together 27, 38, or 49 useful tips for your audience? Would that be a blog post they would be interested in reading? And what if we inserted teasers for your complete step-by-step system multiple times throughout the post? Do you think a few people might just subscribe or buy to get the system? Listing a bunch of tips is definitely valuable, but having a cheat sheet or complete system to follow is even better.

What if you put together a video or a webinar that contained those same tips? You would want to bring in your Hero's Journey story to add credibility, proof, and personal engagement. You'd mention some case studies from clients to add additional proof. And when you came to the end of the video or webinar, you could offer them your product or service to get results.

Grabbing and holding a prospect's attention is at least 80% of the work of advertising. And with all the ads we're inundated with online, it's easy to get lost in the shuffle. Many of your potential buyers are even using ad blockers so they don't even see your advertising. The biggest secret to success with cold advertising today is to NOT look like advertising!

What is Native Advertising and Why Is It So Effective?

The David Ogilvy ad is called an Advertorial. It's an ad which looks like an editorial in a magazine. The most effective way to advertise in a magazine is to make your ad look like the content. This means copying the font and style of the headlines and subheads the magazine uses for their articles. It means using the same font for your text. And you could even position your photos in the same locations. The more your ad looks like the rest of the content, the more likely readers will actually see it. There is so much advertising today that they're literally blind to it in many cases.

Advertorials have proven so effective that most magazines require advertisers to stick a disclaimer at the top or bottom that says "Paid Advertisement" or something similar. Otherwise their readers don't know the difference and think the ad actually is content.

Product placements in movies are also a form of this. How many times have you noticed your favorite actors having a Coke or driving a Chevy? There's a scene going on in the kitchen and in the background you can see the brands of cereals they're eating and a coffee cup from Starbucks they picked up yesterday. Movies are FULL of product placements today because they're so effective.

One of the famous stories is about the Harley-Davidson Fat Boy. Sales surged the moment Arnold Schwarzenegger rode it in 1991 in Terminator 2: Judgement Day. Harley has rotated in and out other motorcycle models as they updated them, but the Fat Boy has been in constant production even during updates. That movie helped establish their brand. And it's easy to see why. It told a story. Of course Harley could never say it, but their customers felt more powerful while riding that motorcycle. They could be Arnold. They could be the unstoppable terminator. That's the power of story in influencing buying decisions for decades into the future.

Native advertising is the online form of advertorials. This is where you disguise your ad to match the form and function of the site you're advertising on. Let's say you're advertising on a blog that accepts ads. One of the ad formats they accept is a 'blog post' where you can write a blog post that also sells your product and looks just like any of the other content.

You're going to get a much higher readership rate of this type of ad because it doesn't look or feel like an ad (*if you do it correctly*).

The FTC has decided native advertising is so similar to 'content' that you may need to have appropriate disclosures on your advertising letting readers know this was written by another company (and even that it is potentially an ad). You can see their guidelines and examples here: **www.ftc.gov/tips-advice/business-center/guidance/native-advertising-guide-businesses**

Many advertising sources already have a disclosure on your ads. For example, with Facebook, they will post a notice that this is "Sponsored" near the top of every one of your newsfeed ads. Anyone viewing the ad can see that disclosure and know this is a paid ad instead of just a normally shared post. Google does the same in their listings by posting a little "Ad" message beside all the advertising both in their search engine and on Youtube. Twitter posts a little "Promoted by" message at the bottom of sponsored tweets.

There are also advertising networks that are exclusively dedicated to longer form native advertising such as Revcontent, Outbrain, Taboola, Gravity, Nativo, and many more. Going into all these networks and exactly how to use them is beyond the scope of this book. Make sure you're on my list and have claimed my free gifts over at **www.MyMarketingcoach.com** to get all my updates.

Today's NEW Sales Funnels

My preference in online advertising would be to promote a squeeze page directly. Offer a free Lead Magnet gift in exchange for someone's email address. Immediately after someone joins your list, you make them a related offer. In addition, you start sending them frequent email updates using the email methods discussed earlier in this book. Get them on the list. Build a relationship. Make offers.

That method still works in extremely passionate markets. For example, clients in raw foods, bodybuilding, and scrapbooking have recently used cold ads that take visitors directly to a squeeze page. In most markets though, the opt-in rates have dropped dramatically. Where we used to get 30% to 60% opt-in rates, there are markets where I've seen clients struggle with 5% to 10%. That means the cost per lead has increased up to 6 times in those markets over what they would have been just a few years ago?

There is a simple way to bump these numbers back up. Instead of asking for people to give us something first (*their email address or their money*), it's often more effective to give them something first. Give them content and value. This could be a content rich, entertaining video about your subject. It could be detailed 1,500+ word blog post. It could even be a free PDF download without any opt-in required.

Let's say you run a supplement company that offers products related to the Paleo diet. We could create several detailed blog posts. One could be a case study about a lady who lost 42 pounds on the paleo diet. It includes her struggles with losing weight before, how she found the paleo diet, and a few of her favorite meal plans. Perhaps you even talk about a few times she 'fell off the wagon' during her diet. Another of these blog posts is an article from a doctor about some of the science behind the paleo diet and includes 7 strategies for overcoming the common challenges her patients have faced. Your third blog post is a little more 'direct' of a sale and talks about the common mistakes on the paleo diet...and which supplements can be the best choices to solve these problems.

These 3 content pieces were created as test ad campaigns. Throughout each blog post, you insert at least 3 or more opportunities to click a button or banner to opt-in for a free 'content upgrade.' This could be a checklist, recipe book, discount coupon, or even a cooking video designed to give them even more free information. Get the email address. If they register with their email, then you make an offer for one of your best selling supplements (the one most related to the initial content piece).

Instead of going for the email address, you could go directly for the sale of one of your supplements if you have a really strong offer. A great test offer would be free with shipping. They get this Whiz-Band new supplement that will do X, Y, and Z for them. It's Free with a $7.95 shipping charge. You're simply trying to get as close to break-even on the first sale as possible. After someone purchases, you will immediately make at least 2 or more upsell offers for other related products with a discount price only available in the upsell funnel.

You also add them to your buyer's list. This means you can follow-up consistently with email. These buyer emails will be worth considerably more to you than a free email list. At the same time you can insert offers inside your outgoing orders and send out direct mail pieces for related products.

The secret here is creating an irresistible offer to get them to respond. The front-end is not where profits are generated. You're simply trying to generate a buyer. The money is in the backend and everything that buyer purchases in the future.

This funnel is pretty simple. You run a valuable piece of content upfront. Create multiple blog posts or videos so you can test different concepts. Give them several opportunities to either opt-in to your email list or purchase an irresistible offer. Either way, you will give them additional opportunities to purchase from you and you will begin following up with infotainment based emails.

You will also want to 'cookie' all of the visitors to your free content so you can retarget and bring them back to either a squeeze page to get them on your list or your irresistible offer directly. We'll talk more about retargeting in just a few minutes.

How to Use Video Advertorials

At the time of this writing, my two favorite sources of paid advertising are Youtube and Facebook. This could easily change in the future. Make sure you're on my email list at **www.mymarketingcoach.com** to get the newest, updated information on this and other online marketing topics.

Obviously you have to use video ads with Youtube, but my most effective ad campaigns with Facebook lately have also been videos. Most of these have used the advertorial approach. Instead of giving 37 secrets about

X though, I'll cover just one or two tips. You want to keep your videos quick and entertaining. Give them one piece of valuable, contrarian information. Whet their appetite for more.

Face facts. Your audience is having fun on Facebook. They're chatting with their friends, sharing cat pictures, and watching funny videos. You come up in their newsfeed. You could run a boring ad, but they've learned to ignore most of these. They'll gloss right over your advertising. They might even hit the "This is Spam" option, destroying your Relevance Score in the process. But what if you give them a valuable tip quickly and you do it with personality and style? This isn't something they hear every day. Now you have their attention.

You add in a little credibility such as who you are and why they should listen to you. Then you give them a call-to-action to get even more free tips on your website. My clients and I have found putting ourselves on camera has been the most effective way to create these quick videos. It gives us a chance to quickly build the relationship and the viewer is much more likely to subscribe to our list when they get to our site. You may pay more per visitor for leads who come through a video, but you're going to find them much more responsive once they hit the site. You've given value up front.

Here's an example of one of my early videos of this type:
www.mymarketingcoach.com/youtube

As you can see, it's nothing fancy. It has barely any editing, and it doesn't even look very professional. It just gives a little entertaining story, a valuable tip, and a call-to-action to grab your free gift. When you break it down, it's formatted very similar to my style of email. You give the story. You have a lesson in the story. And you ask them to do something.

Anyone can get up in front of a camera and produce a video like this. This video example was produced specifically for Youtube Discovery ads. These ads appear when you search on Youtube. They also appear in the right column beside related videos and they can even have a banner inside of related videos. You can choose to have these video listings appear on keywords you choose, specific topics, or even specific video placements. You only pay for viewers who click your ad to watch your video.

There is a second type of video advertising on Youtube called an In-Stream ad. Those are the ads that appear before the video you want to watch. In some cases, you're forced to watch the entire ad, but the majority of these ads allow you to skip them after 5 seconds. And here's a little secret behind that type of advertising. You don't have to pay for a viewer until they've watched the first 30 seconds of your ad (*unless your ad is shorter than 30 seconds*). You want to do something to grab attention within the first 5 seconds to engage with the viewer and keep them from skipping your ad.

At the same time, you want to make your pitch and get them to click over to your site within the first 30 seconds. My general approach with these ads is to use a pattern interrupt in the first 5 seconds. Grab their attention by doing something unexpected. Tell the watcher to STOP. Say something completely contrarian. Have a cow come flying through the screen. Quickly add in some credibility about why we should listen to you. Then give us a call-to-action for a gift (*with opt-in*) on your site. In fact, I'll often tell people to go to my site and register. Get all of that in about 25 seconds, leaving a little pause for them to take action. They've watched 30 seconds so now you have to pay. At this point you can give them an entertaining tip or story and then go for the call-to-action again.

That's a very simple approach to a Youtube In-Stream ad. You're interrupting them from watching another related video, so you have to make your appeal quick. With a Discovery ad on Youtube or a video on Facebook, you can start off by making a big promise of what they'll get out of the video itself. Build a little credibility of why they should listen to you. Then give them the story and tip. Give them a call-to-action about how they can get even more goodies like this at your website.

I keep talking about 'detailed content' and valuable information in this chapter, but don't forget the lessons we covered earlier in this book. Constipated content doesn't sell. It doesn't matter how useful your content is if it misses that personal connection. Information alone isn't very effective for selling without selling. We're up to our ears in information today. Entertainment trumps information. Infotainment is king in the online environment.

In some cases you might drop the 'information' angle completely. Check out the viral video the Dollar Shave Club used to take themselves from totally unknown into a major player in the men's shaving market. There isn't a lick of valuable information here. It's all 'pitch' but it's wrapped in an entertaining format. Watch this video and see if you can spot all finger of the Golden Glove in action:
www.dollarshaveclub.com

How to Earn 8 to 1 Return Or More On Your Advertising

The single most effective form of paid advertising online today is remarketing/retargeting. You may hear either word used and they are pretty much interchangeable. You install a little pixel on your website and you can track any and all of your web visitors. You can then show them ads as they visit Facebook, Youtube, or hundreds of thousands of other websites.

You've probably already experienced this even if you didn't know what it was called at the time. For example, maybe you looked at a book on Amazon or you were considering some shoes at Zappos. You didn't make a decision at the time and you hopped over to Facebook. Low and behold, there is an ad for the exact pair of shoes you just looked at on Zappos. You decide to check out the weather and those same shoes appear right beside the weather! You can't seem to escape them. Zappos is stalking you!

This is called retargeting. When you looked at those shoes, they dropped a pixel on you. They're advertising in multiple networks around the web. You see their ad in Facebook either because they're using a Facebook pixel or they're using one of the retargeting networks. You see their ad on other websites such as the weather or the news because they're using a retargeting network that includes that website.

A few of the popular retargeting networks include Adroll, Perfect Audience, and Retargeter. Google Adwords has a pretty extensive network also that includes both Youtube and their Adsense system. While these networks also retarget on Facebook, you can pixel your visitors and target them directly through Facebook's system (*I personally prefer to buy the ads directly on Adwords or Facebook since they're networks I'm already using*).

Retargeting campaigns are dollar-for-dollar my most profitable ads. It's not uncommon to see an 8 to 1 return on these ads or even better. In other words, for every dollar I invest, I get back $8. You're not likely to see those numbers on virtually any other kind of advertising.

Why is retargeting so profitable? It all comes back to your ability to deliver multiple messages to a hungry audience. In some ways, it's similar to email. I've already mentioned that the goal for the over two decades I've been online has been to get people to give you their email address in exchange for some type of free gift. Once you have that email, you can consistently follow-up with them, deliver your message in multiple ways, and work on the know, like, and trust factor to get the sale.

The reality of advertising is the first time someone sees an ad from you, they likely don't know you from Adam. If you're not a Fortune 500 company, they've never heard your name before. If your promise is exciting enough, they may give you a moment of their attention. But they have little reason to believe you. Sure, you can fill your page with proof. As I talked about in the "Golden Glove" chapter, many websites have proof hiding disease. They underestimate just how important proof is to their sales.

If the problem is desperate enough and your promise is strong enough, they may consider purchasing from you on their very first visit. Your proof has to get you over the credibility hurdle. Your offer has to be so irresistible they just can't ignore it. And there needs to be some reason why they should act now.

In the majority of cases, you just can't make the sale on the first visit. This is where email marketing and retargeting both come into play. Retargeting allows you to pixel your visitors and show them your ads across the Internet. These are visitors who were interested enough in your initial ads to raise their hands by visiting your site. They wanted to see the product you were selling. They wanted to read the content you had available. They've shown an interest in this topic and you've crossed the first hurdle of capturing their attention, even if it was only for a few seconds.

It gets even more exciting! You can pixel all the visitors to your site, but you can also pixel visitors to specific pages. I published a blog post called, *"37 Tips to Create Emails That Sell."* Anyone who visits that page is interested in creating more profitable emails. I could use ads related to email in my follow-up with them. For example, I could offer those visitors my Free Email Conversion Kit if they subscribe to my list. Or I could offer them a course about email marketing.

Compare this to someone who visits my video about installing a Facebook pixel for conversion tracking and retargeting. What do we know about that visitor? They're interested in Facebook advertising. They might not be interested in my free gift or my course about email marketing. They're much more likely to respond if I advertise a free gift that's related to Facebook.

This is especially true with your product pages. When you visit a pair of shoes on Zappos, they don't show you retargeting ads for a pair of jeans. They show you the exact shoes you were looking at in the ad. You can pixel visitors based on which products they looked at and run retargeting ads that take them back to those specific products.

You could even target visitors who visited your shopping cart and left without buying. Shopping cart abandonment is a serious problem online. According to the Baynard Institute, 60% to 80% of shoppers abandon the products they put in their shopping cart without purchasing. Overall industry average is 67.91%. That's just under 7 out of every 10 shoppers walking up to your counter with their purchase in hand, dropping it on the floor, and walking out without buying.

Retargeting gives you the opportunity to go after them. Obviously the online environment is different than a physical retail location. Maybe they were ready to order, but then their 7 year old daughter needed their help. They went to go check on the problem, and completely forgot about you. They could have been shopping on their mobile device during their lunch break, and it was time to get back to work. Even though these shoppers never gave you their email address or any other contact information, you can run retargeting ads to bring them back to your store. In fact, you could even bring them directly back to their shopping cart if your software makes this possible by saving the items they had in it.

You could follow-up with them on Facebook. They could see your ad as they visit other websites. They could even see an In-Stream video ad on Youtube before watching that cool new music video. Since this person already visited your store, you know they're interested in what you have to offer. You're not limited to reaching them just when they're searching about your keywords or topics. You can follow-up with them no matter where they are online.

Don't overdo this or you can look a little creepy. They shouldn't get the feeling you're stalking them all over the web. Keep the volume of ads low to only a few appearances per day per user. Just because you know every page they visited on your site doesn't mean you should share that knowledge with them. It's a little scary just how well we can track our visitors.

For example, you can set-up a retargeting audience in Google Analytics based on just about any metric. You could target people who spend at least 3 minutes on a specific page of your website. They're definitely interested in whatever is on that page. You could target people who've visited 3 or more pages during their visit. You could target people who complete specific goals on your site. The choices are almost unlimited. Think about what actions someone would take if they're considering making a purchase with you. What do buyers do that the average visitor does not?

Advanced Retargeting Campaigns

A few of the common ways my clients use retargeting include:

1. Retargeting general visitors to any page of our site with a free email gift offer on a squeeze page.

2. Retargeting visitors to our content pages such as blog posts and videos and taking them to a squeeze page with a free offer related to the content they were interested in.

3. Retargeting visitors to our product pages and bringing them back to that offer or a related offer.

4. Retargeting visitors who visited our shopping cart but didn't complete check-out. We'll either remind them of their shopping cart or promote the original product they were considering.

5. Retargeting visitors who came to one of our squeeze pages and didn't opt-in. We'll target them with a different free subscription offer.

6. Retargeting subscribers and buyers with other products and services we offer. These campaigns can be run in conjunction with a sale or special discount period you're also running to your lists.

These are simple uses of retargeting, but you can also get much more advanced. I'll use Facebook as an example here because it's easy to set-up multi-touch campaigns on their system. I'm not going to go into all the technical details because Facebook regularly changes their system. And the interface you see today could be quite a bit different from when I wrote this. They make changes to their interface multiple times per year.

On Facebook, you could set-up a sequence of retargeting ads. This would work best for a business owner who has a continuity based sale or a higher ticket sale that needs even more credibility and proof than the average purchase. For example, if you're a consultant and each client is worth $25,000 or more, this would make sense. Or you offer a software program that costs $100/month where people stay for 8 months on average, you know the lifetime value of that customer is $800. Neither of them are likely purchases someone will make on the first visit to your site. They aren't likely to even sign up for your free consultation on their first visit until you've built up more credibility, even if you have a ton of testimonials for your expertise.

You create either a video or a pillar blog post that's full of valuable content for your market. You also install multiple opportunities for a visitor to opt-in to your list and get a free cheat sheet related to the subject. You run your first Facebook ad directing people over to this page. You build value into the page, and they start sharing it with others. And a small percentage of the visitors (*maybe 5% to 10% opt-in to your list*).

You have the Facebook pixel installed on the page so you can retarget all visitors, and you also set up the pixel on the thank you page after someone opt-in so you could target subscribers separately. Your first retargeting ad will go out to everyone who visited this page but didn't join the list. You set-up three case study pages from your previous clients that also share some useful content with the viewers. You run retargeting ads based on how long it has been since they visited your website.

> Day 1 – 4: You send visitors from your original landing page to the 1st of the 3 case studies during the first few days.

> Day 5 – 8: You now send those same original visitors to the 2nd of the 3 case studies during this time period.

> Day 9 – 12: You already know what we're doing here. Send visitors to the 3rd case study.

> Day 13 to 20: Send visitors to a page that describes your free or low cost consultation offer where you'll demonstrate your expertise for their situation and offer your larger consulting package to help them implement your advice. You explain the offer on this page and you include an application form for them to fill out to qualify for a consultation with you.

Each of those pages could be programmed to be shown to visitors on a specific date based on when they first visit your original landing page. The beauty of this system is it can be fully evergreen. The system will run on this schedule whether they visit your website today or 6 months in the future.

Another option would be to provide a step-by-step walkthrough of your content. You could retarget visitors who see your first landing page content and only show them the first case study. You could segment out visitors who go to your first case study and show them the 2nd case study. You continue this on out through the 3rd case study and your final call-to-action to get them to schedule their time with you.

In either case, you're basically putting together an automated sequence with your Facebook ads just as if you were doing an email follow-up sequence. It gets crazy what you can do with retargeting. In addition, we could add a link to your application form throughout all these case study pages. There's no reason why you couldn't be picking up leads throughout the whole process.

Ask yourself what a visitor needs to believe before they become a quality client with you. What do they need to see or understand? What objections will they have? Instead of forcing your entire message down a visitor's throat in just one sitting, now you can spread it over several points of contact. This type of marketing is especially powerful whenever you have a little more difficult of a sale to make.

Action Steps

- If someone is specifically looking for your product, you can sell it to them immediately. Otherwise, you'll want to get them to make a 'safe' first step such as subscribing to your free email list.
- Follow Gary Bencivenga's advice, "Make your advertising itself look, feel, and actually be valuable to your target audience."
- Test using one of your 'epic' blog posts or one of your strongest videos as your landing page in paid advertising. Insert multiple calls-to-action to join your list or buy your product throughout the content to get people on your list.
- Create a simple video advertorial where you share a good tip about your subject, add some credibility, and then do your call-to-action.
- The most profitable form of online advertising is retargeting. You should install a Facebook or Google pixel on your websites, and retarget all of your visitors with additional content and ads.
- You can create a follow-up sequence on Facebook (and other retargeting networks) using a series of ads connected to strong content pieces on your website that handle objections and persuade your buyers.

How to GROW Your Local Service Business

Some readers may skip directly to this chapter. The temptation to go directly to the action plan can be overwhelming. If this is the first chapter you've read, you can gain some insights and even a plan to get started, but you're also likely to feel a little lost. I'm going to be using phrases and instructions we covered throughout the book. You'll need to refer back to those chapters to understand everything covered here.

These techniques work for ANY business, including yours. It doesn't matter what challenges you're currently facing. Perhaps your margins are being squeezed by the ever-increasing cost of goods. You may be losing business to the Internet. Competition is increasing. Advertising doesn't work like it used to. Complicating all these problems could be a decline in your local area. Many cities in the US and abroad are struggling now with increased taxes and lower paying jobs.

Your business is unique, at least to a point. These techniques will work for you. I've helped thousands of clients in hundreds of different markets. I've likely consulted and come up with a plan for a business similar to yours already. Obviously, there isn't room in this book to share all the unique ways you can apply these principles. That's why I've focused primarily on the big picture. These are the strategies you can use to dominate any market.

Your personal application of these strategies will vary depending on your industry, your location, and the skillsets of you and your team. There is really only room to pick one example business here, but these principles will apply to any business. As I cover a few methods for our chosen example, look for ways you can apply these techniques to your business.

Let's focus on a local CPA practice. CPAs (*Certified Public Accountants*) face numerous challenges. Competition has increased dramatically. Software has advanced to the point that many clients now feel accountants are unnecessary. It's a hot/cold business where a large portion of the new business occurs over just a few months leading up to the tax deadlines. This can make it tough to hire and retain good staff when your business may be overwhelmed for 3 months and slow the other 9 months.

Obviously other local service businesses face challenges of their own. Chiropractors are being squeezed by insurance premiums and lower payouts. Dentists also face insurance hassles and are struggling with increased competition from large corporations that are dominating many markets. Real estate agents have a lower barrier to entry and face a large number of poorly trained competitors which bring down the whole industry along with client price pressure on commissions. Home contractors such as painters, pest control, plumbers, and lawn care companies are facing increased competition and their current advertising options don't work like they used to.

There is no way to cover every type of local business. Financial professionals, fitness professionals, and natural health professionals are all facing challenges. The Internet is incredible for providing options and choice for consumers, but it also provides increased competition...and not just from other professionals. You're facing low cost or even free options in many cases.

Some of your peers may have essentially given up. You can hear it in their voices. They talk about all the challenges you're facing in your market. They talk about how much easier it used to be. There is too much competition. Advertising doesn't work like it used to. You've been turned into a commodity.

In their minds, they're simply trying to survive the inevitable decline. That's NO way to live. Yes, you face challenges today. But all of those problems can also be turned into opportunities. Old advertising methods like Yellow Pages don't work because people are using Google as their Yellow Pages today. Newspapers are declining in readership because your audience gets their news on Facebook and other social media sites. They're plugged into their community.

Increased competition means it's vital to illustrate your competitive advantages. Why should someone choose to do business with you over every other option? This not only includes direct competitors, but it also includes software and other DIY options available to your audience today. If you're working harder and harder for less results, you're on the wrong path. Change your direction.

Instead of fighting the trends, use them to your advantage. That's what this entire book is about. Your customers don't like being sold, but they love to buy. Give them the opportunity to buy. Provide them with information that allows them to make their own decision instead of you having to 'overcome their objections' and sell them by brute force.

Who is YOUR Ideal Client?

Let's focus on our local CPA practice. Traditional CPAs are thought primarily as tax preparers, but that is only one of their opportunities. It's limited in scope, and it's the most competitive area to focus on. You're competing with other CPAs, and this includes the big corporate firms such as H&R Block and Jackson Hewitt. They even put up Kiosks in Walmart! Plus, you're competing with all the software options such as Turbotax.

If you target everyone, you'll be competing for the crumbs. Start off by defining your Ideal Client Avatar. Individuals who work a W2 job and rent their home are EASY to file. They may also be low value clients to you. Just about any option will work fine for them. Your help is most needed as returns get much more complicated.

An individual working a higher income job, with multiple investments, especially as you move into real estate, will have a much more complex return. In addition, they will need help throughout the year as they plan for future taxes. They can take advantage of multiple deductions and further reduce their taxes by the actions they take with their investments. They need ongoing advice.

There is an even more lucrative market. Focus on other small business owners. This is where taxes get much more complicated. You can offer additional services. They might need bookkeeping. They might need Quickbooks set-up services. That's right. Some of your competitors are busy complaining about software such as Quickbooks because they see it as invading their business. You're smarter than this. Quickbooks obviously isn't right for every business, but it can be an asset to both the business owner and you if it is set-up correctly. And it's much more difficult than most people expect. You can profit from this by providing services to help business owners set it up.

We're not finished yet. What else do local business owners need? They need quarterly strategy meetings. They need to sit down and review the profits and losses from their business. They need to plan their upcoming quarter. So many CPAs and business owners are simply reactive. You're doing your client a disservice if you sit around waiting for them to simply hand over their documents to you in the beginning of the year for tax time.

Where were you the rest of the year helping them save every penny they could on taxes? Where were you in helping them spot money being wasted in their business?

You're limiting your value and your income if you position yourself as just another tax preparer. They're a dime a dozen. Someone who proactively helps business owners not only save on taxes, but to keep more of their hard-earned money in their pocket every month is a trusted advisor they would want to refer to others. Increase your income by increasing your value.

Focusing on all small business owners is likely still too large of a market though. Think about your favorite clients up until now. Who do you most enjoy working with? Who pays your fees without complaint? What types of businesses do you share the most affinity with?

Let's say a few of your favorite clients are chiropractors and dentists. While you will offer your services to any small business owner, we might identify these two industries as Ideal Clients you will focus your attention on first. Any direct mail campaigns you send out will be targeting local chiropractors and dentists. Online, you may have to target all small business in your local area because the local audiences are too small for chiropractors and dentists only. A personalized approach on Linkedin would allow you to contact them directly though.

Your next step would be to write down everything you know about this audience. What are the biggest challenges they're facing right now? What are their goals? How do they feel about taxes? How can you help them reduce taxes not only during tax time, but throughout the rest of the year? What other ways can you help them in their finances and their systems? What local meetings do they attend? What websites do they visit? What groups do they participate in?

What Is Your Strategic Myth?

Why should someone choose to do business with you instead of the competition? Everyone wants to attract premium new clients, but no one wants to focus on the foundation. The first step is knowing who you're speaking to. The second step is coming up with a unique message that will attract a hungry buying audience. One of the issues of selling your CPA services is that many entrepreneurs will see you as an expense instead of an investment. They already hate paying taxes, since many of them feel they're being unfairly targeted for their success. When they add your fee on top of the taxes they're already paying, it's even more painful.

How can you turn your services into an investment instead of an expense? You will continue to offer tax preparation of course, but what other services will you add? As mentioned previously, you could add a Quickbooks set-up service. Other CPAs may see Quickbooks as cutting into their profits. In your view, you see it as simply a tool to make your job easier. It doesn't reveal deductions or help a client with their tax planning. It only tracks what has already been set-up. Offering this service can give you a doorway into a client's business. After you get them set-up and teach them how to use it, you can tell them how easy it is to have you prepare both their taxes and all the other forms they have to fill out throughout the year.

You also create your ongoing proactive quarterly financial meetings. Every 3 months, you'll meet with a client and go over their books together. You'll help them spot areas where they can save money in addition to reducing taxes. In addition, you'll make yourself available by phone or email for any questions they have in between meetings.

This turns a one-time purchase (doing their taxes) into a yearly subscription. Each client is now worth three times as much money to you. How much more could you spend on advertising if tripled the value of each client? What if you knew the client would keep coming back every year? What if your unique methods were so valuable to them that they referred 2 additional premium clients like themselves? Increasing the lifetime value of every client who walks through the door is a total game changer for your business.

There has to be a story behind this package and why you created it. You've been doing clients' taxes for years, and it hurts you to see all the deductions they're missing out on. You're limited in what you can do for a client based simply on the paperwork they provide from last year. There are so many more ways they could proactively save money. It makes you angry just thinking of all their hard-earned money going to the IRS when they could have been using it to grow their business, invest more in their retirement, and provide for their family.

Make the message personal. You can't stand it when you see an entrepreneur paying one penny more to the IRS than they legally have to. And you were frustrated year-after-year doing taxes for entrepreneurs while being limited to what they did the previous year. Saving money on taxes requires you to make proactive decisions the year before about how you invest your business' profits.

In addition, you've found you have a talent for spotting all the hidden waste that's costing them a fortune. You'll create a custom plan for each of your clients. You'll follow up with them. And you'll help them put the plan into action throughout the year.

Share Your Hero's Journey

Review the chapter on the Hero's Journey. Think back to what led you to be a CPA. Surely, there are other businesses you considered. You might have a childhood story about the business your parents ran when you were little. Or you chose this field because numbers came naturally to you (*obviously this is a talent you can use to your clients' benefit today*).

Perhaps your story picks up later. You're already an accountant working in someone else's office, but you're frustrated with the inefficiency surrounding you. Clients aren't getting the best results, and you have to go out on your own. Since you've been in business for yourself, you've faced many challenges they may identify with. That's the key here. You're not just telling an 'origin' story. You're looking for the elements your Ideal Clients will best identify with. Most chiropractors and dentists went into their practice because of a mission. They understood the value of what they provide to a person's overall health and life. Connect with that feeling in your own story.

You're not just another tax preparer. You saw how understanding the numbers allowed entrepreneurs to do more. They can grow the business, hire new employees, and provide more for their family. Some background story allowed you to see the difference you could make in someone's business and overall life. This story could have been why you became a CPA in the first place. Or it could be the story that caused you to go into practice for yourself. Or perhaps it's a client you met since you've been in practice. You saw what the right advice did for them.

You had an "AHA" moment where you just couldn't do business as usual anymore. That's what this is all about. It's about that moment. It's about the turning point. It's about the story and the emotional impact it had. You made a discovery and there was no going back. Now you have to share this message with others. You have to shout it from the rooftops, *"Why isn't anyone else doing this?"*

I have to be a little general here. I don't know your story or what the Inciting Incident is in your life. There may be several key moments in your life. One of my discoveries was when I first heard about the power of the

Internet, and purchased that computer on my last credit card back in 1996. I faced numerous challenges that first year until I stumbled upon the 'secret formula' of using email to sell without selling.

Another big turning point was after I 'retired' from the Internet for 18 months and decided to come back online and directly coach entrepreneurs one-on-one. My coaching practice was successful right out of the gate, but I initially struggled with getting clients to implement. It was coming up with simple systems such as the Golden Glove which helped my clients start receiving the massive results they do today.

Don't make anything up. You don't have to. You just need to look back at your life and the turning points of your life. Who influenced you? What mentors gave you advice that made a dramatic difference? What challenges did you face and what was the turning point for each? You're looking for a story that helps illustrate your unique message to the audience. Since we're talking about proactive tax planning, you would want the story to illustrate planning ahead instead of just reacting to what circumstances dictate.

How to Come Up With Your Initial Content

There are a lot of ways you could come up with content to distribute. You could write a blog about ways to save on taxes and spot hidden profit opportunities in your business. You could create a series of videos answering the most common accounting questions. You could even run a local business podcast where you interview business owners in your local area to both produce content and create relationships with the local influencers.

One of the best ways to get started would be with local meetings. Come up with a presentation you could deliver in a group such as the Chamber of Commerce. You could also partner with local banks to share a message with their entrepreneurial audience. Your topic needs to be exciting. Taxes put people to sleep. Off the top of my head you could share something like *"7 Common Mistakes STEALING Your Take Home Profits"* or *"How to Find an Extra $10,000 In Your Business This Month."* Either of these subjects would be all about reducing expenses and keeping more money in your pocket. Taxes may be involved, but they would only be one component in the overall message.

You could record this presentation and put it on your website as a video. Use it as your free Lead Magnet to get people to subscribe to your list. Set-up an email list using any of the available email services like Aweber or Constant Contact. Send out at least one email a week (*sending more emails is even better*). Use what you learned about email earlier in this book to create Infotaining emails that share value and content while building a relationship with your reader. Your call-to-action in your initial emails will be for a free *"More Take Home Money Today"* consultation with entrepreneurs.

Set-up a Wordpress blog either on your current site or on a new domain that targets keywords your audience is likely searching for. Use your city combined with the search phrase. If you live in Ocala, it might be OcalaCPATaxAccounting.com or OcalaSaveMoneyOnTaxes.com. Post a copy of each of your emails to your new blog.

Include your origin story in both your presentation and your first few emails. You can make that initial content do double duty and include many of the same tips in your emails which you created for your presentation. The best place to get these tips is directly from your own experience of working with clients. Then you could provide a quick story for each tip and how to apply it.

If you need a memory jogger, you could scan through a few 'tax' books on Amazon. I did a search for "Tax small business" and one of the top books was called *"The Little Big Small Business Book."* I used the Search Inside feature by clicking the image near the top left and scanned through the Table of Contents. Some of the topics that jumped out to me that could fit your presentation include coming up with the right structure (sole proprietorship, s-corporation, LLC, etc.), common deductions, and getting financing.

I then scanned through the related books on Amazon and opened one called *"Accounting for Small Business Quickstart."* It talked about How to Review Bank Statements, budgeting basics and software, and understanding financial statements. That makes me wonder what most business owners will miss on their financial statements? What I'm quickly being clued into by doing this review of the top selling books is just how 'basic' much of your audience will be.

You can't present accounting in a dry, boring manner like most presenters who have gone before you. You have to make it interesting. That's where your personal stories and your Hero's Journey come in. You need to take simple principles and cover them with a more interesting personal interest story. How can what you know equal additional income for them? How can it save them money? And how can it put more take home pay in their pocket? Just being interesting will set you apart from the competition.

How to Expand Your Content Delivery Locally

Since I'm an 'internet marketing' expert, you may be wondering why I suggested public speaking before online marketing. You have to go where your audience is. In a local area, your audience of small business owners are already congregating together. They're attending business meetings. They might be in local Meet-up groups for entrepreneurs. They might attend local networking groups like BNI. I don't make a distinction between offline marketing and online marketing. It's all marketing. Attract your Ideal Clients wherever they are. The same methods that work in an online environment work offline as well.

A live presentation in front of a local audience is even more powerful than running a webinar online. The advantage online is that you can do the meeting from the comfort of your home. In addition, you can speak to hundreds or even thousands of people at once through webinar software such as Gotowebinar, Google Hangouts, or Facebook Live. You'd have to rent a meeting room if you do a presentation in person. You have to deal with the traffic hassles. You have to get dressed and spend time commuting. It's easier to do a webinar online, but it's not as effective as being in person.

You can create a greater connection with the audience in-person. They can see your body language. They can shake your hand. There is built-in credibility when you're standing face-to-face with your Ideal Client. On a percentage basis, you will have a higher conversion of attendee into client in a live in-person environment.

This is true when it comes to publicity also. Getting national publicity for your local business can be difficult. Your message has to be more exciting than the latest celebrity gossip. Getting local publicity is much easier. It becomes a human-interest story. Your competition isn't the movie star or pop star. It's the mayor or school board. That's a much lower barrier of entry.

Just telling your story about how you got started in business and why you do things differently can be enough to get local publicity. Publish a book and you're almost guaranteed publicity in your local area. In fact, I've often told coaches and consultants who can serve worldwide audiences to start their publicity campaigns in their local area. It's so much easier to get featured there. Once they've been interviewed for the local paper and radio station, they can use that initial publicity to move toward larger stations in other areas.

Take your presentation and cut it up into 'segments' that would fit a radio interview. Prepare a list of questions an interviewer could ask that leads you into sharing your message. Focus on telling stories just like in your speech. The first few questions may be your background and how you got started with what you do. As you dig into the meat of the interview, you'll want to share contrarian advice the listeners aren't hearing anywhere else.

As a CPA, you'll want to talk about several unusual ways small business owners can save money on taxes. Unusual is the key word there. Don't talk about normal deductions everyone knows about. Talk about the ones that surprise your clients when you recommend them. What can a business owner do this year to save even more on their taxes next year? Have a story to tell about each of these to keep it interesting. Don't share the name of the client unless they've given you permission to do so first, but do tell the basic story and how much it can be worth to someone.

Make it fun. Taxes are a boring subject. If you start talking about new government regulations, the audience will fall asleep. That's why stories are vital. Be passionate about your topic and what you do for your clients. Talk about how exciting it is for you when you look through a business owner's spreadsheets and find a way for them to save an extra $10,000…or earn an extra $20,000. It's all right there in the numbers speaking to you, even if no one else sees it. People may not be 100% positive what you're talking about, but they'll resonate with your stories and hear your passion.

You can speak at events, attend networking groups, and do interviews. All these methods allow you to tap into someone else's audience. Always offer a call-to-action of either calling you for your free consultation or going to your website and claiming your free online gift. Get people on your email list. That is king. It's almost like money in the bank when you're sending out frequent Infotaining emails like we talked about earlier in the book.

You can build even more authority by creating your own business group. Perhaps it's a Friday morning breakfast before normal business hours. You need to reach critical mass first where you've built up a list of at least several hundred local business owners and attended other people's events till you're known in the area. Then start your own group. Keep it simple. Perhaps you or someone else speaks for 20 minutes. And you have organized group networking for 20 minutes. You've met speakers to invite while attending other local events.

How to Multiply Your Reach Using Linkedin

In-person marketing can be more effective initially, but that doesn't disqualify the online environment. Search Linkedin for local groups. Do a search for "City entrepreneurs" or "City business owners." In Ocala, I'd search for "Ocala entrepreneurs" and "Ocala business owners." I'm looking for groups in my local area which I can join and network with. You can do a similar search over on Facebook, but you'll often find Linkedin has more B2B type groups.

Get in the local groups and look for questions you can answer. You're the expert on taxes and financials of the business. You can't provide direct support for their individual situation. You need to get potential clients on your free consultation for that, but you can answer the general questions they ask.

You can also pursue your Ideal Client through direct contact on Linkedin. Search for local chiropractors and local dentists. Send a connection request. You're building your network. They have to approve your request which could take anywhere from a few hours to a few weeks (*it all depends on when or if they login to their Linkedin account*). Linkedin will let you know when you're connected and you can send them an initial message.

Since you're following the Sell Without Selling approach, you're not going to immediately offer your services. That's way too pushy for online marketing. Instead, you'll provide value to them. You should already have a Wordpress blog set-up and several pieces of great content on your blog. Choose two or three of your BEST content pieces that not only share valuable information but they also illustrate how you're different from the competition. At least one of them tells your origin story.

Send a short Linkedin message to each new contact that thanks them and offers this free content. Here's an example of what this message may look like...

HI [First Name],

I'm glad we connected on Linkedin.

As a respected chiropractor in Ocala, I thought you might enjoy these recent articles I created to help you save money on taxes and put more money in your bank account:

www.yourwebsiteaddress.com/Ocala-Chiropractor-Saves-10000-In-Taxes

www.yourwebsiteaddress.com/3-Most-Common-Tax-Mistakes-Chiropractors-Make

I still have room for a few more clients in 2017.

If you'd like to explore how I help chiropractors proactively save money on taxes while putting more money in their pocket, reply to me for a "How to Find Free Money" consultation.

Thanks for connecting.

Talk Soon!
YOUR NAME

This is a promotional message but you're delivering content first. They will get value out of the message whether they ever contact you directly or not. That's part of this whole system. Everyone you come in contact with is better off just for having met you. You're a giver first.

There are two key aspects to the link URLs for your content pieces. Each one uses a benefit rich title. They can "*Save 10,000 on Taxes*" or they can see the "*3 Common Tax Mistakes.*" The 2nd aspect is these are customized for the audience you're speaking to. Chiropractors are in both of the URLs. Would a chiropractor be more likely to read a tax saving article written for all business owners or one that's specifically for chiropractors? The chiropractic specific article will grab their attention first.

All you have to do is modify one of your 'general' tax articles to refer directly to chiropractors. Do the same thing when you contact dentists. You create another copy of your article and modify it to be dentist specific. Edit the email to match the dental market.

Your goal will be to get people OFF the Internet as soon as they reply. Schedule a phone consultation. Or ask them to come into your office. Linkedin is only good for the initial contact, but you'll convert much better if you get them into direct contact and provide customized advice for their situation.

Let's take a step back before we make all these new connections and send all these messages. You'll want to have your blog set-up and content on it. You'll want to have chiropractic and dentist specific articles on your blog you can refer to in your messages. And you'll want to create a kick-butt profile for Linkedin itself. Most of your competitors will just put that they're a CPA. That's BORING! Come up with something more exciting for yourself. You're "The Expert At Saving Thousands of Dollars in Taxes and Tapping Into FREE Money Hidden in Your Business."

In your summary, talk about your experience and how you help clients. Remember to focus on the benefits you provide to clients and even talk about your call-to-action, how they can get their free gift on your website or their Free Money Consultation. You can add to your credibility by asking a couple of clients if they could share their experiences with you on your profile. That will add extra social proof to your profile. In addition, you can create your first few Linkedin connections by sending out connection requests to clients and other local business owners you already know.

How to Tap Into Facebook Advertising

You probably invested a little money in getting your website up and having your Wordpress blog installed, but you haven't spent a penny on advertising yet. There are hundreds of options online, but one of the best choices for you will be Facebook advertising. Google Adwords is a possibility, but clicks are usually pretty expensive there. And Youtube may not have the volume you're looking for in your local area. That brings us to Facebook advertising.

I wouldn't limit your ads to chiropractors and dentists unless you're in a large area. There won't be enough volume. Instead I would target local business owners who are above a certain income level. One of the beautiful things about Facebook advertising is how specific you can get with your targeting.

Refer back to the chapter, *"How to Sell Without Selling With Paid Advertising."* Install the Facebook Pixel on your blog and use it to create a custom audience of those who visit your blog.

The best way to get started with Facebook ads is by sending visitors initially to one of your content rich blog posts. This way you're giving them something they can share instead of going 'hard sale' on them with an offer for your services upfront. You have to build your authority before they're willing to take the next step of contacting you directly.

Facebook is constantly changing their system so setting up your ad could change by the time you read this. Start off with the option of "Send people to your website." This is an ad where you're paying for clicks to your website. Now you have to choose your audience. The 'default' selection if you're in the US is to target the entire US. Hit the X button and remove the US. Type in your city name and Facebook should help you autocomplete the name of your city. You can also choose how far outside of your city you want to advertise. The default here is 25 miles but you can change it to whatever distance your clients will travel to you.

You're now targeting everyone in your local area. That's way too general since we want business owners. Click on the "Browse" button under Detailed Targeting. Facebook gives you a world of options. We could target people by what type of industry they're in such as Healthcare and Medical, but we're specifically looking for small business owners. I could choose the category of Demographics > Work > Job Titles and type in both "chiropractor" and "dentist." That selection gives me less than 1,000 people to target in my city of Ocala, and that's just too small of an audience. I tried the same selection in San Diego and it was still too small of an audience.

Next I selected the Business and Industry interest of "Small business." This gave me an audience of 13,000 potential prospects in the Ocala area. This is a small audience, and I'm not really happy with all small business owners. I want people who have a profitable business. So I choose "Narrow Audience." I then choose "Demographics > Financial > Income" and I select all the categories from $75,000 and up.

That gives me an audience of only 1,400 people in my local area. That's a TINY audience. On a practical basis, you'll often find you can only reach around 10% of a specific audience at any time with your ads. This means there is only an audience of around 140 real viewers of my ad. This is much smaller than I would like to see. That's one of the negatives of living in a small area.

If I add the Interest 'entrepreneurship' in addition to "small business", my audience goes up to 3,200. That's a little better, but still tiny for Facebook ads. You will want to keep your advertising to a small budget, likely never more than $5 a day, and possibly just a couple of dollars a day. Otherwise, you're going to show your ad way too often to this small audience.

As a comparison, my clients who advertise nationwide are often looking for an initial audience that is 500,000 to 1,000,000 in size. That gives us a large enough audience that we can expand our advertising significantly if it performs well for us.

You'll have to keep your ad sizes small, and you'll want to rotate different content pieces regularly. Perhaps you advertise one blog post for a week. Then rotate to another blog post for the same audience the 2nd week.

You use a third blog post for the 3ʳᵈ week. And you do another blog post the 4ᵗʰ week. Then you rotate those same four blog posts over again the next month.

This small audience size is another one of the reasons I recommend getting out in the 'real' world and contacting their audience there. You have a smaller universe in your local area than those who have a nationwide or worldwide audience. And you can get better bang for your buck by meeting them in person where they already are.

How to Use Direct Mail to Attract Your Ideal Clients

Direct mail is one of the most effective tools for reaching a small, targeted audience. We selected chiropractors and dentists as our Ideal Clients to start. You can find a compiled mailing list of your audience on **www.Infousa.com**. Or you could simply have one of your staff members do a search on Google for "Ocala chiropractor" and write down the contact information for every chiropractor in your area. We'll use the InfoUSA path to demonstrate this.

I choose "business mailing lists" and now I get to select my audience. I choose chiropractic and choose doctors of chiropractic (DC). Then I choose Ocala Florida under Geography and cities. This gives me a total list size of 45 leads in the Ocala area. Obviously if you're in a larger city, you may have a much higher number. There are 372 leads in San Diego. If my audience was larger, I could even choose larger practices by selecting the number of employees or the annual sales figures of the practices. With this small local audience, I'm going to select all 45 leads here in Ocala.

Next I search for dentists. There are 153 leads in Ocala. With the combination of these two lists, there are only 198 leads in my local area. You could do a multi-step direct mail campaign to all these leads for less than $1,000. You'd separate out the chiropractors from the dentists so you could prepare letters that spoke directly to their unique challenges, shared industry examples, and used their language.

Create a series of 3 to 5 touch points. The first direct mail piece may be a straight letter for a free consultation and an offer of "FREE MONEY." That's your hook for all the money they're currently overpaying to the government and the hidden holes in their bucket which they're losing. You tell a quick story of how you've helped another chiropractor (*or dentist*) in the local area save money…and how you could do the same for them. You're currently accepting a few new clients and you have open slots for a a "Free Money" consultation if they'd like your help in finding the free money available in their business.

Keep this initial letter to one page front-and-back which will give you room to insert another couple of pages in with it for one first class stamp. Add a print out of one of your best blog posts (*one of the same ones you're using in your Linkedin contacts*). This way you're giving value upfront. And since you already contacted many of these leads through Linkedin, this is actually your second point of contact (*and it's possible they've seen you at a local event also*).

Your next touch point by direct mail will be the same letter with an audio CD of either an interview you've done recently or your speech. The only thing you'll change in the letter is letting them know about the included CD and how it can benefit them immediately.

Your 3rd touch point may be your second blog post printed out along with the same initial offer. You continue the sequence and send out a postcard inviting them to your upcoming speech at a local event or the breakfast group you've created for business owners. If you had your staff compile the list yourself, you might even send an email follow-up at this point similar to your LinkedIn message.

Perhaps you compile a newsletter for your current clients, and you include this targeted mailing list in the next time you mail out your newsletter. Instead of spreading yourself wide and trying to reach everyone, you narrow down your market and go deep with content delivery. That's how you create an effective direct mail campaign with a small local audience.

How to Apply These Techniques In Your Local Practice

I used CPAs simply as an example. These techniques apply to any local service business. The first step isn't to immediately jump into online advertising. Instead it's to come up with what sets you apart from the competition. Look for your 'story.' If all you are is simply another commodity in an over-competitive market, you won't be able to cut through the clutter.

Cutting-edge Internet techniques won't save you if you have a bad overall strategy. Follow the system. Identify your Ideal Clients. Compare yourself to the competition and find your competitive advantage. Come up with your story and your Hero's Journey. Create your Golden Glove offer.

From here, create content that will appeal to your audience, build your authority, and persuade them to contact you for more. You have to use the right bait for your audience. Instead of jumping on the Latest Flavor of the Month in online advertising, go to where your prospects already are. Look for influencers who already have them on their list.

Speak in front of hungry audiences. Contact your Ideal Client through Linkedin. Send out customized direct mail pieces to specialized audiences. We didn't go into joint ventures in this chapter, but you could also partner with others who already serve your audience and persuade them to send your content out to them. Go through the rest of the book, and you'll find additional strategies and techniques you can apply based on these proven principles.

Action Steps

- Don't try to sell equally to everyone. Identify your Ideal Premium Client. While competitors compete for the scraps, you'll actively attract the hungry higher ticket clients into your practice.
- Come up with unique offers that stand out from the competition. In addition, share the story behind these offers and why they're so important to you.
- Share elements from your "Hero's Journey" that your Ideal Clients will identify with. Find the "Inciting Incident" that forced you to change direction and do business differently from the competition.
- Create an attention grabbing and interesting presentation for local meetings. This can be recorded and added to your website as a Free Preview Lead Magnet. Some of the stories can be pulled out and used as emails.
- Contact your Ideal Clients on Linkedin and use a value-first approach by sending them access to at least 2 high quality blog posts customized for them or their industry.
- You may be able to target your Ideal Client with Facebook ads. Don't go directly for a pitch. Instead, send your first ad to a content piece on your blog that fits them personally.

How to GROW Your Consulting/Coaching Practice

I've been an online business coach since 2006. To me, this is the perfect Lifestyle business that gives me the freedom to work from anywhere and set my own hours. Plus, I love my clients. The system I've shared with you throughout this book will help your clients preselect themselves. Those you will enjoy working with are attracted to you and your methods. Those who conflict with you never make it through the hurdles of doing business with you. This is an incredible way to run a coaching or consulting business of any type.

These methods work for you whether you're a consultant or a business coach. People define a 'coach' as someone who simply asks questions and allows their client to guide themselves. There are times I do this. A client is much more likely to implement your advice consistently if it was their idea...or they at least think it was their idea! I use questions not just to gauge the situation but to also help my clients make the right decision.

Consulting has a little more of a done-for-you component to it. My coaching is a mixture of both coaching and consulting because I'll often help clients write ad copy, edit emails, create scripts for videos, review their ad campaigns, and more. In addition, I provide direct advice on how to create their products, attract new clients, and share their stories.

A consultant is someone who simply provides professional advice and/or help with implementation. It includes marketing consulting, management consulting, technology consulting, healthcare consulting, and so on. It doesn't matter what field of consulting you're in. This system can and will work for you.

You might not even consider yourself as a consultant at all. Maybe you're a copywriter or an investment advisor. Clients come to you for your expertise, advice, and even implementation. You could be a life coach or an executive coach. This could mean coaching people to find the right career, helping them get fit, or grow functional teenagers (*that's got to be a hard market*).

You may think your practice is unique, and you'd be correct. It is unique. Your audience will be different than mine, but they'll respond to the same system. You'll answer different questions that your audience is asking, and you might even use a different core method for delivery of your content. It all comes back to your audience, their interests, and your own skillsets. Don't create a Youtube channel if you hate being on video. Build your business with written content. If you hate writing, do a podcast and let your audience hear your voice.

Write Out a Detailed Description of Your Ideal Client

You're going to see a LOT Of similarities between this chapter and the previous one. This system has been proven to work for thousands of clients. There are little variations on the system based on what you do and who you serve, but the basic principles stay the same no matter who you're trying to reach.

Human nature doesn't change. The Golden Glove formula works to persuade people to buy consulting just as well as it does for physical products. My Infotaining Email Formula has sold supplements, chiropractic, membership sites, cosmetics, dresses, and $100,000 consulting packages.

Your Hero's Journey applies whether the business is done under your personal name or a company brand name. There is always a reason why a business, product, and/or service were originally created that helps illustrate what it does for your clients.

Who is your ideal client? I have several coaching clients who have been with me for a decade or more. One of my clients joined the very first month I offered coaching, and he is still a client to this day. In addition, I've since partnered with him on several projects worth considerably more money. He will likely be worth a million dollars or more to me over the lifetime of doing business with him.

That's the type of client you're looking for. Twenty percent of your clients drive 80% of your profits. Often you can break it down even further and 5% of your clients drive 50% or more of your profits. Who are those clients?

What is their desperate problem? What keeps them awake at night? What else have they tried to solve their problem? Who else could they contact to help them solve their problem? What are the end results if they don't solve the problem? How much is it costing them? While I've helped both beginners and experienced online marketers, my IDEAL client is someone who already has a website up and traffic going to it. They're making money, but they know they could be doing better! Often they're overwhelmed in their business and aren't sure which direction to turn next. They're working too many hours and they need to put systems in place.

Often this means more than just money to my clients. Yes, they'd love to take their six-figure business to seven figures and beyond, but it's even more important that they get their life back. Maybe they're working 60 or more hours per week. Their marriage is suffering. They've gained an extra 40 pounds and their health is suffering. They don't get to spend time with their kids growing up. They don't feel like a good mother or father anymore. They want the FREEDOM they were promised.

I work with clients who are just starting out, but it's much easier to multiply the results for a client that already has traffic coming through. It's possible to bump their sales by an extra 30% to 50% simply by making a few changes to the headline on their site. Getting them to run an email special out to their list could be worth an extra $30,000. Create results like that for a client the first month and they'll stick with you for years (*or possibly even decades*).

How can you give your Ideal Client a Quick Win that will excite them to continue the relationship and possibly even upgrade to other services you have available? Who is the perfect 'set-up' for you to apply your magic? What other qualities do your Ideal Clients have in common?

Start thinking about where these people congregate. What books do they read? What experts do they follow? What podcasts do they listen to? What Youtube channels are they watching? What Facebook pages do they visit? What Facebook groups and other discussion groups are they participating in? What keywords are they searching for on Google and Bing? What blogs do they read? What magazines do they read?

If you can't identify what your audience is already doing online, you're not going to be able to reach them. One of the advantages you have in a location independent business is the ability to attract customers from around the world. Currently I have one-on-one coaching clients in the US, Canada, UK, Germany, Japan, Malaysia, and Australia. I've helped clients in dozens of countries around the world and the client list for my group programs and my print newsletters have stretched into hundreds of countries. There truly are no borders for an online business today.

You can't attract 'everyone.' Only the big Fortune 500 companies like Coke and Pepsi can use mass advertising in today's market. As a small business owner, we have to laser focus on what our Ideal Clients are reading and doing.

There are influencers online right now who have your target audience already on their list, listening to their podcast, and reading their tweets. There are Youtube channels you could advertise on to attract your Ideal Client. There are interests in Facebook which hold those $100,000+ clients for you. The more you know about them, the easier it is to reach them affordably.

Find Your Golden Glove & Story

Having a unique promise that stands out from the competition is even MORE important when you're competing with a worldwide audience. How many other consultants or coaches claim to do what you do? Take my situation as an example. There are hundreds of 'internet business coaches' who claim they can help you increase the profits of your online marketing. "Online marketing consultants" are a dime a dozen today. What sets me apart from them?

First, I narrow down my targeting. I'm not going after large companies. The largest business I've personally worked with was a $50 million-dollar business. That's pretty good sized, but it still had a single decision maker at the top. He started the company and continued to run it as a Lifestyle business for himself. The majority of my clients are under the million-dollar level when they come to me. They're in the start-up stages up to about a million dollars. There are still a lot of consultants going after this market.

My next qualification is I'm looking for those who want Lifestyle type businesses. Entrepreneurs who live for 80 hour weeks are NOT a good fit with me. I've worked with a few and helped them improve their marketing, but we don't gel correctly. Sure, you may have to work long hours in the beginning to get your business growing and systems in place, but our goal is to create a Lifestyle business you can run without giving up the rest of your life.

My slogan is Earn More, Work Less, Enjoy Life! That's a process. First, we get your business earning more. That's going to take some time and effort. Then we put systems in place so you can Work Less. Finally, the end goal is to ENJOY LIFE...not to build a business which consumes your life. That slogan is important to me and motivates me in what I do.

Another quality that sets me apart is my focus on selling without selling. The goal of my business is to make money, but I'm not willing to give up my integrity to do it. We can share content and value that makes our audience's lives better whether they ever purchase from us or not. Everyone you come in contact with is better off for having met you.

In addition, I focus on proven methods that work. I've tested the 'content only' approach that some will tell you to follow. It doesn't work. You can send out the best tips and advice, and you won't make any sales from it unless you mix in the story behind the message. I'd prefer it if you could persuade people with logic and reason, but human beings don't make rational decisions. We make decisions based on emotions, and we justify those decisions with logic. That's why your story is so important. This includes both your big Hero's Journey story and little personal stories and tidbits.

My story has adapted and grown over time. I first started online because I was looking for a way out of my dead-end pizza delivery driver job. There had to be a better way. My wife and I were over $50,000 in debt with nothing to show for it other than a minivan with a dent in the side. The majority of our credit cards were maxed out, and I used one of our last cards to buy my first PC at Best Buy. I went online, visited forums, and started answering questions. I tried dozens of different things over those first months, and the one discovery that set my course in motion was the power of email. Getting people to join my email list was the secret.

As my email list grew, so did my income. Soon I was earning a full-time income online. The Internet was only beginning to become popular for online businesses, and conventions started inviting me to speak and share what I was doing. My business grew. In 2004 I sold off that first business, took 18 months off, and launched MyMarketingCoach, LLC in 2006 to help other entrepreneurs Earn More, Work Less, and Enjoy Life with personalized step-by-step guidance of what works online.

That story is part of my brand. I've already shared it in this book, but I had to share it again because it fits into this section. It's part of my story and who I am. It's part of my message and what sets me apart from the competition. You have a story also. There is a reason why you do what you do. There was an Inciting Incident that set you on the path you're on today. There's a reason why you're driven to help your clients like no one else can.

Combine that story with a Golden Glove offer and you have a winning combination. You have something that will cut through all the hype in your market, and speak directly to the hearts of your Ideal Clients. Spend time here before you move to the next step. Create a story that works and a Golden Glove that attracts hungry buyers. Everything else you do is based on this foundation.

Attract New Clients By Reaching Out to Influential Connections

The fastest way to attract new clients is to go to people who already know, like, and trust you. For example, many consultants start their practices by hiring themselves to companies they previously worked for as a salaried employee. I've helped new business coaches launch their practices by connecting with business owners they already know. It could be a friend or family member. They worked for a reduced rate or even free to get their first case study they could share in their marketing. It can be difficult to build up the credibility initially to attract new clients online. That's why you should take every advantage available to you.

Who do you already know who may need your services? Think about family members, friends, coworkers, clubs, churches, or any other social group you're a apart of. Not only could your initial clients be in this group, but you may also find influencers who can refer other clients to you.

For example, I worked with one of my clients for months before he shared with me that his mother was a reporter for a major newspaper. That was the perfect connection to get some publicity for his business starting out. If you're a business coach or consultant, who do you know who may have business owners on their list? It could be your accountant friend or your uncle who's a business lawyer. It could be the relationship you already have with your local bank.

I helped one of my coaching clients start up a Facebook advertising service by connecting him with another client who serves chiropractors. They ran a webinar together for the chiropractic audience, my client picked up half a dozen new clients immediately out of the gate. Think about how much time and effort he saved by going through the connection I gave him. Sure, he had to share a percentage of all fees with his joint venture partner, but he saved months of time getting launched. And that relationship continues to feed him new clients.

Perhaps you've established a relationship with a consultant or coach you've hired in the past. Or maybe you've attended a conference. You can gain knowledge from conferences, but often the most valuable component are the connections you make at the event. Who do you know already that has your Ideal Clients on their list or in their field of influence? If you serve a business audience, you could connect with people you already know on Linkedin, and then start searching through their connections for who else you can connect with. It's amazing who you can reach out to through your circle of influence.

Here's another little trick for generating referrals. If you call up an accountant you don't know and ask her to refer her clients to you, she's going to think you're crazy. She doesn't know you and there's no incentive for her to do the referral. But what if you contacted that same accountant and asked who her Ideal Client was and whether she would like you to refer clients to her? She'd likely wonder why you were doing this, and jump at the opportunity.

If you position yourself as a specialist, you can reach out to any other non-competitive specialists your audience would be interested in using. Create your own referral network. Write a quick description of what you do, who your Ideal Client is, and what your initial offer is to get that client through the door. Send a letter to influencers asking them if they would like you to refer clients to them. All you need from them is a quick description of what they do, who their Ideal Client is, and what their initial offer is to get that client through the door. They can look at the one page document you included for yourself as an example.

Will everyone fill this out? Of course not. Some will. You're making them an offer they can't refuse. You're giving them free money. You're going to send them over referrals with nothing in exchange. You've become a giver first. They'll read your 'referral sheet' as an example for creating their own to send back to you. They're likely to refer others to you if your offer is good enough just out of reciprocity for you sending referrals to them.

This line of thinking affects everything you do in your business. Give first. Leave everyone better off than before they met you. You'll be on the right path if you come back to these principles no matter what you're trying to do.

Share Your Message To Other People's Audiences

Public speaking is a shortcut to credibility. My client did a webinar for the chiropractic audience. That was his doorway into their world. He didn't have to travel. He didn't have to appear in-person. He put his picture on a couple of his Powerpoint slides to make a personal connection with his audience, but he did the entire one hour webinar for close to 100 attendees from the comfort of his own home.

That launched his practice with a bang. One webinar and he was in business with multiple clients paying him monthly for his services. Do you have any connections that have a stage open to you? This could be a virtual stage through a webinar or it could be an in-person event. There is absolutely no reason why you couldn't start your practice off with local speeches just like I recommend for local professionals. Those local events are easier to get involved with than the national stage. They might not have a large audience, but they're nearby and they're looking for speakers just like you! Get your practice in and perfect your presentation while attracting new clients.

Your additional advantage is not being limited to your local area. You can hold webinars for anyone who has a list, no matter where in the world the audience is. I've held webinars for clients in Russia, Canada, UK, Australia, and others. Start off by contacting people you already have a connection with. They'll be much more open to working with you in the beginning. Those early webinars can become case studies you use to get additional appearances. You could use a tool like Google Hangouts or you could sign-up for a free 30 day trial of **www.Gotowebinar.com** (*their ongoing monthly pricing is very reasonable for unlimited webinars in your account*).

When you contact your 'host' (*the person who has a list of potential attendees to your webinar and your future clients*), make them an irresistible offer. Not only will you deliver amazing content along with case studies of what you can do for the attendees, but you'll also share a percentage of all sales you generate from the webinar. These commissions often range anywhere from 20% to 50%. It depends on the margins available to you, and how valuable your services are compared to what others could deliver. It's just like any other kind of marketing. The more competitors you have with a similar offer, the higher your commissions have to be to stand out. The secret to getting the commission rate down is coming up with a service offer that sells like crazy and doesn't have direct competition.

What if you don't have any connections? I'd start locally since those events are often looking for speakers. Get some experience. Make some sales. Get a few testimonials about your presentation from hosts and audience members. Use the credibility you build on the small stage when you move online.

Refer back to the chapter of connecting with Influencers. Give first to prove your value. Get on the lists of those who regularly email your target audience online. Follow them on social media. Share their content first. Send them a testimonial. Attend their webinars and participate in the discussion. Contact them to ask for an interview.

Use baby steps up to asking for the webinar UNTIL you have the credibility of several events behind you. When you have an irresistible offer and you've produced some strong commissions for others in the market already, then you have the credibility to go directly to asking for the webinar.

The other strategy to use is whenever you have a success in anything, ask for a referral. You interview an expert and they comment on how much they enjoyed it, ask for one or two other experts who would make good guests on your show. When you're the one being interviewed, and they talk about enjoying the content, ask if they know another podcast or two you could appear on. When you do a webinar that makes money for the host, ask who else they know who may want to hold the webinar for their audience. The two natural responses you need to develop to all praise are *"Could I quote you on that?"* and *"Who else do you know...?"*

How My Client Attraction System Works For Me 24-7

Here's where '*How to Sell Without Selling*' comes into its full power. You should NEVER have to sell yourself to a client. They should already be pre-sold on you as the consultant or coach they want to hire before they speak with you. They should be selling you on working with them instead of you trying to sell them on working with you. I've had a waiting list for my one-on-one coaching for almost a decade. People are continually joining that waiting list and I only have spaces in my coaching a couple of times per year at most. Those slots get claimed fast (*in as little as 15 minutes after they've been made available by email*). This system can do the same for you.

The power of my system is in consistent delivery of contrarian content from a confident character. Use contrarian content that appeals to your target audience to attract them to your website. Get them on your list with a free Lead Magnet that helps them while building your credibility at the same time. Send emails that tell your Hero's Journey Story, share case studies, and make a personal connection with your audience. Never forget that part. Constipated content is not enough to make the sale. You've got to build the relationship. You're sitting down to lunch and sharing from your heart just as if you're speaking to your prospects one-on-one.

One weekly email is the minimum frequency. Several times a week or even daily is better in most markets. In each email you're promoting something, whether it's your initial consultation/coaching offer or a waiting list like I have. You could even promote products that share your expertise for additional income and clients. We'll get to that in the next section.

Mix in other forms of content. These could include longer blog posts, videos, podcasts, or even Facebook Live where you answer questions from your audience. People can better hear and feel your passion in video and audio. Reading alone often can't do your passion justice. Plus mixing in audio interviews from others works well for expanding your audience and making connections with influencers.

Any of the traffic generation methods I've talked about throughout this book work for building your email list and promoting your services. Facebook and Youtube are perfect for this because of the personal connection. I've also used Google Adwords, Google Display Network, Bing, Twitter, email advertising, and even direct banner purchases on websites.

There are hundreds of traffic sources available online, and this simple email follow-up system can tap into any of them. Get targeted prospects on a list, follow-up with them, and sell them without selling. Since the best techniques for generating traffic change constantly online, you should join my email list at **www.MyMarketingCoach.com** or my monthly Club at **www.MonthlyMentorClub.com**.

Why Creating Your Own Products Provides a Path Into Your Services

Many consultants and coaches resist creating information products because they're afraid to reveal their systems to the public. Won't people just buy your products and do it themselves? Won't the competition get ahold of some of your secrets? The reality is these products can often become the most effective business card for your services. They create an additional passive income stream for you while attracting your best clients to you.

The information product with the highest level of credibility is a book. You don't write a non-fiction book about your topic to make money. Sure, you might make a few dollars, but the big benefit of the book is the immediate credibility it gives you. A consultant walks up to a prospect and hands her their business card. You walk up to the same prospect and hand her a copy of your book. Which one is more effective? It's not even close. The prospect doesn't even need to READ the book for the credibility boost. Just the fact you wrote the book is enough. You're not just a consultant or a 'writer.' You're an author. And this is your topic of expertise.

Publish your book on Amazon. Send your customers to purchase it there to help drive Amazon sales. The more sales you get for your book, the higher it goes in Amazon's rankings. Searchers find it while looking for your topic and you get additional sales. Those new people who just stumbled upon your information in Amazon may become some of your best clients.

A book takes time to create, and it's often not the best product to start with. You could get started with a simple audio series. That could be created in one day. Or you could produce a series of videos you deliver online through a password protected membership area of your website. Combine your audios or videos with an edited transcript and a few cheat sheets, and you now have a product that can produce extra income while attracting new clients to you.

In addition to the extra passive income from your products, you can often increase the rates on your services. You don't need to 'lower' your fees to make them affordable. If someone doesn't have the money for what you offer, they can purchase your products for the DIY route. Those products will help you create an even better relationship with them, and they'll be first in line to hire you when they get more money and you have available spots for new clients.

One of My Biggest Online Breakthroughs

The power of email done correctly is the biggest breakthrough of my online career. Another one of my breakthroughs is the power of a paid membership site or a print newsletter. I had one of the first membership sites in the online marketing space. It was called Netbreakthroughs. Each week I shared the results of one of my ads I was testing. This could have been a split test between several banners in my ad or it could have been a split test of headlines on my website. As my site grew, members started to submit their own case studies of what was working and not working in their businesses.

In addition to the weekly ad test, I published two articles about what was working in online advertising, and I had a members-only forum where you could get advice on your own websites and campaigns. Members received all of this for just $19.95/month. It attracted over 1,500 members. I eventually sold this membership in 2004 when I 'retired' from my first online business.

I started my new business in 2006 and started publishing my Monthly Mentor Club print newsletter not long after. Every issue of this newsletter is written personally by me and contains 15 to 23 pages. Each of the monthly issues is written directly from my personal experiences and the help I'm providing to my private one-on-one clients. Because of my constant immersion in the market and helping clients, members have often told me how I seem to write exactly what they need at the time. They're facing the exact same challenges my private clients are.

At **www.MonthlyMentorClub.com** you can find out more about this club. My previous membership site and the current one have served a very similar purpose in my overall system. At least 80% of my private clients were a member of my private 'club' first before upgrading to coaching with me. I've seen the same results with my private clients who offer consulting and coaching. Their memberships provide consistent, reliable income each month, and their members upgrade into working directly with them.

This works not only with consulting and coaching, but it also works with workshops, clinics, services, and higher ticket products. Your best buyers upgrade from your membership.

This is even more powerful than email alone. Email allows you to continually show up in your prospect's email box. You're building a relationship. They're hearing your stories and identifying with your case studies. They click your links and buy your products. My print newsletter allows me to also show up in their mailbox each month. I'm giving them my best information and exactly what is working for my clients right now. And I'm likely ALONE in that mailbox. They're not receiving mail from other coaches. I don't have to worry about spam filters or my email disappearing before it gets to them.

Creating your own Club wouldn't be the first recommendation I'd make to you. Take advantage of any connections you already have first. Build your email list and offer your services. Start helping clients so you have case studies to talk about. As your email list grows into the hundreds and then into the thousands, then create your own membership for an additional source of revenue and one of the best client generators you could ever create.

The beauty of the clients you attract this way is they will already be sold on your methods. They agree with your systems, or they wouldn't have stayed a member. And they definitely wouldn't have upgraded to working with you directly. This is one of the most sure-fire ways to attract clients you LOVE working with!

Action Steps

- Write out a detailed description of your Ideal Client Avatar. The better you can describe them, the easier it is to attract 'perfect' clients while repelling low quality clients.
- Create a 'Golden Glove' and personal story that attracts your Ideal clients. You have to demonstrate your uniqueness in super-competitive markets.
- Start your practice by connecting with people who already know, like, and trust you. Get referrals in the beginning, even if you have to offer your services at a discount to build up case studies.
- Create client magnets such as emails, blog posts, videos, podcasts, and more all designed to attract your Ideal Clients. If you're having to 'sell' your services, you're doing it wrong.
- Put your client attraction on overdrive with your own book or monthly membership of some type. These forms of information publishing create passive income streams for you while preselling your Ideal Clients on your premium services.

How to Start From Scratch Online When You Don't Even Have a Business Idea Yet

What if you're just getting started online and don't have any type of business yet? What if you don't even have an idea for a business yet? That's where I personally started online back in 1996. I didn't have a clue what to sell or who to sell it to. All I knew is I needed a way to make money online to escape that dead-end pizza delivery job.

My favorite business models revolve around information products, coaching, and consulting. In some ways, I would describe those as the "Perfect" business. You spot a problem and you create products or services designed to solve that problem for your audience. This is what the majority of my one-on-one clients do in their business. They sell books, ebooks, online courses, home study courses, workshops, coaching, consulting, and done-for-you services such as copywriting or Adwords management.

Businesses like these require almost no overhead. You can get started with just a laptop. While some clients work at home like me, others prefer to travel and work from coffee shops. I prefer the peace and quiet of sitting on my lanai while you may prefer being surrounded by people going about their day. Coaching and consulting can provide a premium income with a small group of clients. Information products add passive income to your model. Work once and get paid on it forever!

The margins in this business are incredible. Books are a poor information product themselves, but they build credibility for your other products and services. The margins just aren't there in books. It may cost you $3 or $4 to print up a book that sells for $10 to $20. Compare that to a set of 10 DVDs which may cost $30 or less to duplicate-on-demand and sells for $195 to $495. That's with ZERO inventory expenses. You can have the products created and shipped for you completely hands-free.

You could sell digital courses for anywhere from $7 to $997 depending on the subject matter and they cost next to nothing to fulfill. You're talking a few cents in bandwidth per download on your server and a membership script to protect your products. And that's for a product that can be set-up to sell for you 24-7.

If you have the expertise and the desire to go into consulting, coaching, or create your own information product, go for it. The fastest success stories I've seen have come in these fields. You can leverage your life experience and wisdom to create a high 'active' income with consulting and coaching. You can also use that same experience and wisdom to create a steady stream of passive income from information products.

If you're NOT sure what you want to do, you could start with affiliate marketing. You don't have to create your own products. You don't have to write your own 'sales copy.' You don't have to worry about shopping carts, taking credit cards, or setting up a protected members area. There are thousands of people who have already done the work. They've created products. They've tested their websites. They know how to convert visitors into sales. And all you have to do is send visitors to them, and they'll handle the rest. You'll get a share of their profits for each referral you send their way. It's one of the easiest ways to get started online.

I've seen way too many people fall into Analysis Paralysis. There are a lot of moving pieces in an online business, and they get overwhelmed just thinking about all the options. I've received emails from people who have told me they've spent years trying to figure out what market they should get started in. That's crazy! You're much better off getting started on a small scale, and figuring some of this out as you go along. You're not going to have every piece of the puzzle in place when you start. It's just not possible. An often used expression is "Ready, Fire, Aim." Get moving and fix it along the way.

Affiliate marketing is perfect for this. Instead of spending the next month (*or even several months*) putting together an information product, you focus first on the audience. Get a website up. Create a Lead Magnet to get people to subscribe to your list. Send traffic to your site. And start publishing emails. Promote affiliate programs to monetize your website and emails in the initial stages.

As your email list grows, you can send out a survey to your list and ask them what they want to buy. You'll have a built-in audience ready to purchase before you create your first information product. This initial phase of building up your website and sending out emails will also help you refine your message. Maybe you're not sure what you're Hero's Journey story will be yet. You're not positive about exactly what your audience is most interested in. And you haven't figured out what unique promise you can offer. That's OK. You'll fill in all these pieces as you move forward.

You'll need a website and an email list service. I recommend **www.mylowcostwebhost.com** and **www.mymarketingcoach.com/aweber** (*both of those links are affiliate links*). I practice affiliate marketing in addition to earning money from information products and coaching. Even as you grow your business in the future, you'll continue to earn multiple income streams through affiliate promotion in addition to anything else you do.

Find An Addicted Buying Audience

Your first step will be choosing a market to go after. It's impossible to reach 'everyone.' It's counterintuitive, but the more you refine your audience, the easier it is to attract them. You can figure out where this audience hangs out online. You can review what desperate problems they're facing and what language they use to describe those problems. And you can put together a message that attracts them to you.

Since you're starting out as an affiliate, we don't have to fully refine your audience yet. We can choose a 'broader market' and refine your marketing down to a tighter niche as you start putting out content about the subject. Some of the broader markets would include subjects like make money, natural health, weight loss, anti-aging, and relationships. For example, you could focus initially on 'dating for women.' That's a relationship market, but it may not be a fully refined audience yet.

As you continue to research the market and start publishing content, you may discover your best buyer is a 30 to 40 year old professional female who is busy in a corporate career. They're interested in dating and perhaps marriage because they want to build a family. They have money to spend. And they don't have a lot of available time which means they need methods that work and they may be interested in higher ticket services that can shortcut the time.

"Make money" is an extremely broad market, but you may get started there in the very beginning. People want an easy way to earn an extra $1,000 a month. As you start marketing to that audience (*which will primarily be people looking for business opportunities*), you can refine your message. For example, you might find your skillset fits Youtube well. You enjoy creating videos. And you start experiencing success by attracting viewers to Youtube channel and getting them on a list. You refine your message to focus on Youtube optimization and monetization.

There are 3 keys I look for when helping a client choose a market to get started...

1. #1: **Passion**: Is this a subject where you are curious to know more? Are you hungry to read books on the topic? Is this something you would enjoy talking and writing about daily? Don't go into a market where you'd be bored to tears in just a few months. Something you've consistently studied and investigated previously is often a good guideline to help you choose.

2. #2: **Buyers**: Are you speaking to an audience that is proven to buy? You can review bestsellers on Amazon to see if people are buying books about the subject. Are there products you can promote on affiliate directories such as **accounts.clickbank.com/marketplace.htm** or **www.CJ.com** (*you'll have to join their network to see available affiliate programs*).

3. #3: **Value**: Do you have value to share, a story to tell, or any type of proof and credibility? Even if you start out promoting other people's products and services as an affiliate, you'll still need to produce some of your own content. You'll need a Lead Magnet to get people on a list and you'll need to send out regular emails about the subject. Having your own story and experiences are a huge advantage in a market. Those stories grab and hold attention.

This is where many people find themselves stuck. We're so used to downplaying our own skills and experiences because we're supposed to be humble. You might be tempted to say there's nothing you can share value about. You're not good at anything. I've heard that dozens of times from clients, but I've never spoken to anyone where we haven't been able to dig out some experience or skill they could share with the world.

Are you truly saying there's nothing you're good at? You haven't learned anything in school, on the job, or in your personal life? You don't have any hobbies? If I had to choose something outside of online marketing, I'd choose a market in one of my hobbies. I love training my dogs and could specialize in German Shepherds. I have studied a lot about fitness and could talk about weight training or bodyweight fitness. While I'm not 100% Paleo, I could definitely talk about the subject with experience. I enjoy investing

295 of Scratch Online

and could talk about stocks and index funds. I'd could even have fun with a website about doing reviews of strategic board games.

You don't need to be the premier expert on a subject. You just need to know others just getting started. You need to know enough about the subject to sort through the good and bad in the market. As a trusted advisor, you should be able to protect your audience from getting scammed by those who would take advantage of them. You should be able to point to products and services which are a good deal for your subscribers to purchase.

In addition to Clickbank and CJ, you could also promote some of the Cost-Per-Action affiliate networks such as:

- **www.Neverblue.com**
- **www.Peerfly.com**
- **www.Maxbounty.com**

These affiliate systems will pay you for leads you generate, even before a sale is made. The negative here is that many of these networks will NOT approve you to promote until you have a website about the topic. So you may want to wait until you at least have a basic site up and content published before applying for their programs.

Here are three simple questions to ask yourself before you choose your market:

1. Are people buying? You can answer this question by looking at Clickbank, CJ, Amazon, and even the top paid ads on Google (the organic listings are not as valuable as paid ads for this because a company needs to be selling something to consistently pay for advertising).

2. Can you help a customer get results? It's a subject you're interested in and that you have some type of value to share. You can 'protect' your audience by promoting good sellers.

3. Can you reach subscribers affordably? A good way to review this is to look for popular Facebook pages in the market and use **www.facebook.com/ads/audience_insights** to see what Facebook can tell you about those audiences.

Create Bait to Attract Your Audience

Attract an audience by grabbing their attention and delivering value in advance. This value could be a content rich blog post, Youtube video, social media post, or podcast. Once you've attracted their interest you need to move them to the next step of asking for their email address. After you get their email, you'll continue to deliver value and move them toward an affiliate purchase.

Review the chapter about Lead Magnets. Provide a gift in exchange for the email address. It has to be something that hits the benefit and curiosity hot buttons. Two quick lead magnets that work great for affiliates are a Personal Case Study or an Interview With An Expert. Both of these can build your credibility while pointing your new subscribers toward one of your affiliate offers.

A personal case study would be your own experiences with a product or service. For example, let's say you purchased a course on dog training that you've now joined as an affiliate. A personal case study would describe the problems you were experiencing with your dog that caused you to purchase the product. Maybe she was pulling your arm out of joint every time you went for a walk. She was jumping up on people. There might have been additional problems you would discuss.

You bought XYZ course and tried out one of the methods. You share a couple of tips from their 'effortless walk' system. Make sure to share it in your own words and don't give away the entire system. Leave viewers hungry to know more. Then point to your affiliate link where they can get all the details on the complete system.

My outline for a Case Study Lead Magnet is:

- Problems You Were Experiencing Personally
- What Other Approaches You Tried That Didn't Work
- The Solution You Discovered
- One or Two Quick Tips Someone Could Use Immediately to Demonstrate Results
- Tie the Solution to the Affiliate Offer

Your second option is to do an interview with an expert you'd like to promote. You can research your market, especially in forums and Facebook groups, to find the common questions they're asking. You can use other people's questions and other people's expertise to create your Lead Magnet.

Register as an affiliate before the interview and promote the expert through your affiliate link. This method also allows you to tap into the expert's credibility and stories in your marketing. You're promoting the interview about them, instead of yourself.

When you're starting out completely from scratch with no one on your list yet, it can be a little difficult to secure that first interview. You don't have any credibility to show an expert why they should say YES. For all they know, you'll do the interview and never promote it. They'll simply waste their time. It can often be easier to start with your own Case Study in the very beginning until you get up to a few hundred people, get a few sales for the affiliate program, and then use that credibility (*you're making sales for them already*) as a springboard to ask for the interview.

Ask for the Email Address

One of the biggest mistakes online is confusing your visitor. You want to make it clear and obvious what the next most logical step is for each visitor. The most effective opt-in page is a squeeze page. Someone can either opt-in to your list or they can leave. You can see an example of this kind of page here: **www.mymarketingcoach.com/free.**

Some advertising sources such as Google want to see a more substantial site that includes a company logo, about us page, contact us, and some form of content. You can see a website I designed specifically for Google Adwords and Youtube advertising here: **www.theterrydean.com.**

On my main website and blog, I ask for the email address front and center on the home page: **www.MyMarketingCoach.com.** When you visit the blog, you will see there is an opt-in form at the top right of each page and often another opportunity built into the content itself: **www.mymarketingcoach.com/blog.**

The type of page you use depends on the traffic source you choose. As you can see, since I have multiple streams of traffic I'm using all these types of opt-in pages in my own business. When I'm being interviewed for a podcast, I send people to a squeeze page. If I'm sharing content on social media, I'll point people to one of my blog posts.

The first goal is to get the email address. That's your audience. You can promote affiliate programs to your list and you can also survey your list to create products or services of your own in the future. You don't own any of the social media sites you participate in, but you own your list. It's your business.

Promote An Offer Immediately

If you use a Case Study or an Interview with an expert who has their own affiliate program, it makes sense to link over to the affiliate program immediately. Some people will tell you not to sell to your list immediately, but my tests with clients in dozens of different markets have proven you want to make an offer immediately. In some markets, you'll generate close to 50% of your sales in the first 24 hours.

Think of it this way. Someone is searching for a solution to their problem. Your ad grabs their attention and they decide to give it a try. You either go immediately for the opt-in or you provide a little content in advance and then go for the opt-in. They were interested enough to search the subject. Your ad was strong enough to pull them. They read your page and decide to give you a shot and opt-in to your list. You're building on commitment and consistency each step along the way. You throw up a huge STOP sign if you decide to hold off on making an offer. They're interested and excited about the subject now, but you make them wait and cool down. You've just blown it with a portion of your audience.

The two options here are to either immediately deliver the content or go for the sale first and then deliver the content. You could ask them to check their email to download their free Lead Magnet, but here's something to check out before they do. You tell a quick little story about the offer and give your affiliate link. This 2-step approach of asking them to check their email first for the gift would work best when giving an audio gift. It will take a little time to listen to the audio and they might not get a chance to go through your link.

The second option is to build the affiliate link right into your content itself on the thank you page. With the case study, you could tell your story right on the thank you page (*or in a PDF on the thank you page*). And you work your affiliate link into the story itself several times as you introduce the solution you found and describe what it did for you personally.

Either of these methods can work for the thank you page. I've even had a few clients who rotated several different thank you pages as a split test. They endorsed different affiliate programs on each of the tests to see which one would produce the most sales. One affiliate page generated 3 times as much money as the rest! They would have never known this if they didn't test it. Not only did they earn more money, but it also gave them a better understanding of what their audience was willing to spend their money on in the future.

Attract Hungry Buyers

It's easy to get overwhelmed with all the options available for traffic. You could go after paid traffic such as Google Adwords, Google Display Network, Youtube, Facebook, Instagram, Twitter, Banner Networks, Solo Ads, and so much more. Or you could go for free traffic sources such as Blogging, Youtube, Podcasting, Joint Ventures, Social Media, and more. The right traffic source for me might not be the right source for you.

It's all about finding a hungry audience you can target cost effectively. Combine that with your own skill set and assets. If you're limited on time, but you have the budget to advertise, you'll want to go with paid advertising. If you have time, but you don't have money to advertise, you'll go for one of the free methods.

If you're in a passionate market where people want to share your message with others, Facebook may be a good bet for your initial paid advertising campaign. For example, if you are in the dog training market, pictures of puppies are almost guaranteed attention grabbers on Facebook and Instagram. The only other method that may be nearly as effective for that market would be Youtube. Videos of puppies are even more fun than pictures! If you're in a more business related market, Facebook might not be as valuable to you. Google Adwords may be a better choice in the beginning.

For free traffic sources, it all comes back to your personal skillsets. It's often easier to rank on search results with video on Youtube compared to blog posts on your own site. If you enjoy the interaction with others, podcasting could be a stronger choice. Blogging has the lowest barrier to entry since all you need is a Wordpress blog to start writing.

Don't try to do everything. You'll just drive yourself crazy! Focus on one traffic source in the beginning. It takes time to tests ads that work and optimize your campaigns. If you try multiple traffic sources all at the same time, you'll divide both your attention and your budget. You'll sabotage your own results because each traffic source requires its own set of steps. Once you have your first source of traffic working for you consistently, then you can expand out to others.

Find Your Voice With Email

You're going the affiliate route for simplicity. It shortcuts the learning process because you don't have to get everything in place first. You can get started and refine your message along the way. You might know what the best offer is for the audience. You can test multiple affiliate offers. You might not know how your story stands out from the competition.

As you tell your story through a series of emails, you'll interact with your audience and identify what resonates best with them. They'll ask you questions. You can monitor your open and click rates. You can pay attention to which emails bring in sales for the affiliate products you offer.

Don't be lazy by just sending out the emails provided to you by your affiliate merchants. Everyone is using those emails. You'll just be another me-too parrot in an already crowded marketplace. Instead, look at the benefits they focus on in those emails and use them in your own themes. Tell a story from your life and connect it to the benefits of their offer. Post your own review of their product, using a few of the ones they show for inspiration.

Be a confident character who delivers contrarian content with clear consistency. Talk about the myths, mistakes, and misconceptions in your market. What lies are others telling? What mistakes have you personally made? And what do people believe about the problems or the solution that's just plain wrong? One of the emails that got the most negative feedback early on was about how business opportunities which promise income for zero work are lying to you! Dozens of people complained about that email even though it's common sense. They bought into the outrageous hype in the internet marketing that promises an easy button without thinking or work.

Did that get me to back off my message? No way! It made me want to talk about it even more. Some people unsubscribed. They weren't my audience anyway. Those same emails were appealing to my target audience. My message confirmed what those subscribers already knew.

Become a voice for your buying audience. Say what they're already thinking. Give voice to what they can't put into words for themselves. Integrate your personality into your message. I'm a quiet, laid back individual so my writing often flows in a logical, step-by-step manner. It's how I think. Don't try to be me. Be who you are.

What if I could wave a magic wand and turn you into a bolder, more outgoing version of yourself? What have you been afraid to say? What is your audience saying in their heart but can't quite put into words? Become their voice. Tell stories from your daily life. Who or what influenced you growing up? Who is important in your life today? What is your origin story...the reason you got started in this business? What are you hobbies? What happened to you yesterday that can illustrate your message?

It's impossible to produce enough 'amazing content' to hold interest today. We're overwhelmed by content. You have to mix your content with a personal connection. Your audience will continue reading your emails because they identify with you personally, not just based on your content alone.

Practice writing emails. Create a rant about a desperate problem in your market. Maybe you're a little limited in the beginning because you're not quite sure who you are yet. That's OK. Keep writing. You'll make the connection soon enough. Each of your emails will connect to one of your affiliate offers. You may rotate through several offers, promoting one for several days, and then switching to another. If you're emailing correctly, you'll begin seeing results. Some emails work. Some offers sell. Others don't.

You'll get feedback directly from your audience. Don't get upset when you get negative comments. If you're not getting any negative feedback, you're not bold enough with your message. You can't please everyone. When you try to please everyone, you end up pleasing no one. Let them love you or hate you. You've lost them if you become easy to ignore.

How to Multiply Your Income

Your list is growing. You're making money from affiliate offers. You've written enough emails that you're finding your unique voice. You could continue with the affiliate model. It's a great way to create a mostly passive income. You generate traffic and build a list. Let other people worry about creating products, taking orders, and paying out commissions.

If you want to multiply your income, now is the time to create your own information products, coaching, or done-for-you services. Having your own products allows you to earn more from every sale. Instead of getting 10% to 50% of the price on every sale, you keep 100% of the money minus product costs, customer service, and fulfillment. But even more important, you're able to tap into affiliates and joint venture partners who promote your products and services for you.

The first step is to look back at what is already selling to your audience. Which offers produce the most income for you as an affiliate? Compare this to the emails you've sent which have produced the best result and the emails you've received from your subscribers. What is it they want to buy? How can you create an even better version of your bestselling offers?

Don't make the same mistake I've often made. I've wasted months before creating an encyclopedia type product containing every answer to every question I could imagine. I put together an overwhelming offer that was too much for my audience. Start out with the quickest and easiest product you can produce. Perhaps it a 2-hour audio series on the subject. Maybe it's a series of short 5 to 10 minute screen capture videos you produce with Camtasia Studio. Show them a quick step-by-step system to get from where they are to where they want to go.

For example, a project like this book is a pretty major undertaking. It took a long time to create even though portions of it were pulled from other materials I've written previously. A much easier product that sold extremely well for me was a 90 minute video I did with Glenn Livingston called "How to Choose Your Market." We took one aspect that held people back and just focused on that to produce a low cost product which sold well when priced from $7 to $19.95. It would be perfect for a 'beginner' type of project.

One of my tricks to producing a product you know will sell is to use a webinar service such as **www.GotoWebinar.com**. Come up with your subject and write bullet benefits about what you'll cover during the training. Advertise it to your list. They get the webinar plus the recording when it's over, and you'll give them a full money back guarantee if it's not everything you promised it to be and more. All they need to do is pay the fee you've set through Paypal. After they pay you take them over to the registration page for the webinar. You teach your class. Answer whatever questions they have at the end of the class. Email them all the download at the end of the event.

You've now produced your first product. If no one buys your webinar, you don't hold the event. You would have created an outline for the content before you advertised the event, but you won't finish the product if it doesn't sell. In addition, this forces you to get the content done. There is a deadline. You can't put off the event for months into the future. You have to hold the event when you've promised it.

If you want to teach a subject that will require multiple sessions, you can set-up a series of weekly webinars such as every Tuesday night at 7 PM for the next 2 to 8 weeks. Don't go over 8 weeks, or you'll find way too many people drop out during the event. Focus on the audience and give them an easy action challenge to complete each week to keep them involved. This type of 'group coaching' program could sell for anywhere from $197 to $5,000 depending on the subject you're covering. B2B subjects that focus on attracting new clients often sell for premium prices while consumer subjects will have lower prices.

This system allows you to make money before you create your product. Since you've already been tracking your emails and making sales of affiliate offers, you'll have a pretty good idea of what your clients want to buy. After the event, you can package up your product and put it behind a membership site such as Wishlist member. You're now in the information business...and you can continue to expand with more products and services in the future.

Action Steps

- The easiest way to get started online is by focusing on building a list of hungry buyers. Monetize your list initially with affiliate offers, and expand into information products as you get feedback from your list.

- Consider the 3 most important factors of choosing a new market: passion, buyers, and value. The most important aspect of your new business is a hungry, buying audience.

- Create a Lead Magnet based on a Free Preview such as a case study about the affiliate product you will promote first to your list. Build your list.

- Focus on one traffic source in the beginning. Facebook advertising is a good choice for paid advertising, and blogging or Youtube are good choices for free advertising.

- Practice your 'voice' by writing emails based on the Infotainment model. Write a rant. Publish contrarian content. Tell personal stories. Monitor opens, clicks, and sales.

- One of the easiest ways to create your first product is by holding a paid webinar. Prepare your presentation, put together your "Golden Glove" web page about the offer, and sell it to your list. Make money before the product is even created.

Attract More New Clients, Income, and Prestige

The strategies and techniques you've learned throughout this book work for any business. Just because I didn't cover your industry specifically doesn't mean the methods won't work for you. There is only so much space to share in a book without it becoming a multi-volume encyclopedia.

For example, I didn't cover much about ecommerce businesses which sell thousands of individual products. The Golden Glove can be applied to the home page of your ecommerce store, and it can also be applied to each product page individually. Start off by focusing on your top selling products. Refine your message. Communicate your problem, promise, and proof. Give people an irresistible offer and tell them why they should take action now.

Maybe your store doesn't have a 'face' for the company, so you're not sure how to create an Authority Architecture in your business. Even Fortune 500 corporations can have a face for their business. Apple was built on Steve Jobs as the brand. They built their brand on innovation. That extended not only throughout their products but also into their stores with the Apple Genius Bar and the employees they hired to help their clients.

It's tough to compete with the giants in your industry as a small ecommerce business. One of the advantages you can tap into is the personal feel. It's something we've lost in today's digital world where much of the customer support is provided by overseas companies. Create an About page on your website. List the key employees in your business. Show pictures of your employees and provide some details about them.

Provide content on your subject in your own name. You could have others write under your name. Or you could use a pseudonym for the 'expert' voice in your company (*this pen name would be better for the main content creator so you don't 'lose' the name when an employee leaves your company*).

Brainstorm with your team to come up with the 'voice' of your company. Is it an experienced mentor providing insights to her students? Is it a wizard who comes up with magical and innovative ways to solve current problems? Is it a bold champion who rushes headlong into challenges and defeats them? There is an origin story behind why you started this business, and it helps illustrate why your solution is so much more valuable than the competition for your portion of the market.

It's not about your products or services. It's about your story. Products and services can be copied. The story behind your company and the stories about your clients are what sets you apart. It's not about building a better mousetrap. It's about creating and continually communicating a more engaging story of the benefits you provide your clients.

It's not about your content. That is easy to reproduce. Content is cheap. Some websites follow the model of paying peanuts to writers who produce thousands of pages of content. They're trying to attract visitors simply based on the volume of keywords they write about. That strategy worked for a time, until Google started rewarding those who build a brand in their market. While keywords still matter, it's even more important to be seen as an authority by the influencers in your marketplace.

Your audience is looking for consistent, contrarian content from a confident character. That's one of the reasons you need to focus on getting people on your email list. Selling today is not about overwhelming people with an in-your-face sales pitch. Instead it's about communicating multiple facets of your story. It's about building a relationship with people who know, like, and trust you. Some visitors buy immediately, but others need multiple contacts.

Giving value in advance sets you apart from all those quick hit sales people. You give first and prove your worth. You improve the lives of everyone you come in contact with even if they never cross the hurdle and make a purchase with you. You're a guide who points out the root desperate problems they may never have even fully realized themselves. You're a mentor who can show them the way to a unique promise. And you back up everything you do with proof of others who have overcome similar problems.

Where to Get Started For Fastest Results

If you already have a website, one of the fastest ways to get results is with the Golden Glove. Everyone wants more traffic, but attracting more visitors to your site isn't going to do much good if your site can't convert those visitors into subscribers and sales. It's like trying to collect water with a leaky bucket. Maybe if you run fast enough, you can make it to your destination with enough water, but you'd be much better off repairing the holes in your bucket first.

I originally used the Golden Glove while doing website reviews at workshops. At times I only had 10 to 20 minutes during a webinar or conference to help a website owner increase their sales, and that required me to come up with a system that worked quickly every time. The Golden Glove helped me reveal the conversion cracks in just a few minutes...

1. **Desperate Problem**: Who is this for and what problem are you solving for them?

2. **Unique Promise**: Why should someone choose your solution over every other available option?

3. **Overwhelming Proof**: Why should they believe the solution is for real, you're a credible person to purchase from, and the solution will work for them personally?

4. **Irresistible Offer**: How can you make it more painful for them to walk away than to purchase your offer?

5. **Reason to Act Now**: Why must they take action today?

You can use the five fingers of the Golden Glove on any of your websites or individual pages. It doesn't matter whether you're asking people to join your list or buy your product. Ask yourself each of the questions above.

How will a visitor know you're speaking to them specifically and what problems you can help them solve? Don't underestimate just how important the "Desperate Problem" is to the sale. You may have heard someone say they could sell ice to an Eskimo. That expression is a lie. Either that salesperson is so deceitful that they make up problems customers don't have, or they're simply so good at identifying hungry buyers that you never see them speak to someone who isn't interested.

You want to enter the conversation already going in the head of your visitor. They feel a desire. You tap into that hunger and you expand on it. You let the visitor know they've come to the right site.

You tell them how your solution is different from other options they've considered. This can be difficult if you're in a super-competitive market or everyone offers the exact same product.

This is where your story can give you an advantage. Your story can make your solution feel unique. A good story can mix in the Problem, Promise, and Proof in an easy to swallow format. Another option is to focus heavily on your guarantee and why it's stronger than everyone else in the industry (*again there can be a story behind your guarantee and why you're offering it when no one else comes close*).

You back up your promises with proof. This includes your story, case studies, testimonials, scientific studies, demonstrations, and anything else that adds credibility to what you do. Your visitors have been disappointed before. They're suspicious. Why should they believe you?

What makes your offer irresistible? Why is it such a good deal? Review the chapter on the 5 Step Persuasion Formula to see how you can use soft offers, trials, payments, bonuses, and other methods to create an offer that's irresistible.

Finally, why should the visitor choose to take action now? What will they miss out on if they decide to wait? How many times have you made a decision because time was running out? You were on the fence, but took action because a sale was going on. It's like being back in school. How many times did you cram for the test the night before? Most of us have the tendency to procrastinate and we need that incentive to move forward and take action now.

Combine all five of these fingers and you have a proven persuasion formula that works for any offer. It doesn't matter whether you're giving away a free report, selling a t-shirt, or asking people to make an appointment for your office. Fix the conversion cracks and the results will be multiplied from every penny you spend on advertising and every minute you invest in online marketing.

What If You're Struggling to Identify Your Ideal Client and Their Desperate Problem?

Many businesses struggle because they're trying to force a square peg into a round hole. They came up with a brilliant idea for a product or service, but they haven't identified what is most important to the buyer. That's a losing game. It's much easier to find a hungry buyer and deliver them what they want. It makes the whole sales process smooth. You don't have to sell the customer on anything. They're already ready to buy. You simply have to explain the Golden Glove to them, and watch them reach their own buying decision. Remember, no one likes being sold, but we all love to buy.

Identify your Ideal Clients. Review the buyers who have been with you the longest and invested the most money with you. What separates them from the average client? What do these Ideal Clients have in common?

Get on the phone and talk to them. Find out why they originally purchased from you and what they were trying to accomplish. What other solutions did they try? What made you stand out from the competition? You're trying to gain insights into what helped them make a buying decision.

If you're just starting in business and don't have any clients yet, you can do some of this research online. Scan the reviews on related products in Amazon. Join forums and Facebook groups about your topic. What questions are they asking? Check out Facebook's Audience Insights and review the demographics and other interests for some of your top competitors. Visit top competitor websites and reverse engineer their Golden Gloves. You can see what causes a client to buy by analyzing several top selling competitive websites.

Create an Ideal Client Avatar. This is your client. This is who you're writing your website for and who you're sending your emails to. Great marketing puts the audience first. It's about their problems, hopes, desires, dreams, and goals. Avoid industry jargon that will confuse them. Speak to them in their language. It's vital you understand your client's story and where they're coming from.

How can you share a story that resonates with your audience if you don't first know their story? What are their beliefs, especially about your topic? What do they think in their heart that they might even be afraid to express in words? All of our experiences from the moment we're born until the day we die influence our character and our view of the world in general. You could share the same story with two different audiences. One grabs it as a lifeline. It's the most powerful, life changing thing they've ever heard. The other audience isn't moved by it at all. It all comes down to making a connection with the hearts of your audience.

Share Your Story And Create Your Authority Architecture

You'll be tempted to jump right into creating content since you now know the questions your visitors are interested in, but that would be a big mistake! Constipated content doesn't sell. That's the normal boring content people can find on any website. It's disconnected from your 'celebrity' personality. Instead, first come up with the story that will resonate with your Ideal Clients.

Go through the Hero's Journey and look for the pieces to your story puzzle. Your origin story demonstrates why you got started in this business.

You either personally experienced the Desperate Problem your clients are going through or your heart was moved when you saw what others were going through. You had to make a difference. You faced challenges trying to overcome the problem, but eventually this solution was created. Your business is unique because no one else has your story!

Once you have your story, you can fill in the other pieces of the Authority Architecture. You have a vision for your world. It's about more than just money to you. Your clients don't care about how much money you make. They care about the mission and the hope you inspire in them. You have a villain you defeated. Usually this isn't another person. Instead, it's a faceless enemy that's easy to hate. For example, many entrepreneurs in natural health use the pharmaceutical companies as a villain. They're easy to hate. Doctors are NOT the villain because many clients have met them in person and usually like at least one or two of them.

Look for common interests with your audience. Perhaps you love dogs or spend time with your children. You live by the ocean (*water is often popular*). You enjoy the great outdoors. Mix in little personal elements like these that make you a real person to your audience. We live in a celebrity culture where everyone wants to know the intimate details of their favorite celebrity. You won't have any paparazzi outside your door, so you get to choose what you share.

Create personal parables which are little stories throughout your life that illustrate principles you teach. These won't come all at once. You'll develop them over time. Look for little stories you can share when you're creating content pieces such as emails. You'll know the ones which resonate with your audience because of the response you receive, including sales that come in. Keep using the stories that work and let the others fall to the side. Over time you'll develop dozens of personal stories that communicate your message to your audience effectively.

Make complicated principles simple. That's a secret of success in today's overwhelming world. Come up with 'rules' to follow. Create your own language and terms. Create that feeling of being part of the 'in-crowd' for those who are in your audience and understand your rules and language. Share both your super powers and your personal flaws. You don't come right out and say how awesome you are. Instead you demonstrate how you and your company have helped clients succeed. And many of those case studies will share a common thread of the unique promises you deliver to your clients.

You don't need all of these pieces in place before you start. You'll develop them over time. Reread through the story and authority chapter multiple times as you're producing content. You'll find new ways to integrate in your story. You'll add more depth and emotion to it. You'll find your voice as you continue producing content.

Why It's About Free Previews Instead of Content

Get your story and authority positioning correct and you're already ahead of 95% of your competition. Combine that with a strategic free preview model instead of just randomly delivering content, and you have a proven system for attracting hungry buyers to your products and services.

How are free previews different from random content? Random content simply teaches what you think customers need to learn. Free previews demonstrate how your products and services can improve the lives of your clients. Always think about where the story may fit. Bring in case studies to share your methods whenever possible. A case study can reveal tips while sharing what your clients have accomplished with your products and services.

Another effective free preview model is to teach your audience the hard way of doing things, and provide your product and service as the easy way. For example, you could teach your clients how to create their own Adwords ads, or they could simply hire you to do it for them.

You could give people useful but incomplete information. You teach them step one in your system, but leave them hanging on what they need to do next. Curiosity can be as strong of a buying motivation as benefits, especially in an information or coaching business.

You could redefine the root problem. Everyone else thinks the problem is X, but the real problem is Y. None of the other methods are valid because they're all solving the wrong problem. For example, chiropractors can teach their audience why migraines can be caused by their neck being out of alignment. Keep it simple, but provide scientific evidence and demonstrate that the problem is something different than they've been told. Their services become the natural solution to the root cause of the desperate problem.

The goal of free previews is to position your products and services as the easiest solution to the desperate problem. Your goal is to disqualify other solutions while giving value and tips your audience can use to see at least partial results (*the faster they can see these results the better*).

301

It's About Your Audience and Your Email List

Social media can play a role in just about everyone's business, but the money is in your direct relationship with your audience. When you build up a Facebook page, you're building on Facebook's brand. When you build your email list, you're building your brand. Concentrate on getting visitors to your websites, your blog, and your social media profiles onto your email list.

Offer an Attention Grabbing Lead Magnet as a bribe to get people to join your list. That's a high value free preview of your products and services. It doesn't matter whether it's a PDF Cheat Sheet, an audio interview, a video, or a discount coupon for your store. The purpose of the gift is to attract more subscribers, build your authority, and guide people to making a wise buying decision.

Once people are on your list, follow-up with them consistently with emails that mix in your authority, your personality, and your message. Think of each email as a quick chat with a friend over lunch. Be personable. Be yourself. And move the sale forward.

Plan your call-to-action before you start writing the email. That's the most important element. What are you asking your reader to do today? Do you want them to click over to your website and buy a specific product? Should they register for a webinar? Should they fill out your application for a free consultation? Or perhaps you simply want them to share your video with their friends on Facebook? The vast majority of your emails should have a specific call-to-action. Otherwise, what's the point of investing your time in writing it.

Once you've decided on the call-to-action, come up with a case study, personal story, or some other top-of-mind hook to begin the email. Remember, you're making a personal connection with your audience. You can do this by sharing something that happened this week or when you were growing up. It could be about your children or the person you met at the store. Or you could simply connect to major news. Connect to major sporting events, elections, movies, or celebrity news.

Tell your story quickly and then share a piece of advice or a few tips that apply to your subject. That's the 'lesson' and content section of your email. Then transition from there into your call-to-action. Those 3 steps are the basic model for writing effective emails.

Of course you can break this mold and create emails where you answer questions from your subscribers or give multiple tips. There are no 'definite' rules of what you have to do in each email. The trick is to grab their attention, keep their interest, and transition into an offer that's connected to the message.

Get Multiplied Value From Every Piece of Content

Set-up a Wordpress blog where you can post archives of your emails. I post almost every email except for a few exclusive specials that are for my list only. You could use your email as the script for a video. If you do podcasts, you could use your email as a jumping off point into a longer discussion. If you prefer podcasting instead, you could pull clips from your podcast to create your emails and your blog posts.

It all comes back to using whatever medium works best for you. Some of my clients have created entire books straight from their blog content over several months. Others have used the interview method to write a book or create all the content they share online for the next 6 months. Don't struggle and beat your head against the wall doing something you hate. Online business is FUN when you do it correctly!

Make a list of every question your audience is asking to create your initial content. Spend 10 to 15 minutes writing out those questions. Take a short break and then make a list of every question they should be asking. Visit Amazon and look through the Table of Contents of some of the most popular books on your topic. Write down ideas as they come to mind for additional topics to cover. These three assignments can help you come up with all the content you'll need getting started.

Find the best time and method for your personality and/or team to create this content. Some of my clients prefer investing 30 minutes each morning writing an email for the day. Others are more like me and prefer working in 'time blocks' where you might create 4 or more pieces of content over several hours. My favorite place for writing is out on my lanai, but yours could be in a busy coffee shop. It isn't about what works for me. It's about doing what works for you!

Connect With Others to Expand Your Reach

Don't go it alone. The fastest way to grow your audience is by connecting with those who already have your Ideal Clients on their list or on social media. Partner with them. Go back to our core philosophy. Add value to these influencers' lives even if they never do business with you. What can you do to help them first?

You could interview them for your podcast. That would of course provide you with content and add to your credibility to be seen with this expert. At the same time, it can give them additional exposure for their projects. You could share their content on your social media sites. You could create a 'link' post where you link to the best blog posts from different influencers about a specific subject. You could purchase from them and send them a testimonial. You could join their affiliate program and promote their product.

Make small requests first. Ask if they would like you to write a guest post for their blog about your specialty. If you've used their product or service, you could even write a case study for their blog. Do the interview with them. If they have a podcast, you could promote yourself as a guest on their podcast. Send them a free copy of your product to try out for themselves.

Run Paid Advertising to Create a Consistent Flow of High Quality Clients

I love free marketing, but it's often hit-or-miss. One guest post may give you 300 new subscribers, and another one is a complete dud. You send out press releases and nothing happens. You send out another press release and all of a sudden you're in major media. There are of course ways to improve your odds on each of these, but it still sometimes feels like you're shooting in the dark.

Paid advertising is fast, consistent, and convenient. You can start generating visitors to your website within the next 60 minutes. The negative of paid advertising is it can be expensive, and it can be difficult to convert cold leads into sales. They don't know you and they don't trust you.

That's why it's so important to put the Sell Without Selling methods into action. You can make your advertising itself useful to the viewer. The more specialized and the better you target your Ideal Client, the easier it will be to create a hook that grabs their attention. Move them to your site with the enticement of free value, and focus on getting them on the list first.

Install the codes provided by the advertising source into your website so you can track the leads and sales generated from each visitor. It's unlikely your advertising will be profitable right out of the gate. It takes time to cut out the keywords, interests, and ads which aren't working. You have to optimize each step in your funnel from the audience to the ad to the landing page to your thank you page and on down the line.

Install the retargeting pixels from any advertising source you're using including both Facebook and Google. In many cases, your initial ad campaign won't be profitable on its own. It's too hard to profit from cold visitors who don't know you. By installing retargeting pixels, you'll be able to follow-up on those visitors with additional ads and offers to bring them back to your site.

The money in advertising is often found in the retargeting, not the initial ad campaigns! If you're not using retargeting, you may be wasting money with your ads. We couldn't get into all the intricacies of retargeting in this book, but you can check out **www.MyMarketingCoach.com** for more information on this and how to use it.

Also make sure to visit **www.MyMarketingCoach.com** and join my list to get up-to-date advice on my favorite advertising methods. At the time of this writing, Youtube and Facebook were two of my favorite ways to advertise, but that can quickly change in the future.

Focus on the Lifetime Value of Each Client

The model I've laid out for you in this book isn't about making a quick sale. It's about building long-term relationships where you add value to everyone who comes in contact with you. This is how you build a business that not only profits today but continues to grow and multiply in value for decades to come.

Your list will grow. Your subscribers will know, like, and trust you. They'll follow your recommendations. You'll create long-term relationships with clients. You'll make connections with additional influencers who expose you to even more clients in the future.

Expand your products and services. If you're a consultant, look for ways to communicate your expertise in information products. Train team members who can deliver services for you. If you're in an information products business, create a membership or ongoing monthly continuity of some type. Add in higher ticket products and services such as workshops and coaching.

An ecommerce business can have an ever growing product line. Amazon is an example of this. They started with books, but have now expanded into almost every product possible. They were never in the 'book-selling' business. They're in the Amazon Prime business. And they've continued to add to this core subscription offer with memberships for ebooks, audio books, movies, and music.

A local business owner can provide higher level services or yearly service packages. You can put a systematic referral system in place. You can bring in additional practitioners to serve even more clients. Eventually you can grow a practice that sells for a premium price when you choose to retire or move in another direction.

The 'Sell Without Selling' model attracts Premium Clients. Treat them well. Protect them. Value them. And they'll provide an incredible Internet Lifestyle to you.

Action Steps

- It's NOT about your products and services. It's about your story. Keep that in mind no matter what business you're in. You're selling experiences instead of products and services.
- Use the 'Golden Glove' right now to review your most important website landing page. How can you improve each of the 5 fingers of persuasion on that page?
- Identify your Ideal Client Avatar. If you don't know who you're trying to attract, then you're likely not very appealing to anyone. Focus your attention on your hungry buying audience.
- Share your story and the other pieces of your Authority Architecture. Constipated content doesn't sell. Produce Infotainment instead of information.
- Build your email list. Communicate with them consistently. Share personal stories, contrarian content, and offers. Your income is in your relationship with your list.
- Create advertising that's useful and valuable on its own. Mix in Infotainment all along the sales process. That's the core secret behind how to 'Sell Without Selling.'

About the Author

Terry Dean started his first online business from scratch in 1996. He went from delivering pizzas for Little Caesars for $8 an hour to creating a full-time income online. He has been called one of the grandfathers of Internet marketing and was one of the first online marketers to demonstrate the power of email, generating $96,250 from an email to his list in front of a live audience.

Terry sold his first business in 2004 to semi-retire at 30. In 2006, he returned to his passion of coaching entrepreneurs on how to Earn More, Work Less, and Enjoy Life using the Internet. He mentors his clients both one-on-one and in small groups. He has been publishing the Monthly Mentor Club letter since 2007 and it has helped thousands of entrepreneurs profit from online marketing: **www.MonthlyMentorClub.com**.

Terry's main website is **www.MyMarketingCoach.com**. Claim your copy of his Free Email Conversion Kit which includes 64 story shortcuts, 5 proven subject line templates, 10 email introduction starters, and his 7 step system for creating effective emails. In addition, you can access his blog, one-on-one coaching, and group coaching options at this site.

Made in the USA
Middletown, DE
25 August 2019